Right-Wing in the Civil War Era

Soldiers of God and Apostles of the Fatherland, 1914–45

EDITED BY

ALEJANDRO QUIROGA AND

MIGUEL ÁNGEL DEL ARCO

continuum

Continuum International Publishing Group

The Tower Building	80 Maiden Lane
11 York Road	Suite 704
London	New York
SE1 7NX	NY 10038

www.continuumbooks.com

First published 2012
Chapters 1, 2, 3, 5, 6, 7 and 8 were originally published in Spanish by Comares in *Soldados de Dios y Apóstoles de la Patria*, Granada, 2010

British Library Cataloguing-in-Publication Data
A catalogue record for this book is available from the British Library.

ISBN: HB: 978-1-4411-7914-2
PB: 978-1-4411-8176-3

Library of Congress Cataloging-in-Publication Data
A catalog record for this book is available from the Library of Congress.

Typeset by Fakenham Prepress Solutions, Fakenham, Norfolk NR21 8NN
Printed and bound in India

Contents

Introduction: Soldiers of God and Apostles of the Fatherland in Interwar Europe

ALEJANDRO QUIROGA AND MIGUEL ÁNGEL DEL ARCO

This book is concerned with the leading figures of the Spanish right in the turbulent period 1914–45. By adopting a biographical approach, the volume aims at providing a new insight into the origins, development and aftermath of the Spanish Civil War. The focus here is on how key individuals experienced the political and social crises of interwar Europe. The book's main arguments can be encapsulated in two key propositions. The first is that the Spanish conservatives, far from being an isolated, monolithic block, were a heterogeneous force profoundly influenced by German Nazism, Italian Fascism and French Traditionalism. The second is that the interaction of Spanish nationalism and Catholicism was the ideological driving force at the heart of the right's political cultures and actions. If we are to understand the radical solutions that the conservatives chose to halt the threats that they saw in a rapidly-changing, post-First World War society, then we have to explore the right's religious perception of the Spanish nation and its patriotic concept of Catholicism. In doing so, the book also challenges the idea that Catholicism hampered the consolidation of fascism in Spain.

The chronological framework of this work is delimited by the two world wars. Between 1914 and 1945, Europe experienced revolutions, the collapse of empires, ethnic cleansings, unprecedented social struggles, and the rise of fascist regimes and genocides. These cataclysmic events can be understood as part of a 'European Civil War' that brought into conflict forces of the right and the left throughout the 'Old Continent'.[1] On many occasions this European Civil War was a 'cold war' with low levels of physical confrontation.

It was a domestic struggle that took the shape of strikes, lockouts and skirmishes between trade unionists, on the one hand, and policemen, military men and members of right-wing gangs, on the other. In other instances, however, the European Civil War turned into one that was far from cold. The civil wars in Finland (1918), Russia (1917–22) and Greece (1944–5), together with the myriad infightings all over the continent under Nazi occupation, are good examples of hot conflicts in which the domestic socio-political clashes were directly influenced by international disputes and vice versa. Within this wider picture, the Spanish Civil War of 1936–9 has to be considered a central episode of the European Civil War.

It was in this context of European Civil War that the Spanish right's ideas, social anxieties and political decisions were shaped. The mental universe of the characters analysed in this volume was forged in a context of continuous struggles among Europeans, and the ideas and fears that led to the political mobilization of the Spanish right were heavily influenced by thinkers, politicians and events beyond the Iberian Peninsula. Thus, Antonio Maura, the leader of the new right in the last years of the Restoration regime (1875–1923) was a good friend of the French traditionalist chief Charles Maurras and understood the need of modernizing Spanish conservatism following the dramatic changes brought by the Great War. General Miguel Primo de Rivera befriended Marshall Petain and was always very fond of paralleling his dictatorship (1923–30) to that of Benito Mussolini. Like his father, José Antonio Primo de Rivera was a great admirer of Mussolini, and his Spanish fascist party *Falange* drew heavily from the Italian radical right. José María Gil Robles, the leader of the Catholic right during the Second Republic (1931–6), travelled to Nuremberg to learn first-hand from the Nazis how to organize parades, rituals and propaganda. Juan Tusquets, Franco's daughter's private tutor and one of the nationalists' key propagandists, visited the Nazi concentration camp of Dachau. Juan Antonio Suanzes, Franco's minister of Industry and Trade, took fascist Italy as the model to follow when implementing his project of national modernization. Antonio Vallejo Nágera, head of the Psychiatric Services of the Francoist army, learnt some of his methods in Germany before developing a programme of experimentation on Republican prisoners. Even Francisco Franco, a man seldom inclined to intellectual activities, was an avid reader in the 1920s of the anti-communist propaganda generated by the *Entente Internationale contre la Troisièmme Internationale*, an anti-Bolshevik organization founded by White Russians and Swiss reactionaries. More important in terms of international influence was, of course, the fact that Franco's rise to power within the rebel ranks and, ultimately, his military victory in the civil war, were mainly due to the aid of Hitler and Mussolini.

In most of the literature about the 1920s and 1930s Spanish right there is little place for individuals.[2] The historiography of the subject has largely concentrated on the study of diverse conservative parties and political cultures. As a result, scholars have produced a number of typologies to differentiate between conservative groups depending on their discourses and practices.[3] At the heart of many academic studies on the Spanish conservatives there has been an attempt to define the nature of the Franco regime, for the political personnel of the dictatorship was made up of a myriad of veteran right-wingers of the 1920s and 1930s. Broadly speaking, it is possible to differentiate between those scholars who emphasized the impact of the European conservatives, including fascists, on the Spanish right, and hence on the Franco regime, and historians who have minimized foreign influences and highlighted the weight of Catholicism as an ideological buffer that prevented fascism from having a real impact on the Spanish right.[4] The former wave of interpretation underlines the fluent relations between Spanish and European radical conservatives; the latter school relies on a rigid concept of fascism and argues that Francoism was never a genuinely fascist regime.

By employing a biographical approach, this volume aims at shedding some new light on the subject. Beyond the broad purpose of ascribing substantial ideas to protagonists through biographical narrative, the analysis of the lives of these leading right-wingers allows us to historicize the Spanish right in a more comprehensive manner. Instead of studying a figure or a movement confined to a particular political regime, we explore the lives of our protagonists in the interwar period. This chronological framework allows us to follow the lives of these historical subjects over the last years of Restoration, the Dictatorship of Primo de Rivera, the Second Republic, the Civil War and the early years of the Franco dictatorship. The goal here is to overcome the traditional chronological structures linked to political regimes. In this manner, we are able to focus on the way diverse social and political transformations impacted on our characters throughout different historical periods. Rather than a motionless picture of historical subjects, we provide the reader with a film in which the lives of the principal protagonists go through different political eras.

As Ian Kershaw reflected when writing on Adolf Hitler, biographical analysis can easily fall into the trap of 'over-personalizing complex historical developments [and] playing down the social and political context in which the actions of the protagonist took place'.[5] In the chapters of this book, we have sought to historicize the lives of our figures by exploring their dialectic relationship with the multiple social, political and cultural worlds of interwar Europe which they inhabited. Studies of individuals can make visible the social and political constraints that different historical subjects lived with and how they reacted to particular crises. The larger aim is to understand how our protagonists lived, gave meaning and attempted to transform a series of particular historical contexts.[6] How did they see a given political system? How did they come to a particular idea? Why did they choose to take a certain decision?

What triggered a precise action? All these are very specific questions that need to be answered taking into consideration the historical context in which the actions of the individuals took place. This biographical approach does not minimize the importance of social and political context but restores a sense of human agency in the interpretation of the past.

Political biography also facilitates our understanding of how individuals experience historical events and ideas. Chris Ealham and Michael Richards have pointed out that the Spanish Civil War was shaped by a number of strains, some of them strictly political and some others 'that were to do with people's ways of comprehending the social events around them'.[7] In the case of the Spanish right, the issue of perception was paramount throughout the entire interwar period. The analysis of lived experiences illustrates the way the Spanish conservative leaders perceived and acted upon events and crises that, in some cases, they themselves had helped to create. Fear of social change, or rather anxiety produced by the possibility of it, dominated conservative mentalities. For example, the anti-communist craze that was to sweep Europe following the Bolshevik Revolution had more to do with the perception of a threat, even if clearly exaggerated for political aims, than with the actual challenge posed by revolutionaries in many parts of Europe. It is also worth noting that biographical studies are useful to deconstruct the myths associated with important historical figures. Biographies of political leaders should be able to humanize their subjects, in the sense of stripping them of any aura of supernatural greatness. After all, greatness linked to important historical figures is a political and cultural construction too.[8] By looking at the topic through the lense of biography, we have sought to de-mythologize our protagonists, while producing a more nuanced and fluent picture of the Spanish right.

A common theme running through all the contributions to this volume is the central role played by the complex interaction of Spanish nationalism and Catholicism in the conservatives' political cultures. As in the rest of Europe, it was in the post-First World War era that different groups of a new radical right emerged in Spain. Whether monarchists, fascists, authoritarian Catholics or traditionalists, they broke with the old liberal conservatism of the Restoration regime. What all these groups had in common was a penchant for placing the nation at the centre of their political universe, together with a tendency for advocating dictatorial solutions against democratization and social reform. Crucially, these different political groups of the Spanish right had very fluid relations between them, which facilitated the exchange of political personnel, money and ideas.[9] Additionally, Spanish conservatives developed close ties with French, Italian, Portuguese, British, German and Austrian members of the radical right. It was against this backdrop of domestic and international influences that many on the Spanish right gradually entered a process of 'fascistization', by which elements of Mussolini's Italy and Hitler's Germany were selectively incorporated into their ideological and action repertoire.[10] This process of fascistization was, it should be noted, a European phenomenon, as conservatives all over the continent adapted ideas, rituals and tactics from the fascist dictatorships to their domestic political arenas. By the same token, strictly fascist movements borrowed ideas, personnel, symbols and money from different conservative groups.[11] Even if conservatives of all sorts always put the nation-state at the centre of their political discourse, there can be few doubts that a transnational European right emerged in the interwar years.[12]

Catholicism, or rather a particular reading of it, became the second common denominator of the Spanish right in the interwar era. The study of religion as a constituent element of the ideological and symbolic universe of the European radical right has revived historiography on the subject. The understanding of fascism as a 'political religion', the evaluation of religion as a device of mass indoctrination and mobilization in counter-revolutionary dictatorships and the recent debate on the influence of Christianity on Nazism have shown the paramount role religion played in shaping the political cultures of conservatives of all hue in Europe.[13] Spain was no exception here. All the chapters in this book suggest that Catholicism was central to the various ideological formulations, especially in shaping Spanish nationalist articulations. Catholicism did not hamper the Spanish right's process of fascistization. On the contrary, religion stalwartly contributed to the ultranationalist adoration of the fatherland and became a direct means to the 'sacralization of the nation', that is, to the transformation of the patria into a divine entity. Although the process had begun before the First World War, interwar Spanish conservatives verbalized a new political discourse that equated Catholicism with Spanishness and fostered a process of 'sacralization of the fatherland' in which the myth of the nation became the supreme political value. This new organic canon of Spain had its political implications, not least in terms of the violent actions taken against those considered to be 'internal enemies' of the nation, such as republicans, socialists, anarchists, regional nationalists and communists. The Francoist brutal repression of political enemies during and after the Civil War was integral to this sacred concept of the nation developed by the Spanish right in the previous years.[14] In a discourse saturated with Catholic terms, mass killings, widespread torture, slave labour and concentration camps were portrayed as a necessary sacrifice to 'purify' the nation and 'redeem' the vanquished.[15]

In most cases, the 'sacralization of the nation' was not based on an application of theological principles to politics, but rather on a political manipulation of Catholicism. As in the case of French Traditionalism, Catholicism was significant for the Spanish right not as a religious creed, but as a structure of order linked to the nation. Family values, hierarchy, discipline, authority and dogmatism were the main political merits that the Spanish conservatives found in Christianity. The words of General Primo de Rivera on his dictatorship are telling:

> '[My] government bases its actions on religious sentiments. It does so because we believe that religion is a very useful educational means for social aims. The government intentionally avoids any attempt of theological definition, as this is a responsibility that belongs to a different power.'[16]

In an era in which politics went through a process of sacralization all over Europe, Catholicism became not only the ideological glue of the Spanish conservatives but also a tool of indoctrination and social mobilization.

As the old nineteenth-century mechanisms of social control became increasingly inefficient, many conservatives found nationalist indoctrination to be the most useful tool to integrate the masses into politics without having to pay the price of democratization. Antonio Maura, the conservative Prime Minister, was one of the first figures to realize the need to modernize the Spanish right and politically reach the masses in the last years of the Restoration regime. Francisco Romero Salvadó explores in chapter 1 the career, impact and ultimate failure of this polemic and extremely complex politician. Maura tried to reform the Restoration system from within and place it on sounder foundations like no other dynastic leader: he believed that the monarchic regime needed to be overhauled or it would be eventually brought down by revolution. Maura's project of a 'revolution from above' was never fully implemented but he became the leader of a heterogeneous movement that adopted the name of *Maurismo* and has been interpreted as the cradle of both modern Spanish Christian-democracy and authoritarian nationalism. In 1923, Maura advised King Alfonso XIII to let the army take power. In fact, Maura's tacit acceptance of a praetorian takeover was the recognition of his own political failure.

Chapter 2 analyses the life of General Miguel Primo de Rivera. Contrary to some traditional interpretations which emphasize the good nature and naivety of the dictator, Alejandro Quiroga shows a manipulative, ambitious and repressive military leader, who perfectly understood the social transformations brought about by the Great War and attempted to create a new authoritarian Spain. Primo de Rivera's dictatorship was one of the first counter-revolutionary regimes established in interwar Europe. Like his friend Benito Mussolini, the Andalusian general combined repression with mass indoctrination, fully aware of the fact that sheer coercion would not be enough to maintain the new authoritarian political edifice. Primo de Rivera orchestrated several propaganda campaigns and 'educational programmes' seeking to create fear of international and, above all, domestic enemies and to promote patriotic feelings among Spaniards. Nationalism was thought to be the panacea against democratic demands and social reform. The Primo de Rivera regime made official a sacralized idea of the fatherland that divided Spaniards into real nationals and anti-Spanish, depending on their political values. This divisive National Catholic concept of Spain was later used by the extreme right in the Second Republic and, ultimately, incorporated into the Francoist ideological arsenal during the Civil War. In this respect, Francoism was built on the nationalist legacy of Primo's regime.

In chapter 3, Eduardo González Calleja explores the complex twists and turns in the life of José María Gil Robles. A highly controversial figure, Gil Robles was an enthusiastic supporter of the dictatorship of Primo de Rivera in the 1920s and the leader of the Catholic right during the Second Republic. González Calleja takes a thematic approach to discuss Gil Robles' positions on democracy, the Second Republic, monarchy, fascism and political violence. González Calleja's work shows the ambiguities of a man who tried to combine his authoritarian beliefs with his participation in a democratic system; his monarchical inclinations with his active partaking in the Second Republic; and his penchant for fascism with the idea that the state should not enter certain political areas reserved for the Catholic Church. The last part of the chapter assesses Gil Robles' responsibility in the outbreak of the Spanish Civil War and his political manoeuvres during the first years of the Franco regime. González Calleja debunks the myths built around Gil Robles and portrays a conservative leader full of contradictions whose discursive radicalism did not match his political actions.

Chris Bannister assesses the political life and afterlife of José Antonio Primo de Rivera in chapter 4. Following his death, José Antonio Primo de Rivera was to become one of the key symbols of early Francoism. His name was carved into church walls across Spain and his resting place in the Valley of the Fallen is beside Francisco Franco himself. Yet Bannister argues that to view José Antonio as a proto-Francoist is to misunderstand his political thought. The leader of *Falange Española* shared the same reverence for the nation and Catholicism as his father General Miguel Primo de Rivera and Franco, but Jose Antonio's ideas were informed by Italian fascism more than they were by Spanish reactionary thought. The chapter defines José Antonio's Spanish brand of fascism as a political concept in its own right; not as a means to continue his father's work or as a precursor to Francoism. Bannister's work details José Antonio's early life up to the fall of General Primo de Rivera, his monarchist period between 1930 and 1933 and the formation and politics of *Falange Española* (1933–6). In keeping with the themes of this book, the main topics of examination are nationalism and religion and how these ideas, so integral to the traditional Spanish right, were incorporated into José Antonio's Italian fascist model. The chapter concludes with a discussion of the use and abuse of José Antonio's ideas by the Franco regime, following the execution of the fascist leader in a Republican prison in November 1936.

Franco's intentional misuse of José Antonio's legacy to build a political base for his regime gives us an idea of the manipulative nature of the Spanish dictator. The cunning and unscrupulous qualities of the general are dealt with in Enrique Moradiellos's biography of Franco in chapter 5. Moradiellos debunks the myths fabricated by Francoist hagiographists about the general's ability to protect Spain from a communist threat in the 1930s and to safeguard Spain's neutrality in the Second World War, by not giving in to Hitler's pressure. This chapter is also critical of those interpretations that have explained Franco's political career and the longevity of his dictatorship by a combination of sheer luck and international support – Hitler and Mussolini, first, and Winston S. Churchill and Harry S. Truman later. By focusing on the general's colonial experience in Spanish Morocco and political manoeuvring during the Second Republic and the Civil War, Moradiellos shows that *El Caudillo* was a complex and simplistic character at the same time. His political career and military victories cannot be explained by fortune and foreign aid alone, but rather by a good deal of prudence, numerous machinations, relentless brutality and unremitting selfishness. Simultaneously, Franco's intellectual mediocrity led him to believe in banal and absurd ideas, such as the existence of a Jewish–Bolshevik-Masonic international conspiracy that aimed at destroying the Spanish nation. In the last analysis, Franco was a figure shaped by the tensions of interwar Europe, guided by a crass Spanish nationalism and a solid religious zeal, whose atrocities combined a lack of ideological sophistication with a strong sense of political self-preservation.

Miguel Ángel del Arco Blanco explores in chapter 6 the life of Juan Antonio Suanzes, Francoist Minister of Industry and Trade and one of the architects of the 'New State' that emerged from the Civil War. A childhood friend of Francisco Franco, Suanzes began his political career with the Civil War when he was invited by *El Caudillo* to join the rebel government. A naval officer and an engineer, Suanzes's words and works epitomizes the compatibility of Catholicism and fascism. He was a devout Catholic but his trips to Italy to broker Mussolini's aid for the Francoists put him in direct contact with fascism. Convinced that Spain needed radically to modernize, he advocated a government-controlled industry and a state-run economy. The 'New State' was to be the primary force in the nation's moral and economic rebirth. Individual and private interests were to be subordinated to those of the nation, and the state was to foster consumption of national products and to decrease imports. The fascist dream of the autarkic nation was well embedded in this Francoist minister. Moreover, Suanzes defended a complete indoctrination of individuals and proposed the creation of agencies similar to the German *Kraft durch Freude* and the Italian *Dopolavoro* to nationalize the Spanish masses.

He also participated in the drafting of the *Fuero del Trabajo*, the law closely inspired by Mussolini's *Carta dil Lavoro* which was to regulate labour relations in the early years of the Spanish dictatorship. For all his fascist tendencies, however, Suanzes always believed that the state's indoctrination should be both religious and patriotic. Thus, in 1941, as director of the Spanish National Institute for Industry (*Instituto Nacional de Industria*, INI), an agency created in the image of the Italian *Istituto per la Riconstruzione Industriale*, Suanzes promoted Christian spiritual exercises among its workers. Suanzes found no contradiction in blending Catholicism and fascism: national and spiritual salvation came hand in hand.

Like Mussolini's Italy and Hitler's Germany, Franco's Spain was built on the myth of the dying nation in need of chirurgical action to survive. Domestic and foreign enemies were portrayed as the cancerous cells which had to be extirpated and the operation on the fatherland's body became the sine qua non condition for an eventual national rebirth. In chapter 7, Paul Preston explores how the accusation that the Second Republic was the anti-Spanish instrument of a Jewish–Masonic–Bolshevik conspiracy was created. With this aim, Preston focuses on the life of Juan Tusquets, one on the main propagandist of the conspiracy theory and a figure with massive influence within the Spanish right. A Catalan priest from a well-off family, Tusquets was a best-selling author whose books were serialized in traditionalist newspapers. Crucially, Tusquets had an important sway on General Franco, who eagerly read his anti-Semitic rants in the years of the Second Republic. Tusquets belonged to those on the right who not only justified political violence but, in fact, theorized the extermination of the political opponent. His message was uncompromising: Spain and the Catholic Church could be saved only by the annihilation of Jews, freemasons and socialists. In the spring of 1936, he himself tried to help in this task and sought to collect funds in Barcelona for a military uprising against the Second Republic. Months later, when Tusquets became a collaborator with Franco during the Civil War, he used his files on alleged freemasons to provide an important part of the rebels' organizational infrastructure for the repression. In the case of Tusquets, theory and practice of the destruction of the anti-Spain enveloped each other.

In chapter 8, Michael Richards deals with one of the most sinister characters of the Spanish right, the military psychiatrist Antonio Vallejo Nágera. Richards casts the figure of Vallejo as representative of an important strand of intellectual Catholic resistance to Spanish democracy in the 1930s. This resistance was expressed through scientific and political discourse during the Second Republic and culminated in active support for the 'purification' of Spain through the categorization, segregation and physical repression of Republicans during and after the Spanish Civil War. The chapter analyses the programme of experimentation on prisoners conducted under

Vallejo Nágera's authority during the Civil War, as part of the Francoist process of national purification. Richards focuses on Vallejo Nágera as psychiatrist, explaining the role of heritage in his conceptualization of 'racial hygiene', the impact of German theories on his thought and the development of biological typologies as the basis of his psychiatric practices. In his experiments Vallejo tried to draw lines between the 'bio-psychological qualities of the prisoners' and their 'democratic-communist political fanaticism'. He was convinced that those with democratic tendencies suffered from a hereditary condition. In his experiments, Republican men were considered 'degenerated' and 'mentally retarded', while female prisoners were treated as 'pathological criminals' and 'Marxist delinquents'. Here too there was an important influence of European fascism. Gestapo officers and Nazi doctors visited the Francoist concentration camps, where they carried out joint experiments with their Spanish colleagues.

The experiments of Francoists on Republican prisoners were one of the multiple forms of national purification implemented during the interwar period. The universe of concentration camps that was created in these years all over Europe, where alleged enemies of the nation were sent for political, ethnic or sexual reasons, was the brutal outcome of a rationale of segregation and extermination based on a sacralized and biological concept of the patria. By 1945, the European Civil War had left a continent riddled with mass graves and concentration camps. The fascist dream of a sacred, purified, biological nation lay in ruins. Unlike Hitler and Mussolini, however, Franco was never defeated militarily. Following the fall of the German and Italian regimes, the Francoists undertook a few cosmetic changes, so the dictatorship could be integrated into the Western camp of the Cold War. Yet the Spanish dictatorship persisted in perpetrating violence on a scale so vast that, in effect, the regime continued to wage war against defeated sectors of society.[17] The Spanish 'Soldiers of God' and 'Apostles of the Fatherland' that emerged in the interwar period were not fundamentally different from their European contemporaries. The survival of Francoism after 1945 marked Spain apart from its Western European counterparts. The fact that Francoism maintained the Manichean discourse of the endangered nation eternally battling domestic and international enemies and prolonged its ideological mobilization through the four decades of the regime led to the perpetuation of the division between victors and vanquished.

The division among Spaniards was promoted on nationalist and religious bases until the very end of the regime. Made public after the dictator's death on 20 November 1975, Franco's political testament called 'to unite God and Spain' and warned young generations about the 'enemies of the fatherland' and the multiple perils to 'Christian Civilization'.[18] It was, broadly speaking, the same message used during the Spanish Civil War. Nevertheless, the interwar Europe in which that nationalistic and religious rhetoric had emerged did not exist anymore. The death of Franco was the beginning of the end of the anachronism that the Spanish dictatorship meant in European terms after 1945. Only once the dictator was buried, could Spaniards attempt to regain a democratic regime and begin a process of national normalization vis-à-vis Western Europe. The divisions created and promoted by the dictatorship, however, have affected Spanish society in the democratic era. The recent 'memory wars' over the historical meaning of Francoism and its crimes are testimony to a toxic dictatorial legacy that still corrodes the social and political landscape of twenty-first-century Spain.

Endnotes

1 Paul Preston, 'The Great Civil War: European Politics, 1914–45', in Timothy C. W. Blanning, ed., *The Oxford Illustrated History of Modern Europe* (Oxford: Oxford University Press, 1998), pp. 148–81.

2 There are, of course, some important works on the life of General Franco. See Paul Preston, *Franco: a biography* (London: Fontana Press, 1995); Gabrielle Ashford Hodges, *Franco. A Concise Biography* (London: Weidenfeld and Nicolson, 2000); Geoffrey Jensen, *Franco: Soldier, Commander, Dictator (Military Profiles)* (Dulles: Potomac Books, 2005). However, biographical studies in English on other leading Spanish conservatives are scarce. Some figures are dealt with in Paul Preston, *¡Comrades! Portraits from the Spanish Civil War* (London: Harper Collins, 1999); and the chapter devoted to Mecedes Sanz-Bachiller in idem, *Doves of War* (London: Harper Collins, 2002), pp. 203–93. See also Geoffrey Jensen, *Irrational Triumph: Cultural Despair, Military Nationalism, and the Ideological Origins of Franco's Spain* (Reno: University of Nevada Press, 2002); and Dillwyn F. Ratcliff, *Prelude to Franco. Political Aspects of the Dictatorship of Primo de Rivera* (New York: Las Americas Publishing Company, 1959).

3 See Paul Preston, *The politics of revenge: fascism and the military in 20th-century Spain* (London: Unwin Hyman, 1990); Javier Tusell, 'Presentación', in Javier Tusell, et al., (eds), *Estudios sobre la derecha española contemporánea* (Madrid: UNED, 1993), pp. 9–13; Stanley G. Payne, *A History of Fascism, 1914–1945* (Abingdon: Routledge, 1996); Pedro Carlos González Cuevas, *Historia de las derechas españolas* (Madrid: Biblioteca Nueva, 2000); Ismael Saz Campos, *España contra España. Los nacionalismos franquistas* (Madrid: Marcial Pons, 2003).

4 Among those works emphasizing the impact of the European right on Spanish conservatives, see, for example, Francisco J. Romero Salvadó, *The Foundations of Civil War. Revolution, Social Conflict and Reaction in Spain, 1916–1923* (London: Routledge, 2008); Michael Richards, *A Time of Silence. Civil War and the Culture of Repression in Franco's Spain* (Cambridge: Cambridge University Press, 1998); Alfonso Botti, *Cielo y dinero. El Nacionalcatolicismo en España, 1881–1975* (Madrid: Alianza, 2008);

Sholomo, Ben-Ami, *Fascism from above: the Dictatorship of Primo de Rivera in Spain 1923–1930* (Oxford: Clarendon Press, 1983); Raúl Morodo, *Acción Española. Orígenes ideológicos del franquismo* (Madrid: Alianza, 1985); Paul Preston, *Las derechas españolas en el siglo XX: Autoritarismo, fascismo y golpismo* (Madrid: Sistema, 1986); idem, *The Spanish holocaust: inquisition and extermination during the civil war and after* (New York: W. W. Norton & Co, 2012); Martin Blinkhorn, 'The Iberian States', in Deflef Mülberger, ed., *The Social Bases of European Fascist Movements* (London: Croom Helm, 1987), pp. 320–48. Among the studies which play down the impact of European influences, in general, and fascism, in particular, see Stanley G. Payne, *Falange. Historia del fascismo español* (Madrid: Sarpe, 1985); idem, *Fascism in Spain, 1923–1975* (Madison: University of Wisconsin Press, 1985); Pedro Carlos González Cuevas, *Acción Española. Teología política y nacionalismo autoritario en España (1913–1936)* (Madrid: Tecnos, 1998); idem, 'Tradicionalismo, catolicismo y nacionalismo. La extrema derecha durante el régimen de la Restauración (1898–1930)', *Ayer*, 71 (2008): 25–52.

5   Ian Kershaw, *Hitler, 1889–1936: Hubris* (Harmondsworth: Penguin, 1998), p. xxi. On the issue of contextualization in biography, see Patrick O'Brien, 'Is Political biography a good thing?', *Contemporary British History*, 10 (4), (1996): 60–6 and John Derry, 'Political Biography: A Defence (2)', *Contemporary British History*, 10 (4), (1996): 75–80.

6   David Nasaw, 'Historians and Biography', *American Historical Review*, 114 (3), (2009): 573–8.

7   Chris Ealham and Michael Richards, 'History, Memory and the Spanish Civil War', in Chris Ealham and Michael Richards, (eds), *The Splintering of Spain. Cultural History and the Spanish Civil War, 1936–1939* (Cambridge: Cambridge University Press, 2005), p. 13.

8   Lucy Riall, 'The Shallow End of History? The Substance and Future of Political Biography', *Journal of Interdisciplinary History*, 40 (3), (2010): 375–97.

9   Paul Preston, 'Alfonsist monarchism and the coming of the Spanish Civil War', in Martin Blinkhorn, ed., *Spain in Conflict 1931–1939. Democracy and Its Enemies* (London: SAGE, 1986), pp. 160–82; Gonzalo Álvarez Chillida, *José María Pemán. Pensamiento y trayectoria de un monárquico* (Cádiz: Servicio de Publicaciones de la Universidad de Cádiz, 1996); Alejandro Quiroga, *Los orígenes del nacionalcatolicismo. José Pemartín y la Dictadura de Primo de Rivera* (Granada: Comares, 2006).

10 For the fascistization of some sectors of the Spanish right in the 1920s, see Alejandro Quiroga, *Making Spaniards. Primo de Rivera and the Nationalization of the Masses (1923–1930)* (Basingstoke: Palgrave-Macmillan, 2007). For the process of fascistization and its limits in the 1930s, see Eduardo González Calleja, 'La violencia y sus discursos. Los límites de la "fascistización" de la derecha en la II República', *Ayer*, 71 (2008): 85–116. For the fascistization of Francoism, see Francisco Cobo Romero, 'Franquismo y los imaginarios míticos del fascismo europea de entreguerras', *Ayer*, 71 (2008): 117–51.

11 Martin Blinkhorn, 'Introduction. Allies, rivals, or antagonist? Fascist and conservatives in modern Europe', in Martin Blinkhorn, ed., *Fascist and*

Conservatives. The Radical Right and the establishment in twentieth-century Europe (London: Unwin Hyman, 1990), pp. 1–14; Aristotle Kallis, '"Fascism", "Para-fascism" and "Fascistization": On the Similarities of Three Conceptual Categories', *European History Quarterly*, 33 (2), (2003): 219–50.

12 Arnd Bauerkämper, 'Transnational Fascism: Cross-border Relations between Regimes and Movements in Europe, 1922–1939', *East Central Europe*, 37 (2010): 214–46; idem, 'Interwar Fascism in Europe and Beyond: Toward a Transnational Radical Right', in Martin Durham and Margaret Power, (eds), *New Perspectives on the Transnational Right* (Basingstoke: Palgrave Macmillan, 2010), pp. 39–65; Markku Ruotsila, 'International Anti-Communism before the Cold War: Success and Failure in the Building of a Transnational Right', in Martin Durham and Margaret Power, (eds), *New Perspectives on the Transnational Right* (Basingstoke: Palgrave Macmillan, 2010), pp. 11–37.

13 See the interpretation of Italian fascism as a political religion in Emilio Gentile, *The Sacralization of Politics in Fascist Italy* (Cambridge, Massachusetts, & London: Harvard University Press, 1996). The concept of political religion is also used in Michael Burleigh, *The Third Reich. A New History* (Londres: Macmillan, 2000). The relationship between fascism and religion has been hotly debated by academics. See, for example, Richard Steigmann-Gall, *The Holy Reich. Nazi Conceptions of Christianity, 1919–1945* (Cambridge: Cambridge University Press, 2003); Roger Eatwell, 'Reflections on Fascism and Religion', *Totalitarian Movements and Political Religions*, 4 (3), (2003): 145–66; Emilio Gentile, 'Fascism, totalitarianism and political religion: definitions and critical reflections on criticism of an interpretation', *Totalitarian Movements and Political Religions*, 5 (3), (2004): 326–75; Hans Maier, ed., *Totalitarianism and Political Religions, Volume 1: Concepts for the Comparison of Dictatorships* (London: Routledge, 2004); Roger Griffin, ed., *Fascism, Totalitarianism and Political Religion* (New York: Routledge, 2005); Hans Maier, 'Political Religion: a Concept and its Limitations', *Totalitarian Movements and Political Religions*, 8 (1), (2007): 5–16. See also the special issue on clerical fascism edited by Matthew Feldmann and Marius Turda, *Totalitarian Movements and Political Religions*, 8 (2) (2007).

14 Francisco Sevillano Calero, *Rojos: La representación del enemigo en la Guerra Civil* (Madrid: Alianza, 2007).

15 Michael Richards, *A time of silence*.

16 Miguel Primo de Rivera, *El pensamiento de Primo de Rivera. Sus notas, artículos y discursos* (Madrid: Sáez Hermanos-Junta de Propaganda Patriótica y Ciudadana, 1929), p. 276.

17 Helen Graham and Alejandro Quiroga, 'After the fear was over? What came after dictatorships in Spain, Greece and Portugal', in *Oxford Handbook of Postwar European History* (Oxford: Oxford University Press, 2012), p. 503.

18 *ABC*, 21 November 1975.

1

Antonio Maura: From Messiah to Fireman

FRANCISCO J. ROMERO SALVADÓ

The Two Mauras

When a national government headed by Antonio Maura was established in March 1918, the Socialist Luis Araquistáin wrote an editorial in the prestigious journal *España* entitled 'The two Mauras'. After years of being the main target of left-wing opprobrium as the symbol of clerical reaction, Maura was now described totally differently. He was someone with a previously unknown side; that of a liberal politician who had just saved Spain from the threat of dictatorship.[1]

Amongst a governing elite of mediocre politicians happy with the status quo, Maura stood out as one of the most influential, versatile and polemic statesman of the Restoration era. Neither the demon made out by his political enemies, nor the Messiah worshipped (and often misunderstood) by his followers, Maura was much more complex:[2] authoritarian in style but utterly liberal in ideology; a lucid leader often isolated by his messianic arrogance, scathing speech and dismissive manners; a devout Catholic but not a zealot; a principled politician in an era of compromise; and a profound monarchist who was systematically scorned by a young king who resented having to deal with someone not prepared to act as the traditional court lackey.

Such was Maura's impact in the early twentieth century that the Republican rabble-rouser Alejandro Lerroux noted in 1910 that `Spanish politics largely consisted of being for or against Maura.'[3] In 1913, however, he had become almost a political pariah. By 1918, still silently respected by the entire monarchist political spectrum, the hitherto Conservative Messiah had to fill a new post; that of 'fireman' or last bulwark of an ailing Liberal regime.[4]

The Conservative Messiah who came from the Liberal Party

In October 1909, Alfonso XIII accepted a resignation that Maura had never tendered. His son Gabriel wrote that that day he saw his father in tears for the first time.[5] Maura's fall from power marked the end of a meteoric rise that had begun in 1881 when he was first returned as Liberal deputy for his native Mallorca.

'To dignify political habits', 'to foster citizenship' and, above all, 'Revolution from above' were mottos espoused by Antonio Maura. They were anathema to a governing class that since the Bourbon Restoration in December 1874 had seemingly found the holy grail of systematically sharing power and its subsequent spoils of office in the rotation (*turno pacífico*) of two dynastic

Figure 1.1 Maura's speech in Baranga (Cantabria), 10 September 1916.

parties, Conservatives and Liberals, manned by notables and starved of genuine grass-roots support.[6]

Following the colonial disaster of 1898 and the loss of the remnants of the once largest colonial empire, blame was above all directed at the incompetent governing 'oligarchy'. As the regime widely came to be seen as an impediment to modernization, Spain's cultural elite led the call for *Regeneración*, or the rebuilding of the country in order to restore its prestige.[7]

Regeneración turned out to be a chimera: a catch-all term even lukewarmly embraced by the governing oligarchy since it ultimately meant little more than a few cosmetic patches so as to carry on with business as usual. There were, nevertheless, some important exceptions. Francisco Silvela, who took charge of the Conservative party after the murder of its founder Antonio Cánovas del Castillo in 1897, made the cleansing of the political system one of his main objectives. His counterpart in the Liberal party and eventual successor as Conservative leader was Antonio Maura.

Having initially travelled to Madrid intending to become a science teacher, Maura ended up studying law. He entered politics with the help of one of the Liberal leaders, Germán Gamazo, whose sister he had married. In a party where anticlericalism (in rhetoric more often than in practice) and free trade were key components, the protectionism and Catholicism espoused by the Gamazo's faction led to its increasing alienation within the party. Maura's own disenchantment grew when, as Minister for Colonial Affairs in 1893, he sought to introduce a comprehensive programme of decentralization for Cuba. Whether Maura's plans might have been too little and too late to stop the outbreak of the revolt in that Caribbean island is arguable. Nevertheless, they were the first attempt to tackle the scandalous state of Spain's colonial administration and yet were utterly rejected as 'anti-patriotic' not just by the Conservative opposition but also by his own party.[8]

Following the death of Gamazo in 1901, Maura took the remnants of the latter's faction into a Conservative party that, headed by Silvela, appeared more in tune with his calls for national regeneration. In July of that year, he warned in parliament that unless a revolution was carried out from above, a more formidable challenge would come from below.[9] Maura's particular brand of regeneration was, however, ultimately deeply flawed. Anchored still in nineteenth-century liberal philosophy, his democratic leanings were more than matched by his 'fear of the masses'. Thus there was relatively little time in his programme for the social question.[10] Instead, his 'revolution from above' was mostly a call to mobilize sectors of the Catholic middle classes who were glaringly disconnected with politics.[11] His projects never envisaged a radical transformation of the existing socio-economic foundations. Furthermore, they were based on the naïve belief that once the pertinent administrative and political reforms had been introduced, the so-called *masas neutras* (the many

Spaniards alienated from the political process) would be naturally inclined to rally around the monarchy and the social order. In reality, all dynastic politicians, even Maura for all his rhetoric, found it difficult to swim in the sea of mass politics. They were aware that genuine democracy was a dangerous path that threatened to end their political hegemony.[12] Hence Maura's attempts to tinker with the status quo alienated him from a governing class, including the bulk of his own party, reluctant to imperil its monopoly of power.[13]

Ultimately, the political class had to contend with a monarchy that had immense leverage in the running of the country. Crowned in 1902 in the shadow of the colonial disaster of 1898, Alfonso XIII showed impatience with his politicians and often used his executive prerogatives to appoint and dismiss cabinets (these crises were known as 'orientales', as they were produced at the Palacio de Oriente, the royal residence). Eager to restore Spain's prestige, he identified readily with the army corps and was fully behind a new imperialist affair in Morocco.[14]

In fact, the relationship between the king and Antonio Maura, whose strong personality made him much more difficult to manipulate than others, was fraught with tension. Ángel Ossorio, one of the closest of Maura's collaborators, wrote: 'the king regarded him with profound respect and with unrepressed antipathy'.[15] Notwithstanding his many bitter experiences with the king, described by Gabriel Maura as 'petulancias augustas' ('royal whims'),[16] Maura's political career, nevertheless, was always marked by profound monarchism.

Indeed, royal disfavour was blatantly displayed from the beginning. Having joined a Silvela administration in December 1902 as Minister of the Interior, Maura supervised one of the cleanest elections to date. The result was a significant return of Republicans deputies, despair in the palace and the fall of a government accused of leaving the crown defenceless. Soon thereafter a weary Silvela abandoned politics and thrust Maura as his chosen successor into leading the Conservative party.[17] One year later, Maura's first experience as Prime Minister was cut short by a new crisis oriental: Alfonso's opposition to the government's suggestion for the role of Chief of the General Staff. In reality, the young monarch's real resentment was at Maura's criticism of his roaring displays of audacity in his new sports car.[18]

Back in power in January 1907, Maura enjoyed a longer spell in office. This was the moment in which he sought to carry out his programme: the uprooting of the caciquista foundations of politics and the fostering of national consciousness and citizenship. It basically consisted of a thorough reform of the electoral law, the system of justice and above all the local administration, the stronghold of the cacique.[19] A crooked suffrage was the price paid for the 'ulterior good' of ensuring the passing of reforms through an overwhelming parliamentary majority. Thus, Maura relied on the services of Juan de la Cierva, a stereotypical heavy-handed *cacique* that he professed to loath, to supervise the elections through the usual chicanery. Maura achieved in the short term the huge majority (253 deputies) he sought. However, it led to a close relationship with Cierva, who was to become the albatross around his neck for most of his career.[20]

This administration was unprecedented in terms of the intensity of parliamentary work. However, Maura's emphasis on *luz y taquígrafos*, or the transparency of the process, and calls for all minorities to participate in this national enterprise did not pay off. His arrogant style and sharp tongue earned him powerful enemies. The result was the frustrating collapse of the bulk of his proposals. After nearly three years of debate, his bill for local administration never left the chamber and ironically, his attempts to reform the electoral law only reinforced the power of the *cacique* as one of the few clauses passed was the so-called Article 29 that allowed for the automatic election of a candidate in the absence of rivals.[21]

Maura's downfall (as indeed that of the Restoration regime) was brought about by dynastic intrigues combined with the social powder keg that was Barcelona and the poisonous effect of the colonial misadventure in Morocco. His attempts to introduce a corporate franchise in local elections and administrative decentralization sought to broaden the appeal of the monarchy. This process initiated a fruitful collaboration with the Catalan social-conservatives of the *Lliga Regionalista* but enraged the Liberals. After all, the shake-up of the foundations of the system offered the Conservatives the possibility of becoming a modern party based on the mobilization of the Catholic middle classes, but the Liberals could hardly aspire to lure the urban petty bourgeoisie and the working classes from republicanism, socialism or anarchism with their programme of timid social reforms and anticlericalism. Therefore they opted for stopping Maura's revolution from above by joining forces with the revolution from below.[22]

Maura's strong emphasis in his programme on fighting political subversion paved the way for the collaboration between Liberals and the anti-dynastic left. It also confirmed the profound divisions in political society between those who perceived the Conservative leader as the epitome of tyranny and those who regarded him almost as deity.[23] Indeed, Cierva's introduction of a tough Bill for the Repression of Terrorism caused massive uproar and was finally scrapped.[24] Yet it was the excuse the Liberal party needed to break the rules of dynastic collaboration and join in platforms and rallies as part of the so-called Leftist Bloc (*Bloque de Izquierdas*). The campaign to dislodge Maura from office ('¡Maura No!') had begun in earnest. This objective was finally accomplished due to an unexpected factor – Morocco.

Maura had accepted the international compromises that in 1904 and 1907 granted Spain control of a small strip of land in northern Morocco but always made clear his aversion to undertake any policy of military conquest. To his chagrin, in 1909 he had to face an upsurge of unrest that actually initiated the sinking of Spain into the Moroccan quagmire. As Prime Minister, he was ultimately responsible for decisions which were actually not personally taken by him. The War Minister, General Arsenio Linares, perceiving the deterioration of the situation, called for reinforcements that included many reservists. They belonged to the lower classes that did not have the 1,500-peseta fee necessary for exemption from conscription. As news of rising casualties began to filter back and with the dreadful memories of 1898 still fresh, protests against the war began in earnest. The clash between the heavy-handed Cierva and the more moderate Civil Governor of Barcelona, Ángel Ossorio, resulted in a power vacuum when a general strike broke out in that city on 26 July 1909.[25] A largely spontaneous antiwar protest became a week of riots (`Tragic Week'), barricade fighting, church burning and even macabre scenes such as the exhuming of nuns' corpses. It was followed by heavy army repression, hundreds of arrests, the establishment of military courts and the execution of five people, including the anarchist director of *La Escuela Moderna*, Francisco Ferrer Guardia. Condemned largely by his anarchist record, the belief that he had been the mastermind behind the bombing which had caused massive mayhem on the day of Alfonso XIII's wedding and the deposition of some Republicans eager to pass the blame onto someone else, Ferrer became the easy scapegoat for the entire insurrection.[26]

As an international campaign in the main European capitals resurrected the myth of a repressive clerical Spain, the Liberals finally saw a chink in the armour of the administration. These were the same Liberals that in the person of their leader, Segismundo Moret, when consulted about granting Ferrer a reprieve, claimed that to do so was 'to renounce the attributes of virility'.[27] Amidst an atmosphere of confrontation, the Cortes opened in October where Cierva's intervention further exacerbated animosities.[28] In a genuine democratic system, Maura's position with a large majority was safe. However, these were neither normal times nor was Spain a real democracy. The king, who recently had promised his total support, accepted a resignation that Maura never submitted. As the historian Joaquín Romero Maura noted, 'By supporting the Liberal veto, Don Alfonso bought civil peace and stopped political modernization.'[29]

A Messiah in the Wilderness

Maura's downfall in October 1909 not only initiated his political alienation and eventual ostracism four years later but also put an end to any serious debate

Figure 1.2 Maura with his wife, Constancia Gamazo, with the King and Queen of Spain.

on the issue of *caciquismo* and eventually led to the triumph within the Conservative ranks of those averse to any kind of political revisionism.[30] These were four years of bitterness characterized by a puzzling contradictory stance. Maura mercilessly attacked the Liberal party, describing their activities to depose him as having descended 'into the sewer' (*'la turbina a la cloaca'*).[31] Nevertheless, he refused point-blank to participate in a bloc with the extreme right-wing parties (Carlists and other Catholic fundamentalists) to fight the Liberal government with the same ferocity as he had faced from the Leftist Bloc.[32]

In January 1912, Maura referred contemptuously to the Liberals' rule as an 'ongoing saga of trickery' (*'ciclo de golfería andariega'*).[33] In fact, once in office, the Liberals' stance appeared to validate Maura's cynicism about their real motives for their previous fierce opposition to his government. Segismundo Moret, who thought he was doing the monarch a favour by helping him get rid of Maura, was himself, in February 1910, the victim of a plot hatched between party barons and the king.[34] Having re-established cordial relations with Maura, a few months before his death, in January 1913, Moret met the Conservative leader who confided to him that 'neither of us will ever regain power again. In your case, because the king does not want you, while in mine, because he does not trust me.'[35] This prediction was proved wrong.

Moret's successor, José Canalejas, failed to heed Maura's advice and instead endorsed the king's interventionist plans in Portugal following the ousting of the Braganza dynasty and dramatically increased military activities in Morocco.[36] Furthermore, despite his programme of timid social and anticlerical legislation, Canalejas failed to achieve social peace. Instead, faced with a wave of industrial action, he resorted to traditional methods of suspension of constitutional guarantees and closing of workers' centres. Ironically, while Maura lectured in Congress on the right to strike, Canalejas was ordering the conscription of workers during a massive railway dispute in 1912.[37]

The target of so much vitriolic hatred, Maura survived two attempts on his life.[38] Canalejas, however, was shot dead by a lone anarchist in November 1912. Maura was certain that the Liberal Prime Minister's tragic death meant his return to power. Enraged that after a brief squabbling amongst the Liberal barons, the king had offered power to Count Romanones, Maura decided, as Silvela had ten years before, to abandon political life. Consequently, he wrote a scathing note confirming that the Conservatives could no longer rotate in office with the existing Liberal party. The *turno* could only be recreated if one of the two dynastic parties evolved into a new *idóneo* (suitable) force to alternate with the other. Simultaneously, he announced, on 1 January 1913, his intention to resign as leader of the party and even to quit his parliamentary seat.[39] An avalanche of support from fellow Conservatives dissuaded him from taking that step.

The Conservative leader became victim in 1913 of his own inflexibility combined with political intrigue. Bending to his demands meant that the Liberals, and indirectly the monarch, had to disown their behaviour in 1909. Rumours circulated from the royal palace that the king was fed up with Maura's haughtiness.[40] Maura's error was to believe that his party was different to the Liberals. With his Cabinet on the verge of collapse, Romanones dreaded his replacement by a new government led by a rival Liberal baron who could then challenge his leadership of the party. On 26 October 1913, the day after Romanones' fall, Maura realized his isolation. Behind his back, Eduardo Dato, a former minister known for his compromising attitude, had agreed to lead an *idóneo* party. As the historian Fernández Almagro wrote, 'Walking on tiptoe, Dato was going far; Maura walking firmly was on his way to [political] exile.'[41]

The Year 1917: The Great Opportunity

The establishment of the Dato administration triggered off a genuine grass-root mobilization that heralded the birth of right-wing mass politics in Spain.

Mostly young middle-class students and white-collar workers heeded Ángel Ossorio's calls to rally around the vilified Maura. Taking the name of their admired leader and ready to rival the left in the streets, the *Maurismo Callejero* was born.[42] Given their position on the margins of the regime, the *Mauristas'* electoral results were encouraging but not a serious challenge to the main dynastic factions.[43] Furthermore, *Maurismo* always remained a broad umbrella of Catholics and Conservatives who adhered fervently to Maura's 'Revolution from Above' but interpreted it in different ways. A minority like Ossorio espoused social-reformist and Christian-democratic ideas. Others, like the leader of the *Maurista* Youth, Antonio Goicoechea, and the editor of the *Maurista* organ, *La Acción,* Manuel Delgado Barreto, increasingly adopted nationalist and anti-liberal principles.[44] The fate of *Maurismo* was ultimately crippled by the attitude of Maura himself.

With the country rocked to its foundations by the impact of the First World War, Maura adopted an attitude of aloofness. He had great influence over the *Mauristas* but never was nor wanted to be their *Caudillo.*[45] A despairing Ossorio, who tried on numerous occasions and always failed to persuade Maura to give *Maurismo* a real leadership, wrote: 'What shall we do? ... You [Maura] must not leave millions of youngsters who look up to you without direction.'[46]

In fact, the First World War proved a catalyst for rapid socio-economic transformation and mass mobilization; a process that undermined the basis of traditional liberal states. Spain, in particular, experienced an economic boom due to its ability to supply both camps as well as move into markets that the warring nations had vacated. Unfortunately, the other side of the coin was widespread social distress due to shortages and galloping inflation.[47] The war also produced polarization around the neutrality question. In general, right-wing forces including the *Mauristas* were Germanophiles. They identified the Central Powers with traditional values such as monarchism and authority, while the left were Francophiles since they considered a triumph for the Allies a victory for democracy and secularism.[48]

Maura finally consented to abandon his semi-retirement in order to speak at three conferences organized by the *Mauristas*: at the Royal Theatre in Madrid (21 April 1915), Berlanga in Santander (20 September 1916) and Madrid's Bullring (29 April 1917). In general, his three speeches contained a mixture of his typical verbose and condescending rhetoric with significant doses of hostility towards the ruling system.[49] With regard to foreign policy, Maura's message was disappointing for most *Mauristas*. Having applauded Dato's position of official neutrality,[50] he engaged in a curious balancing act. Although carefully tuned for his overwhelmingly Germanophile audience, Maura still came across as supportive of neutrality; but of a type of neutrality in which Spain, due to its cultural, economic and natural affinities, had to move closer to the Western powers and, thereby, widely divergent from the leanings of most of his supporters. The journal *España* even suggested that the *Mauristas* soon would be subscribing to 'Maura No!'.[51] A pleased British ambassador, Arthur Hardinge, noted that Maura's only deviations from his overall pro-Allied message were basically attempts at playing to the gallery since his natural supporters were obviously depressed by what they heard.[52]

In the field of domestic policy, Maura's speeches showed no evolution from his traditional rhetoric: the need for citizen's mobilization and the regeneration of politics. Of course, he obtained the loudest cheers when denouncing the existing politics of nepotism which had miserably failed to connect with public opinion. It sounded as if Maura had not recently been the leader of one of the dynastic parties. His lambasting of a political system that had refused his prescription resembled the diatribes of a preacher who knows he has already lost the spotlight. Events were, however, to offer him a last chance to conduct Spain's political renovation.

The unmitigated social havoc triggered by the war resulted in the two bitterly rival labour organizations – the socialist *Unión General de Trabajadores* (UGT) and the anarcho-syndicalist *Confederación Nacional del Trabajo* (CNT) – sealing a historic pact in Zaragoza in July 1916 to coordinate their activities.[53] Crippling inflation and shortages not only hit the working classes but also savaged the hitherto fairly secure living standards for those working in the public sector including the armed forces. Consequently, from 1916, anxious army officers up to the rank of colonel began to join *Juntas Militares de Defensa*, a kind of military trade union that sought to defend the collective interests of the corps. All hell broke loose when, terrified by recent events in Russia, the government, under pressure from King Alfonso XIII, ordered the dissolution of the *Juntas*. The officers' insubordination, in June 1917, provoked the collapse of the Cabinet then headed by the Liberal Marquis of Alhucemas and effectively set off a chain of revolutionary events.[54]

In June 1917, the belief that the regime was in its death throes appeared borne out by the constant assertions in the *Juntas*' mouthpiece, *La Correspondencia Militar*, that the governing oligarchy was leading Spain to moral and economic ruin and called for new men and new political methods.[55] Amidst the reigning chaos, the Catalan Regionalists emerged as the leading force marshalling the opposition by calling for thorough renovation and summoning a parliament or assembly to gather in Barcelona on 19 July in order to initiate that process. This initiative was quickly welcomed and supported by republicans and socialists.[56]

Maura was suddenly catapulted into the spotlight. It was commented that the old statesman was so sure of returning to office that he had even drawn up his list of ministers. On learning that the king had instead chosen to recall Dato to power, Maura wrote to the monarch asking to be freed from all future responsibilities. The country was asking for a complete change he said but, unfortunately, those who were to blame for the national collapse had received the vote of confidence.[57] The *Mauristas* orchestrated vociferous demonstrations outside the royal palace.[58] According to Gabriel Maura, a good deal of the right in June 1917 would have been prepared, if necessary, to follow his father against the king.[59]

Both *Juntas* and *Lliga* turned to Maura for support. Neophytes in the world of politics, the army officers respected and sought guidance from the veteran Conservative statesman. A Catalan *Maurista*, Gustavo Peyrá, acted as go-between with the central *Junta* in Barcelona and encouraged his leader to seize office with the backing of the officers who 'were neither rebels nor anti-monarchists, [but] just loathed the governing oligarchy as much as the *Mauristas*'.[60] At the same time, other leading *Mauristas*, such as Ángel Ossorio and the Catalan Joaquín María Nadal, were eager to take part in the Assembly that they regarded as a similar initiative to the revolution from above preached by Maura. In addition, Cambó wrote to Gabriel Maura asking his intercession with his father to persuade him to join forces with the Assembly. He was aware that without Maura's involvement, the Assembly would be depicted as a project masterminded by separatists and left-wing revolutionaries and hence unlikely to win any sympathies in military barracks.[61]

At this crucial juncture, Maura epitomized the greatest contradiction of Restoration politics: even though he saw the need for political reform, he was unwilling to sanction it. His nonchalant attitude not only paralysed his followers but also sabotaged his remaining hopes of presiding over a revolution from above. He could have become the vital link between parliamentarians and officers against the governing oligarchy. Yet, notwithstanding the constant prompting by his followers, including the requests of his sons Gabriel and Miguel,[62] Maura's legalism proved far stronger than his criticism of the ruling order.

A firm believer in the supremacy of civil power, he described the *Juntas* as an '*engendro monstruoso de añeja depravación*' ('monstrous freak of ancient depravity') and even refused to receive a messenger from Barcelona, leaving him waiting in heavy rain.[63] Maura wrote to Peyrá stressing that he was averse to receive power other than through the legal channels.[64] Equally, he was adamant against lending his support to an initiative, the Assembly, which he compared with a '*zoco profesional*' ('professional flea market'). As he explained to Ossorio, it was a 'subversive road for which he did not have the vocation'.[65] He stuck to that position even when, after the gathering of deputies in Barcelona, Ossorio insisted that the Assembly had been a success and was the best solution for the future. The other two alternatives were a Maura administration or a revolution. The first was not forthcoming and the second was becoming more desirable each day.[66] Maura simply replied that he would not participate in an initiative that could endanger the throne. However, if the Assembly was indeed seeking the same objectives he had preached for years, he had no objections to standing aside.[67]

Maura's passive stance helped the government to regain the initiative. In late July, the Dato administration took advantage of the outbreak of a violent transport dispute in Valencia to provoke the labour movement into launching a revolutionary strike. The plan was to scare the middle classes and to push the army towards crushing the disturbances.[68] This cunning plot paid off in the short term. Encouraged by the recent fall of Tsarism in Russia, the socialists accepted the gauntlet and on 13 August, they staged a general strike.[69] As the government expected, the military put down the revolution. However, Dato's strategy ultimately backfired. Unleashing the might of the army against the workers opened a Pandora's box that could not be closed again.

During the turbulent month of October, the gap between Maura and some of his hard-line followers widened. The veteran leader, in a clear display of liberal values, published a note, on 21 October, forewarning of the dangers of capitulation before the *Juntas* and accusing the government of refusing to seek genuine popular backing and associating the crown with vile factional interests.[70] By contrast, *La Acción*, kept urging the army to overthrow the governing oligarchy. On 26 October, it called for a miracle. It ran a cartoon of a huge broom sweeping away the main dynastic politicians. However, as Gustavo Peyrá described it the next morning, it was not divine intervention but the 'bayonets speaking'. The army submitted a message to the monarch demanding the removal of the existing administration. In return, it guaranteed the dissolution (by force, if necessary) of any new parliament that challenged the dynasty.[71]

The Liberal Monarchy's Fireman

With both Liberals and Conservatives thrown out of office in the space of a few months, constitutional politics was in disarray. The Liberal regime survived in 1917 but the political interference of the officer corps struck an ominous note for the future. After eight days of political vacuum, the solution was the establishment of a monarchist coalition led by Alhucemas that included Juan de la Cierva as War Minister. He had accepted what Maura refused: to be the *Juntas'* political voice.[72]

By March 1918, Cierva had brought the coalition to the verge of collapse. Without consultation, he had sought to introduce by decree a Bill of Military Reforms designed to please the *Juntas*. Simultaneously, alleging that he was saving Spain from the Soviet threat, he ordered the militarization of the postal and telegraph services whose staff had gone on strike.[73] Rumours spread about the *Juntas* planning to back a Cierva administration. *El Socialista* described the situation as 'Living under the Sword'.[74]

However, on 21 March, jubilant crowds gathered outside the royal palace and for once even the left-wing journals cheered at the news of the establishment of a national Cabinet headed by Antonio Maura that included all the

Figure 1.3 Antonio Maura in his Madrid office.

dynastic leaders and even Cambó at Public Works.[75] Suddenly hailed by those who had denigrated him a few years earlier, a sceptical Maura confided to Gabriel that he did not believe this charade (*monserga*) could last.[76] He was not entirely wrong.

Given the outstanding profile of its members, the record of the national government was very poor: settlement of the conflict with the bureaucracy (something easy with Cierva out of the way); the introduction of the *guillotina* (or time limit) in parliamentary debates; a revamped military reforms bill; a general amnesty for the events of the previous August; and very little else. For all their supposed authority, the government had feet of clay. In the crucial field of foreign policy, as German submarine attacks on Spanish vessels reached alarming proportions, Maura noted that Spain's dignity was at stake and informed Dato (his Foreign Minister) that a drastic resolution was needed without further delay.[77] The Cabinet ran into the royal and military veto.[78]

It was not, however, the shambles of foreign policy but internal bickering that brought down the administration. As soon as the imminent praetorian threat seemed overcome, the glue that held the Cabinet together began to become unstuck. By early November, amidst extraordinary wrangling amongst fellow ministers, the government simply dissolved.[79] Maura chuckled: 'let us see the smart guy who takes power now'![80] Little did he know that dramatic circumstances were soon to recall him to office. Nevertheless, as in 1918, he was no longer a natural-born Messiah in a quest to regenerate the system but a fireman on call to save the regime from its final implosion.

In April 1919, civil sovereignty was again in the gutter. One month earlier, faced with food riots in several capitals and massive upheaval in the southern countryside, a Romanones Liberal administration had conceded defeat in a massive industrial dispute conducted by the CNT in Barcelona's key Anglo-Canadian hydroelectric concern, *La Canadiense*.[81] For sectors of the ruling classes, particularly in Catalonia, Bolshevism was knocking at the doors facilitated by the capitulation of the government.[82] As Conservative newspapers, including *La Acción*, began to argue that only a dictatorship could save the country, the incensed Catalan industrialists found a willing ally in the local garrison led by Captain General Joaquín Milans del Bosch.[83] A vicious conflict resumed in earnest in Barcelona when the military refused to free the militants still held from the *Canadiense* episode. In April, infuriated by the conciliatory strategy pursued by the local authorities, the army 'invited' the Civil Governor and the Chief of Police to catch the train to Madrid. Romanones resigned and suggested the king recall Maura to office as the best hope to appease the military-led reaction.[84]

Maura rightly stressed that he had not sought, let alone manoeuvred, his return to office but had only accepted in order to consolidate civil sovereignty endangered by circumstances which had caused the collapse of the previous government.[85] However, he paid too high a price for his success in 'normalizing' the situation: his government embodied a dramatic shift to the right that, as in 1909, rallied the whole political spectrum against him.

Diehard industrialists hailed the return of Maura to power. In a private letter, the President of the *Fomento del Trabajo Nacional*, Jaume Cussó, even called it 'a ray of light on the horizon'.[86] The government did not let them down. Despite containing the `reformist' Ossorio at Public Works, the Cabinet was dominated by hard-liners such as Goicoechea at Interior and Cierva at the Treasury. Emergency measures such as the continuity of martial law in Barcelona and the suspension of constitutional guarantees remained in place. Also, General Manuel Barrera was sent to put an end to southern rural disturbances at the head of an army of 20,000 troops.[87] Emphasis on authority went hand-in-hand with arch-clerical extravaganzas such as the consecration of Spain to the Holy Heart of Christ presided over by the king and attended by over 12,000 people at the *Cerro de los Ángeles* in Getafe (Madrid).[88]

Socialists and Republicans regarded this Cabinet, not surprisingly, as the epitome of all-out reaction.[89] The Liberals were initially delighted to pass temporarily the onerous task of governing in such dreadful circumstances but changed tack when the king granted a decree of dissolution of parliament to Maura on 3 May. Presiding over an electoral process with constitutional guarantees suspended lost Maura much of his political prestige.[90] *Mauristas* and *Ciervistas* doubled their representation to some 104 seats together but this was the first time in Restoration Spain that a government lost the elections.[91] The government was dependent on the support initially promised by the Conservatives. But despite widespread calls for the collaboration of all right-wing tendencies under the umbrella of `forces of order', this was not forthcoming. When, on 15 July, the government, twice in a row, lost the vote over a disputed seat due to Conservative abstention, Maura merely tendered his resignation and was replaced by a Conservative government led by Joaquín Sánchez de Toca.

The governmental experience of 1919 widened the disparities within *Maurismo* and of that movement with its leader. Many of his hard-line followers, headed by Goicoechea, increasingly rejected the constitutional route to power and eventually the movement split when its Christian-democratic wing led by Ossorio departed in December 1922.[92] In turn, Maura returned to his contemplative state. Full of gloom and frustration, he pondered in his private notes about the 'betrayal of 1909'. The result had been the present state of affairs in which governments, bereft of any glimmer of popular backing, only sought to satisfy their factional interests. According to him, the dire situation could only be solved by broad coalitions of the type of 1918 in which politicians could work together above petty party disciplines. Still, he insisted that he wanted henceforth to abide by a position of 'hygienic abstention' and would not be requisitioned a third time to lead a government.[93]

Maura was mistaken. By 1920, Spain was rocked by a dramatic surge in social violence. The cycle of terror helped the Catalan employers to persuade the then Prime Minister Dato to appoint in November the hard-line General Severiano Martínez Anido to the post of Civil Governor of Barcelona. The CNT suffered an unprecedented onslaught: its militants were arrested, its centres closed and many of its activists murdered under the infamous *Ley de Fugas* – the shooting of prisoners while they were allegedly trying to escape. Anarchist groups retaliated in kind and accomplished the spectacular assassination, on 8 March 1921, of Eduardo Dato.

It was not the spiral of social violence but a different catastrophe that catapulted Maura back to power in 1921. Dato's murder shocked Spain's political spectrum but the expectations of a new Maura Cabinet (and even of his heading a reunited Conservative party) were foiled by the main Conservative barons. Instead, they backed a government under the *Maurista* Manuel Allendesalazar with Cierva at Public Works and rallied around the leadership of José Sánchez Guerra.[94] In July, the Spanish people awoke to devastating news from the half-forgotten Moroccan adventure: the advancing Spanish army had been defeated at Annual. The hasty retreat turned into a rout. Some 9,000 soldiers were killed and hundreds captured. In a few days, all the territory conquered since 1909 was lost. As in recent years, Maura became the man to save the nation at its moment of gravest danger.[95]

Dreading a replay of 1909, Maura was initially sceptical about the national response: 'Confidence? God be with us!', he wrote.[96] On 13 August 1921, he formed a new national government with representatives from the dynastic spectrum including heavyweights such as the *Romanonista* Manuel González Hontoria at the Foreign Office, Juan de la Cierva at the War Department and Francesc Cambó – the person who, above all, Maura felt he needed as his deputy – at the Treasury.[97]

At least in the short term, not only the political class (including some Republicans) but also the nation at large rallied behind his administration. Spurred on by the catalytic role of the crisis, the national government undertook a comprehensive number of crucial reforms. In particular, Cambó, with Maura's full backing, introduced a vast package of economic projects: he issued new public debt bonds to finance the burdensome cost of the war (the first on 4 November 1921 was covered in less than 24 hours), reorganized the banking system, instituted a new commercial tariff and sought (though ultimately failed) to reform the tax structure in a more progressive manner.[98] Nevertheless, the government devoted most of its energies to Morocco and regained in the process some prestige for the mauled governing class.

By portraying the Moroccan campaign as a necessary campaign of revenge together `with the decision to mobilize all reservists' (including the *soldados de cuota*),[99] a genuine collective effort was created. Soldiers were sent off amidst enthusiastic displays of patriotism while all over the country subscriptions, raffles and lotteries were organized to raise money for the troops.[100] A veteran of former colonial campaigns, General Juan Picasso, was given the task to investigate the causes of the debacle. On 20 October, Maura reconvened parliament.[101] Banking on widespread support, the government even took on the *Juntas*, refusing to remain in office until they had been subjected to the strict control of the Ministry of War. With much hesitation, the king finally sanctioned that initiative (16 January 1922). It represented a momentary strengthening of civil power vis-à-vis the army.[102]

The Last Services of a Frustrated Fireman

The ever-sceptical Maura wrote: 'let us see how long the wedding cake lasts'.[103] It lasted until the military objectives pursued by the counteroffensive initiated in September 1921 were completed. As in 1918, once the immediate danger had passed and the territory lost in the previous summer recovered, the government began to crumble.

By February 1922, ministerial disagreements about how to proceed next in Morocco were glaring. The vehement Cierva, supported by sectors of the army, believed that the military offensive should continue until the total conquest of the Protectorate. By contrast, Maura was – neither in 1909 nor now – a stalwart supporter of a protracted military operation. In his own words, he was against an unproductive 'peregrination' through Morocco. He agreed with his Foreign Minister Hontoria that Spain should consolidate its position on the coast and from there exert its political influence on the hinterland. Given his control of the purse, Cambó insisted that the country could not afford to be drawn into a weary campaign maintaining an army of 150,000 men in the field.[104]

On 7 March 1922, the national government collapsed. The final blow was the Liberals' demand for the restoration of constitutional guarantees that had been suspended since March 1919. Maura confided to Cambó that the king had encouraged him to stay in power with the Catalan politician remaining as his deputy. But Maura had lost the will to remain in power.[105] He had failed again to put out the fire that was consuming the ruling system.

The two administrations that succeeded that of Maura – firstly a Conservative government led by Sánchez Guerra and then a coalition of Liberal factions headed by the Marquis of Alhucemas – succumbed before the devouring flames fuelled by the unabated social violence and the Moroccan war. Sánchez Guerra bravely attempted to restore constitutional normality. His measures of social normalization included the restoration of full constitutional guarantees (30 March 1922), the legalization of the CNT and the rejection of state-sponsored terrorism (with the removal of Martínez Anido on 24 October 1922). Coinciding with Mussolini's takeover in Italy, the editor of La Acción, Delgado Barreto, under the pseudonym of the 'Duke of G', published a series of vicious editorials in which he combined admiration for fascism with vitriolic attacks against the turno parties. In turn, the enraged Catalan employers found a willing champion in Miguel Primo de Rivera, Captain General of Barcelona since March 1922.

A detached Maura still had two more important contributions to make. First, amidst the tense discussion of the Picasso report in parliament, he unconsciously helped pulverize the Sánchez Guerra administration. On 30 November, he reminded his fellow deputies that Article 45 of the constitution indicated that the lower chamber should formulate any charges against particular individuals deemed responsible for the colonial disaster and the Senate should then act as a supreme court.[106] The following day, Cambó astonished the chamber when he declared that Maura's words had persuaded him to formally accuse the Allendesalazar government in power at the time of Annual.[107] This accusation mortally wounded the incumbent administration since three of its members had been ministers in the accused government. The final implosion came when Cierva (himself Minister of Development in the Allendesalazar Cabinet), rose to criticize with his usual passion first Maura and then Cambó, whom he accused of having used his post at the Treasury to prop up the Bank of Barcelona. As insults and threats were hurled across the benches at recent political allies, Sánchez Guerra merely ran for the exit while announcing he was resigning.[108]

Maura's second crucial intervention was a delicate enterprise. He was prompted to act after his son Gabriel informed him, in August 1923, that the king, obsessed with the Bolshevik threat and enraged by being implicated in the issue of responsibilities, had confided to him that he was toying with the idea of establishing a personal dictatorship.[109] In an attempt to dissuade the monarch from such a risky adventure, the veteran politician agreed that the existing parties were incapable of solving the grave situation but advised the king that instead of him assuming power, 'it would be less harmful that those who have imposed their will in critical situations assume the responsibility of government themselves'.[110] That is what the monarch did. Once Primo de Rivera staged his coup in Barcelona on the night of 12 September 1923, the monarch simply condoned the ousting of the constitutional order.

Like most of the governing class, Maura thought that the Dictatorship was a temporary measure. A largely misunderstood and maverick politician throughout his career, Maura had tried as no other of his dynastic counterparts to reform the system and place it on sounder foundations. Still, accepting the inevitability of a praetorian takeover was an open recognition of his failure first to regenerate the political order and then to save it in its most pressing moments. It is beyond the scope of this work to argue whether the Spanish monarchy could have gradually constructed safer and more far-embracing foundations had his political leadership not been cut short in 1909. What can be argued is that neither the ruling parties (including the bulk of his own) nor the crown were prepared to countenance risky political innovations. Despite his critical stance since 1913 and the demands of his *Maurista* followers, Maura's profound constitutional and monarchist convictions prevented him from endorsing any initiative that could endanger the supremacy of parliament and the safety of the crown. While many *Mauristas*, following the coup, joined the new political cadres of the Dictatorship, Maura's initial tolerance soon became undisguised censure. In February 1925, a few months before his death, he carried out what turned out to be his last service to the crown. Maura called it his civil and inevitable duty to warn that the persistence of the existing situation of abnormality and interference with the popular will constituted a counterproductive, inefficient and dangerous path.[111] Alfonso XIII paid a high price for not heeding Maura's final advice.

Endnotes

1 *España*, No. 155 (28 March 1918).

2 María José González Hernández, 'Neither God nor Monster': Antonio Maura and the Failure of Conservative Reformism in Restoration Spain, 1893–1923', *European History Quarterly*, Vol. 32, No. 3 (July 2002): 309.

3 Gabriel Maura and Manuel Fernández Almagro, *Por qué cayó Alfonso XIII* (Madrid: Ambos Mundos, 1948), p. 268.

4 One of his followers, Cesar Silió, coined the term 'fireman' to describe how Maura was only recalled to power in those very grave situations in which 'a fire needed to be put out'. Cited by María José González Hernandez, *Ciudadanía y Acción. El Conservadurismo Maurista, 1907–1923* (Madrid: Siglo XXI, 1990), p. 118.

5 Maura and Fernández Almagro, *Por qué cayó*, p. 155.

6 Gabriel Maura, *Recuerdos de mi vida* (Madrid: Aguilar, 1934), p. 86.

7 José Luis Abellán, *Sociología del noventa y ocho* (Madrid: Biblioteca Nueva, 1997), p. 27.

8 Rafael Pérez Delgado, *Antonio Maura* (Madrid: Tebas, 1974), pp. 410–14.

9 Maura and Fernández Almagro, *Por qué cayó*, p. 40.

10   Mercedes Cabrera, 'El Conservadurismo Maurista en la Restauración', in José Luis García Delgado, ed., *La España de la Restauración* (Madrid: Siglo XXI, 1985), p. 59.

11   González Hernandez, *Ciudadanía*, pp. 1–2.

12   Biblioteca de la Real Academia de la Historia (hereafter BRAH), *Natalio Rivas's Papers* (hereafter ANR), Leg. 8904 (29 October 1917).

13   González Hernández, *Ciudadanía*, p. 11.

14   An example of the king's early disposition to bypass his ministers is well illustrated in Count Romanones, *Notas de una vida* (Madrid: Marcial Pons, 1999), p. 161. Some very competent analyses of Alfonso's complex personality can be found in Javier Moreno Luzón, ed., *Alfonso XIII* (Madrid: Marcial Pons, 2003). For his meddling in politics and siding with the army against his politicians, see especially the chapter by Carolyn P. Boyd, 'El Rey-Soldado', pp. 216–18, 223.

15   Ángel Ossorio, *Mis Memorias* (Buenos Aires: Losada, 1948), p. 67.

16   Maura and Fernández Almagro, *Por qué cayó*, p. 47.

17   Maura, *Recuerdos*, p. 64.

18   Joaquín Romero Maura, *'La Rosa de Fuego'. El obrerismo barcelonés de 1899 a 1909* (Madrid: Alianza, 1989), pp. 382–3.

19   The most thorough analysis of Antonio Maura's projects can be found in María José González Hernández, *El universo conservador de Antonio Maura* (Madrid: Biblioteca Nueva, 1997). According to this author (pp. 133–5, 409), Maura was the only dynastic politician with a global project (described as 'conservative socialization') to foster citizenship and popular participation in public life. See also by the same author, 'Las manchas del leopardo: la difícil reforma desde el sistema y las estrategias de la socialización conservadora', in Manuel Suárez Cortina, ed., *La Restauración, entre el liberalismo y la democracia* (Madrid: Alianza, 1997), p. 167.

20   On the deadly fixation of Maura with Cierva, the stereotype of the worst *caciquil* manners of the system, see the interesting letter by the Professor of Law at the University of Madrid, Fernando Pérez Bueno, in Fundación Antonio Maura (hereafter AAM), Leg. 81, Carp. 80 (9 August 1919). See along these lines, Javier Tusell, *Antonio Maura* (Madrid: Alianza, 1994), p. 121.

21   González Hernández, *El Universo*, p. 137. A negative view of the electoral reform sought by Maura is in Teresa Carnero, 'Élite gobernante dinástica e igualdad política en España', Historia Contemporánea, No. 8 (1992): 59–64.

22   See the very incisive appendix by Joaquín Romero Maura, in R. Carr, *España, 1808–1975* (Barcelona: Ariel, 2nd edn, 1983), pp. 468–74.

23   González Hernández, 'Neither God nor Monster', p. 319.

24   This law, introduced in January 1908, provided the government with the power to close anarchist newspapers and centres as well as to deport those spreading subversive ideas. Presented as the necessary weapon to consolidate civilian power and so avoid the constant resource to military repression, it was utterly repressive and a clear setback for the freedom of expression and association. See Pedro Voltes, *La Semana Trágica* (Madrid: Espasa Calpe, 1995), pp. 78–9.

25 Against Cierva's instructions, the governor resisted the idea of declaring martial law, since he believed it to be a provocation to use troops to quell an anti-war protest. When the army was called out, Ossorio simply packed up his papers and withdrew to his villa outside the city. Cierva, regarding this as desertion, even thought of ordering the arrest of his governor. See Ángel Ossorio, *Barcelona* (Madrid: Ricardo Rojas, 1910), pp. 48–68, and Juan de la Cierva, *Notas de mi vida* (Madrid: Reus, 2nd edn, 1955), pp. 136–9. See also AAM, Leg. 154, Carp. 6, Cierva to Maura (July–August 1909).

26 The best study of the Tragic Week remains Joan Connelly Ullman, *The Tragic Week. Anticlericalism in Spain, 1875–1912* (Cambridge, MA: Harvard University Press, 1968), pp. 167–282. See also Romero Maura, *La rosa*, pp. 501–42, and Voltes, *La Semana*, pp. 101–33.

27 Maura, *Mis Recuerdos*, p. 139.

28 Cierva, *Notas*, pp. 148–52.

29 Romero Maura, appendix in Carr, p. 474.

30 González Hernández, *El Universo*, p. 174.

31 Maura, *Recuerdos*, p. 139.

32 González Hernández, *El Universo*, pp. 338–9.

33 José Gutiérrez Rave, *Yo fui un joven maurista* (Madrid: Revistas Madrid, 1944), p. 82.

34 Manuel Fernández Almagro, *Historia del Reinado de Alfonso XIII* (Barcelona: Montaner and Simón, 4th edn, 1997), p. 134; Mercedes Cabrera, 'Testamento político de Antonio Maura', in *Estudios de Historia Social*, Nos 32–3 (1979): p. 165. The plot to oust Moret can be seen in ANR, Leg. 11-8895 (30 January–9 February 1910).

35 ANR, Leg. 11-8910 (5 July 1912).

36 For Canalejas's intervention in Morocco and Portugal, see ANR, Leg. 11-8900 (April–June 1911) and 11-8901 (July 1911). Maura opposed involvement in Portugal and the intensification of the campaign in Morocco. According to Fernández Almagro (*Historia*, pp. 189–94) Maura believed that Spain lacked the means to create, let alone maintain, a protectorate in Morocco. Her role should thus be limited to a peaceful presence to ensure her prestige and legitimacy.

37 Harsh socialist criticism of Canalejas's rule can be found in Fundación Pablo Iglesias, *Cartas de Iglesias a Acevedo* (31 October 1910, 6 and 27 January 1912). Maura and Fernández Almagro, *Por qué cayó*, p. 227.

38 He was stabbed in Barcelona in April 1904 and shot and slightly wounded when descending from the train at his arrival again in Barcelona in July 1910.

39 BRAH, *Eduardo Dato's Papers* (hereafter AED), Maura to Dato (1 January 1913).

40 ANR, Leg. 11-8893 (10 and 30 June 1913).

41 Fernández Almagro, *Historia*, p. 191. Other scholars such as Carlos Seco Serrano defend the position of Dato, who only fulfilled his role of protecting the crown, and blame Maura's arrogance for his own downfall: *Perfil político y humano de un político de la Restauración. Eduardo Dato a través de su archivo* (Madrid: Real Academia de la Historia, 1978), pp. 66–73. Cristóbal Robles, *Antonio Maura. Un político liberal* (Madrid: CSIC, 1995), p. 365, also laid the onus on Maura for facing the crown with an impossible challenge. The correspondence in AAM, Leg. 34, between Dato and Maura (12 July, 7 August and 19 October 1913), shows that Dato urged Maura to take over. However, Dato who signed as 'your servant' (*tu súbdito*) did not appear much troubled in bypassing Maura and forming his government at the behest of monarch and Romanones.

42 Ossorio, *Mis Memorias*, pp. 103–4.

43 They returned 21 MPs (March 1914); 16 MPs (April 1916); 27 MPs (February 1918); with Maura in power, they returned a record 60 MPs (June 1919); 20 MPs (December 1920); and 12 MPs (April 1923).

44 For divisions of *Maurismo*, see María José González Hernández, 'Sobre Antonio Maura: el politico, el mito, su política', in *Revista de Occidente*, No. 77 (1987): 108; Ramón Punset, 'Maura y Maurismo. Perspectiva histórica de la revolución desde arriba', in *Sistema*, No. 33 (November 1979): 136; Francisco J. Romero Salvadó, 'Maura, Maurismo and the Crisis of 1917', in *Association for Contemporary Spanish Studies*, Vol. 7, No. 1 (Spring 1994): 18–19.

45 Javier Tusell and Juan Avilés, *El Maurismo y los orígenes de la derecha española* (Madrid: Espasa Calpe, 1986), pp. 106–7.

46 AAM, Leg. 80, Ossorio to Maura (1 June 1915 and 25 August 1916).

47 Instituto de Reformas Sociales, *Movimientos de precios al por menor en España durante la guerra y la posguerra* (Madrid: Sobrinos de la Sociedad de M. Minuesa, 1923), pp. 7, 10–11, 36.

48 For Spain's divisions, see Public Record Office, *Foreign Office Papers* (FO) 371-2471/73,963 and 2760/20,756, Secret reports (29 July 1915 and 17 April 1916). See also Jesús Longares Alonso, 'Germanófilos y aliadófilos españoles en la Primera Guerra Mundial', *Tiempo de Historia*, No. 21 (1976): 38–45; Gerald H. Meaker, 'A Civil War of Words', in Hans A. Schmitt, ed., *Neutral Europe between War and Revolution, 1917–1923* (Charlottesville: University of Virginia Press, 1988), pp. 1–41; and Francisco J. Romero Salvadó, *Spain 1914–1918. Between War and Revolution* (London: Routledge/ Cañada Blanch Studies, 1999), pp. 10–17.

49 Antonio Maura, *Tres Discursos* (Madrid: n.p., 1918).

50 AED, Maura to Dato (27 August 1914).

51 *España*, No. 86 (14 September 1916).

52 FO 371-2762/185,472, Hardinge to Grey (12 September 1916).

53 Andres Saborit, *La huelga de agosto de 1917: Apuntes históricos* (México, D.F.: Pablo Iglesias, 1967), pp. 90–1.

54 Benito Márquez and José María Capó, *Las juntas militares de defensa* (La Habana: Porvenir, 1923), pp. 24, 35–7.

55 *La Correspondencia Militar* (12, 14–15 June 1917).

56 Juan Antonio Lacomba, *La crisis española de 1917* (Málaga, Ciencia Nueva, 1970), p. 201; Jesús Pabón, *Cambó, 1876–1947* (Barcelona: Alpha, 1999), p. 399.

57 AAM, Leg. 401, Carp. 3 (12 June 1917).

58 For the *Mauristas'* reaction, see *La Acción* (11 June 1917) and AAM, Leg. 399, Carp. 18.

59 Maura and Fernández Almagro (*Por qué cayó*, p. 302) describe the king's action as a 'royal slap'.

60 For mail from Peyrá, see AAM, Leg. 389, Carp. 10 (20, 25 and 28 June 1917) and Leg. 402, Carp. 22 (20 June 1917). For the attitude of the officers, see AAM, Leg. 402, Carp. 22 (6 and 22 June 1917).

61 AAM, Leg. 80, Ossorio to Maura (9 July 1917); Leg. 19, Cambó to Gabriel Maura (10 July 1917); and Leg. 185, Nadal to Maura (6 and 11 July 1917).

62 AAM, Leg.390, *Maurista* Centre at Chamberí to Maura (7 July 1917); Leg. 362, Carp. 2, Miguel to Antonio Maura (24 June 1917); and Gabriel to Antonio Maura (26 June, 3, 8, 13 and 14 July 1917).

63 Maura and Fernández Almagro, *Por qué cayó*, Antonio to Gabriel Maura (23 and 30 June 1917), p. 488.

64 AAM, Leg. 389, Carp. 10, Maura to Peyrá (23 June 1917).

65 Maura and Fernández Almagro, *Por qué cayó*, Antonio to Gabriel Maura (6 July 1917), p. 489; AAM, Leg. 397, Carp. 7, Maura to Ossorio (12 July 1917).

66 AAM, Leg. 80, Ossorio to Maura (1 August 1917).

67 AAM, Leg. 80, Maura to Ossorio (7 August 1917).

68 This strategy can be seen in Archivo Histórico Nacional, *Ministerio de Gobernación* (AHN), Leg. 42 A, Exp. 1, instructions from the Interior Minister (8–12 August 1917). See Francisco J. Romero Salvadó, *The Foundations of the Civil War. Revolution, Social Conflict and Reaction in Spain, 1916–1923* (London: Routledge/Cañada Blanch Studies, 2008), pp. 86–7.

69 There was such optimism that, for once, the socialists even opposed their leader Pablo Iglesias, who, from his sickbed, argued strongly against such a strike. See Francisco Largo Caballero, *Mis recuerdos: Carta a un amigo* (México: Ediciones Unidas, 1976), pp. 51–2.

70 AAM, Leg. 389, Carp. 10 (21 October 1917). The profound liberalism of Maura is stressed in Robles, *Antonio Maura*, p. 406.

71 Maura and Fernández Almagro, *Por qué cayó*, Peyrá to Maura (26 October 1917), p. 507.

72 Cierva (*Notas*, pp. 188–9) argued that he only accepted the post when, after being asked by leading *Junteros*, the king begged him to accept or he feared he might have to abandon the throne. However, Márquez (*Las Juntas*, pp. 77–82) claimed that Cierva himself offered his services that were accepted by *Junteros* in Madrid without consulting their colleagues at Barcelona.

73 Lacomba, *La crisis*, pp. 340–3; Cierva, *Notas*, pp. 205–6.

74 *El Socialista* (7 March 1918); Márquez (*Las Juntas*, pp. 114–15) claimed that there was a military plot to create a government presided over by Cierva with eight colonels. See also FO 371-3372/60969, Political Intelligence Department (6 April 1918).

75 The shrewd Romanones (*Notas*, pp. 421–2) claims to have enlisted the vital services of the monarch to argue that he would abdicate unless the dynastic leaders were prepared to bury their differences and to work together to solve the existing deadlock.

76 Maura and Fernández Almagro, *Por qué cayó*, p. 311. Tusell (*Antonio Maura*, p. 180) suggests that his allusion to a potential charade did not contradict a certain feeling of euphoria.

77 AED, Maura to Dato (28 July 1918); Maura and Fernández Almagro, *Por qué cayó*, Antonio to Gabriel Maura (2 August 1914), p. 314.

78 The royal veto can be seen in ANR, 11-8906 (31 August 1918); AAM, Leg. 272, Carp. 1, Dato to Maura (7 September 1918); Romanones, *Notas*, p. 423; and FO 371-3374/153,920, Hardinge to Balfour (9 September 1918).

79 Santiago Alba, the ambitious Liberal Minister of Education, began a domino effect of petty squabbling when his pique with Cambó led to his resignation in early October. See AAM, Leg. 178, Carp. 2 (October 1918). Tusell, *Antonio Maura*, pp. 188–92.

80 Fernández Almagro, *Historia*, p. 267.

81 The *Canadiense* events can be followed in AHN, Leg. 57 A; and BRAH, *Romanones's Papers*, Leg. 20, Exps. 5–6 (February–March 1919).

82 Archivo del Fomento del Trabajo Nacional (AFTN), *Memoria de la Junta Directiva del Fomento del Trabajo Nacional, 1919–1920* (Barcelona: Hijos de Domingo Casanova, 1920), pp. 19, 22.

83 *La Acción* (8 March 1919). Soledad Bengoechea, '1919: La Barcelona colpista; L'aliança de patrons i militars contra el sistema liberal', *Afers*, Nos. 23/24 (1996): 311.

84 Romanones, *Notas*, pp. 434–45.

85 AAM, Leg. 266, Carp. 6 (24 April 1919).

86 Cussó's letter is in AFTN, *Actas*, Vol. 13 (29 April 1919), pp. 312–13. Similar mail from other industrialists is in AAM Leg, 219, Carp. 16 (April–June 1919).

87 For the continuity of martial law in Barcelona, see AAM, Leg. 261, Carp. 4, Maura to Milans (23 May 1919); and AFTN, *Actas*, Vol. 13 (21 May 1919), p. 328. For the measures to fight social subversion in Andalucía, see AAM, Leg. 229, Carp. 12 (April–June 1919); and AHN, Leg. 57A, Exps. 5–6 (April–December 1919).

88 *El Debate* (31 May 1919).

89 *El Socialista* (16 April 1919) and *España*, No. 210 (17 April 1919).

90 Cierva (*Notas*, p. 212), confirms that Maura asked him `to give Goicoechea a hand in supervising the elections'. Complaints from the Liberal leaders can be found in AAM, Leg. 266, Carp. 6 (May 1919). Tusell and Avilés (*El Maurismo*, p. 189) noted that the 1919 elections tarnished the image of Maura.

91 As joyfully commented the editorial of *España*, No. 218 (12 June 1919).

92 Tusell and Avilés, *El Maurismo*, pp. 261–78.

93 AAM, Leg. 178, Carp 4 (March, October and December 1920) and Leg. 266, Carp 7 (undated).

94 Maura and Fernández Almagro, *Por qué cayó*, pp. 339–42. AAM, Leg. 266, Carp. 8 (March 1921).

95 AAM, Leg. 5, Carp. 27. Allendesalazar with the king's concourse resorts to Maura (3 August 1921).

96 AAM, Leg. 250, Carp. 4 (25 August 1921).

97 See AAM, Leg. 19, mail between Maura and Cambó (16 and 20 August 1921); Francesc Cambó, *Memorias* (Madrid: Alianza: 1987), pp. 323–4.

98 Cambó's economic projects are in AMM, Leg. 276, Carp. 11 (undated). Their importance is stressed by Fidel Gómez Ochoa, 'Por una nueva interpretación de la crisis final de la Restauración: el gobierno Maura de agosto de 1921 y la reforma económica de Cambó', *Investigaciones Históricas*, 11 (1991): 260–71. Maura's firm support of Cambó is in AAM, Leg. 278, Carp. 8 (16 February 1922).

99 Maura, in 1909, initiated legislation (concluded by Canalejas in 1912) to introduce universal military service. However, profound divisions remained among the conscripts as the well-off could be released after five months of barracks instruction upon the payment of a 2,000-peseta fee (*cuota*).

100 See reports of these patriotic displays in *La Correspondencia Militar, El Debate*; and *El Diario Universal* (August–October 1921).

101 AAM, Leg. 250, Carp. 4, Maura's notes (25 August 1921). There was a huge gap between Maura's legalism and the editorials of *La Acción* calling for the country to be run by a dictatorship of 'honest men'. See Tusell and Avilés, *El Maurismo*, pp. 237–43.

102 Maura's position is in AAM, Leg. 178, Carp. 5 (14 January 1922). For a detailed narrative of the events, see Fernando Soldevilla, *El año político de 1922* (Madrid: Julio Cosano, 1923), pp. 8–35.

103 Maura and Fernández Almagro, *Por qué cayó*, Antonio to Gabriel Maura (26 August 1921), p. 352.

104 Cierva, *Notas*, pp. 259–61; for Maura's views, see AAM, Leg. 250, Carp. 4, several scribbled notes (August–November 1921). For Hontoria's views and disagreements in the Council of Ministers, see AAM, Leg. 441, Carp. 10 (January–February 1922). Cambó's thoughts are in his work, *El problema del Marroc* (Barcelona: Catalana, 1922), pp. 1–6, 9–16; and AAM, Leg. 276, Carp. 11 (January 1922) and Leg. 441, Carp. 10 (February 1922).

105 The resignation note is in AAM, Leg. 407, Carp. 23 (7 March 1922). Maura's frustration is in AAM, Leg. 273, Carp. 4 (February 1922). See also Cambó, *Memorias*, p. 340.

106 *La Acción* (1 December 1922).

107 Cambó (*Memorias*, pp. 351–2) confessed that a meeting with the monarch, a few hours before Maura's speech, greatly influenced his parliamentary intervention. After confiding to him his anxiety about the country's deplorable situation, the king offered him the premiership in return for Cambó openly renouncing his Catalanist programme. He not only declined the royal offer but, in his own words, saw in Maura's intervention the opportunity to get even with the king.

108 Cierva (*Notas*, pp. 287–9) noted that his rupture with Don Antonio was due to the latter's weakness due to the influence of his son Gabriel Ossorio and Cambó; *La Acción* (6 December 1922) portrayed on its front page a cartoon of Sánchez Guerra's head flying, under the comment: 'He has lost his Head!'.

109 The king's conversation with Gabriel Maura is in AAM, Leg. 259, Carp. 8 (6 August 1923).

110 AAM, Leg. 259, Carp. 7. See also G. Maura, *Bosquejo histórico de la dictadura* (Madrid: Tipografía de Archivos, 1930), pp. 20–1.

111 AAM, Leg. 259, Carp. 10 (11 February 1925).

2

Miguel Primo de Rivera: Overture to Franco

ALEJANDRO QUIROGA*

In the summer of 1929, Julián Cortés Cavanillas, at the time one of the most important leaders of the *Juventudes de Unión Patriótica*, published a book entitled *The Dictatorship and the Dictator*. The work offered an idyllic portrait of General Miguel Primo de Rivera. The young UP member portrayed the dictator as a kindly leader, a patriot close to the people. He described Primo de Rivera as 'a man in every sense of the word' who possessed 'the heart of a child' and who had not wanted to shed blood during his time in power.[1] Cortés Cavanillas also confidently asserted that posterity would remember the Marques of Estella with 'an incredibly high opinion, completely in line with his great merits' and that 'history' should 'bless the new era' which the dictator had initiated on 13 September 1923.[2] Furthermore, the propagandist anticipated a long future for the Dictatorship and predicted that the period of regeneration inaugurated by Primo de Rivera would not end, God willing, 'while Spain was Spain'.[3]

Cortés Cavanillas was mistaken in two senses. The Primo de Rivera regime collapsed seven months after the publication of *The Dictatorship and the Dictator*, and historians' opinions of General Primo de Rivera were anything but 'incredibly high'. Yet strangely enough, the affable image of the Marques of Estella promoted by the men of the Dictatorship has endured. The myth of a kindly, unpretentious dictator close to the people crafted by the Dictatorship's propagandistic machinery was adopted by commentators and historians throughout the twentieth century. Many aspects of the myth have survived into the present day. The following pages call into question this image of Primo de Rivera, presenting a very different picture of the dictator. This vision is based on an analysis of his political writings and actions within the historical context of interwar Europe.

The chapter is divided into five parts. The first section briefly revises the historiographical treatment of the figure of Primo de Rivera from the fall of the Dictatorship up to the present day. The second section analyzes the life of the general between 1905 and 1919, a key period in the Marques of Estella's political formation. The third part deals with the crisis of the Restoration (1919–23) and the formation of a counter-revolutionary mentality in our subject. The final two sections study the figure of Primo as dictator, during the Military Directory (1923–5) and the Civil Directory (1926–30) respectively.

And Who is He?

Cortés Cavanillas was not alone. The image of Primo as an affable, popular and approachable man was promoted in dozens of newspapers which supported the regime, in the official publications of the *Unión Patriótica* (UP) and the *Somatén*, and in the books of a long series of the regime's defenders. Primo appeared in this propaganda as a protective father who 'circumstantially exercises a tutelary dictatorship' and who took great care not to spill the blood of his unruly children.[4] The Dictatorship's propagandists also presented Primo as a providential figure, a divine envoy sent to save the fatherland from the chaos and anarchy into which Spain had been plunged by the Restoration system.[5] Alongside these religious features, the spokesmen of the regime embellished their propaganda with pseudoscientific analyses which spoke of the 'nervous sanguineous temperament' which supposedly endowed Primo with an intelligence superior to that of ordinary human beings, and of his 'intuitionism', apparently a key quality which allowed the dictator to understand his people and rule them with sound judgement.[6]

After the fall of the Primo de Rivera regime, a series of works critical of the dictator were published. These books denounced his repressive character, his complete disdain for the law (including laws which he had dictated himself) and the drastic limitation on all kinds of liberties which marked his time in office.[7] Other works attempted to rescue the figure of Primo de Rivera, merely reproducing the myths of the providential saviour of the fatherland and 'intuitionist' which had been elaborated during his time in office.[8] During the early years of the Francoist Dictatorship, the idea that Primo was a providential man who had saved the country from revolution survived, partly thanks to the writings of the Marques of Estella's old collaborators. Shortly after the end of the Spanish Civil War, César González Ruano published *Miguel Primo de Rivera. The Heroic and Romantic Life of a Spanish General*, a biography in which intuition and love for the people continued to be depicted as the dictator's fundamental characteristics. Primo's political work was presented as the precursor to the regimes of Mussolini, Hitler and Franco.[9] In the same vein, Eduardo Aunós, ex-Minister of Labour in the Primo de Rivera administration and Francoist Minister of Justice, published *General Primo de Rivera. Soldier and Leader* in 1944. The book emphasized that the Marques of Estella's patriotism and Catholicism were fundamental to defining his political and military career.[10] As well as justifying Aunós's own political past, the rehabilitation of the figure of General Primo de Rivera also served as a means of praising the new dictator. In this way, the Catalan politician portrayed Francisco Franco as Primo's intellectual heir and the executor of the redeeming work of the general from Jerez.[11]

As the regime which had emerged from the Civil War shed its fascist apparel after the defeat of Nazi Germany in the Second World War, interest in General Primo de Rivera as the precursor to the fascist dictatorships waned. In 1956, for example, González Ruano published his *Miguel Primo de Rivera* for a second time. As was to be expected, the first edition's references to Hitler, Mussolini and Franco disappeared from the new 'conveniently' revised version. The Marques of Estella would not regain notoriety until the late Francoist period. In 1970, the historian José Manuel Cuenca Toribio published an article in the journal *Historia y Vida* which set out to analyze the dictator from a 'serene and scientific viewpoint'.[12] However, Cuenca did nothing more than reproduce the platitudes generated during the period of the Primo Dictatorship. The author represented the Marques of Estella as paternalistic and kindly, at the same time recognizing his reputation as a womanizer, something which converted him into a kind of 'legendary Sultan of the Thousand and One Nights'.[13] The caricature did not end there. According to Cuenca, the 'arbitrariness and partiality' which Primo 'demonstrated so abundantly in the exercise of power' were so 'to the taste of the timeless Spanish popular soul' that they won the dictator wide social support.[14] If the existence of something akin to a 'timeless Spanish popular soul' is highly debatable, it does seem clear that these kinds of interpretations displayed a large dose of paternalism, not so much in the subject studied, but in the historian who claimed to analyze him 'scientifically'. In the same edition of *Historia y Vida*, Rafael Salazar presented 'Human Profile of Primo de Rivera', an article which repeated, almost point by point, the regime's mythology associated with the dictator.[15] Once again, the Marques of Estella appeared as an intuitive, kind-hearted patriarchal man of action, paternalistic and loved by the people, although divine providence was no longer included as an explanation of his actions. Along very similar lines, the biography of Primo de Rivera published by Ana de Sagrera merely recycled the mythology of the 1920s, using anecdotes and short stories told by the dictator's family members and acquaintances.[16] The biographer, a friend of the Primo de Rivera family, emphasized the Marques of Estella's patriotism and religiosity in order to explain and justify his political actions.[17]

Not all of the studies from the 1970s involve a fairly crude updating of the image of the Marques of Estella created during the Primo de Rivera Dictatorship. Those years also witnessed the first academic debates concerning the nature of the Dictatorship. On the one hand, Marxist historiography interpreted the Primo de Rivera regime as the institutionalization of a Bonapartism, fruit of the crisis suffered by the Restoration's oligarchy.[18] Liberal-conservative historiography, on the other hand, saw the Dictatorship as a regime based on the idea of liberal regeneration of the sort espoused by Joaquín Costa. For conservative historians, the origin of the dictatorship lay in a political crisis and was not socio-economic, as Marxist historians had argued.[19] It was an unusual regime, a kind of swansong of the Restoration elites which, in a unique manner in Europe, had tried to regenerate the liberal system with a temporary dictatorship.

Figure 2.1 General Primo de Rivera addresses the public in the street. His dictatorship promoted mass mobilization and the participation of military officers, clerics and women in patriotic ceremonies.

In the 1980s and 1990s, the work of Shlomo Ben-Ami, María Teresa González Calbet and José Luis Gómez-Navarro compared the Primo de Rivera regime with other European dictatorships and showed that the Spanish case was by no means exceptional. The Primo Dictatorship was one more example of the authoritarian modernization with which conservative groups had tried to face the crisis of interwar Europe. The academic debate centred on analyzing if 'Primo de Rivera-ism' (*primorriverismo*) could be seen as a kind of fascism imposed 'from above' or, on the contrary, if it had to be understood as a regime similar to the dictatorships which emerged in Central and Eastern Europe during the 1920s and 1930s.[20] The object of study ceased to be a caricature of Primo de Rivera, who, according to Ben-Ami, was often portrayed as a good-natured and primitive 'national Santa Claus' or as a 'Mexican style dictator' who lived amid adventures and card games.[21] The Israeli historian focused on the regime's ideologues, the social groups which supported the Dictatorship, and the policies of *primorriverismo*. This new batch of historians openly questioned the postulations of liberal-conservative historiography and maintained that *primorriverismo* was, in many aspects, a clear precursor to Francoism.[22]

Debates about the fascist nature of the Primo de Rivera regime implicitly entailed an analysis of Primo de Rivera's ideology and actions, for the first time almost completely free of the mythological burden which had accompanied past portraits of the dictator. As new studies appeared during the first decade of the twenty-first century, this analysis of Primo de Rivera also became more explicit. Following the path opened by Ben-Ami and Gómez Navarro, Xavier Casals defined Primo de Rivera as a 'mirror of Franco' and saw his regime as having been 'decisive in laying the foundations of Francoism'.[23] In a similar vein, Eduardo González Calleja underlined the 'liquidationist' character of Primo de Rivera's experiment. Primo de Rivera not only destroyed the Restoration system but he also 'provided an authoritarian model which was correctly valued by the victors of the Civil War'.[24]

Faced with this important revision of the figure of the dictator and of the Dictatorship, the liberal-conservative historiography of recent years has stressed the singularity of the Primo regime within the European authoritarian regimes and the absence of connections between Primo de Rivera and Franco. In this way, veterans like Carlos Seco Serrano continue to offer a somewhat sweetened and openly positive vision of the dictator from Jerez. From Seco Serrano's point of view, Primo de Rivera had been, during his entire life, a liberal cut from the same cloth as Joaquín Costa, a lover of his fatherland who was capable of resigning when the king ordered him to do so. At the same time, Seco Serrano's portrait presents an openminded Andalusian who had nothing in common with the reserved and surly character of the Galician Francisco Franco.[25] Other authors, such as Ramón

Tamames, bestow a similarly positive image upon the dictator, above all due to his investments in public works projects. These authors distance Primo's regime from both fascist Italy and Francoism.[26]

In many ways, these authors have perpetuated the myths of the patriotic, paternalistic Primo loved by the people, myths which the historiography of the late Francoist period had already adapted to its own time. In some cases, this adaptation of the mythology of *primorriverismo* in the democratic present day has gone as far as paroxysm. If, as we have indicated, the Primo regime's propagandists arrived at the pseudoscientific concept of 'intuitionism' to explain how Primo made the decisions which he believed to be most advisable for the country, some authors have described the Marques of Estella as a man who, moved by his 'patriotism', ended up concerning himself with the 'social question' simply 'through the deductive method'.[27] Others, like Julio Escribano Hernández, have gone even further, indicating that the dictator's 'naive thinking' and 'emotive character' drove him to act against the 'old politicians [that] had destroyed the nation'.[28] Primo was 'a patriot of the militia' who, 'united with the people', had attempted to restore the Spanish nation with his coup d'état.[29] Furthermore, Escribano presents the Dictatorship as a project in which the Marques of Estella 'harvested the feeling of the citizens of the nation and tried to put it into practice assisted by a group of soldiers who represented the opinion of the army'.[30]

Aside from this author's dubious penchant for coups d'état and military dictatorships dedicated to saving fatherlands, the vision which he offers us seems more typical of the panegyrics of the Primo Dictatorship than of the work of a twenty-first-century university professor. This is precisely because Escribano's work reproduces, in an entirely uncritical manner, affirmations concerning Primo de Rivera's character made by key figures associated with dictatorial propaganda such as Julián Cortés Cavanillas, José Pemartín and Emilio R. Tarduchy. Escribano's work provides a good example of the way in which the collection of clichés created by the men of the regime regarding the Marques of Estella has survived into the present day within certain academic circles.

Sorcerer's Apprentice

Miguel Primo de Rivera was born on 8 January 1870 in Jerez de la Frontera, into the bosom of a family of military men and landowners. His father, Miguel Primo de Rivera y Sobremonte, was a colonel of the General Staff. His uncle José was a commander, and his uncle Fernando was a lieutenant general and the first Marques of Estella. These three men would play a crucial role in the formation of the future dictator. Following his early education in the primary school of San Luis de Gonzaga and in the secondary school of Jerez de la Frontera, in 1882 he went to live with his uncle José in Madrid with the intention of studying for his certificate of secondary education. However, the young Miguel soon changed his mind and began to prepare for his entry into the Military Academy of Toledo. He would finally enter the academy as a cadet in August 1884.[31]

Miguel Primo de Rivera was a mediocre student. In the Military Academy he had to repeat a year of studies, and when he finished he was ranked 70th out of the 191 students in his year.[32] Under the constant protection of his uncle Fernando, who assigned him postings at will, Primo ascended rapidly through the infantry corps. In 1891 he was named first lieutenant and assistant to the Captain General of Madrid, Arsenio Martínez Campos. Two years later he was sent to Africa where he obtained the First Class San Fernando War Merit Cross.[33] In 1895 he was promoted to commander and went back to working to Martínez Campos's orders, who at the time was General-in-Chief of the army in operations in Cuba. The colonial adventure continued and in 1897 Primo went to the Philippines with his uncle Fernando, leader of the Spanish army in the Pacific. In 1898 he returned to Spain, where he received several military postings: to Seville, Barcelona, Madrid and Cadiz. In 1908 he was promoted to colonel. In the years that followed, Primo alternated his stays on the peninsula with his work in Africa, where he went to fight against the Riffian insurgents on several occasions. His labours in Morocco would also bear fruit: in 1912 he was promoted to general of brigade, and in 1914 to general of division. In 1915 he was named Military Governor of Cadiz, and in 1919 he was promoted to lieutenant general. In 1920, he was appointed Captain General of the Third Military region (Valencia).[34]

From Primo's youth, it is possible to highlight three fundamental characteristics: rebelliousness before the established order; a desire to intervene in politics; and an interest in the media. As early as 1895, at the age of just 25, Primo was one of the leaders of the *tenientada*. On 13 March of that year, a group of lieutenants assaulted the offices of the daily newspaper *El Resumen*, which had criticized the officers who had not presented themselves voluntarily to fight in Cuba. The following day, around 400 lieutenants once again assaulted the offices of *El Resumen* and those of *El Globo*, which had criticized the officers' violent actions and defended the right to liberty of expression. The military vandalism had important political repercussions. The president of the government, Práxedes Sagasta, defended the freedom of the press and resigned in protest. Meanwhile, General Martínez Campos attempted, unsuccessfully, to modify the Military Code so that attacks and insults against the army would be subject to military jurisdiction. For Primo, the *tenientada* was a huge professional leap. Martínez Campos evaluated the violent actions of the young lieutenant very positively, asked Primo to be his permanent assistant, and took him to Cuba to fight against the insurgents.[35] Primo learned something important about the Restoration system very early on: military insubordination went unpunished, and what is more, it delivered good professional rewards.

These years spent in the colonies were very instructive for Primo. In both Cuba and the Philippines, the young officer experienced first-hand the fight against the insurgency, the brutality of the war and the miseries of a Spanish army decimated by tropical disease. But Primo also learned the art of negotiation. Both Martínez Campos and Primo's uncle Fernando tried to make agreements with the Cuban and Philippine insurgents respectively. Both men counted on our subject as their right-hand man. Furthermore, Miguel Primo de Rivera personally negotiated the agreement of Biac-Nabató with the leaders of the Philippine insurgency in December 1897. The treaty agreed an end to military activities and the departure of the independentist leaders from the archipelago in exchange for money. As Primo de Rivera would later recognize, the success of the negotiations made him conscious of his vocation for politics.[36] It was quite another matter that the treaty could scarcely be put into practice because some of the Philippine leaders refused to sign it. And when the sinking of the US battleship *Maine* revived the conflict in Cuba, many of the Philippine nationalist leaders who had signed the agreement of Biac-Nabató decided to use the money which they had received from the Spanish to buy arms and initiate a new rebellion. Together with the skill of negotiation, Primo learned what treachery was.

The 'Disaster' of 1898 had an especially strong impact upon Primo. The loss of the colonies overlapped with the death of his father, who died in August 1898. In the same month, Primo wrote to his uncle Fernando: 'God, on taking him away from us, takes the pain of seeing the dismemberment of this fatherland which he loved so much.'[37] Miguel Primo de Rivera's marriage in 1902 to Casilda Sáenz de Heredia, a woman from Guipúzcoa, only consolidated the pain he felt for the defeat. Casilda was a member of one of the great Hispano-Cuban sugar producing families and her father had been the last Spanish mayor of Havana.[38] The Disaster of 1898 also had a long-lasting impact. The fact that the manifesto of the 1923 coup d'état mentioned 'the panorama of misfortunes and immoralities which began in 1898' as one of the motives to justify the insurrection, displays clearly that a quarter of a century later, the wounds of the Disaster had not healed.[39] Furthermore, Primo and many of his comrades in arms shared the idea that the loss of empire had occurred due to the incompetence of liberal politicians and parliamentarianism. From this viewpoint, what came after 1898 was the acceleration of a process of national disintegration which the army saw itself obliged to halt in 1923. To put it another way, we find a distorted vision of

Figure 2.2 Official portrait of General Primo de Rivera. The Dictatorship attempted to promote the cult of General Primo de Rivera as a charismatic, patriotic leader. Thousands of pictures of the dictator were distributed among Spaniards via postcards, leaflets and magazines.

the loss of empire at the base of the ideological justifications of the Primo de Rivera Dictatorship.[40]

It was precisely 'the pain of the colonial catastrophe' which impelled Primo to begin his career as a political commentator, writing a series of articles for *El Liberal* in 1898.[41] Primo had published his first articles in Jerez's *El*

Guadalete before the Disaster, but the new political vocation he discovered in the Philippines would bring him into collaboration with *La Correspondencia Militar*, *Revista Técnica* and *Memorial de Infantería* in the years after 1898. In 1913, Primo embarked upon the venture of founding his own newspaper, *La Nación. Diario Monárquico Independiente*, with a group of friends, while he simultaneously tried to enter politics.[42] *La Nación* barely lasted three months in circulation, but the newspaper already contained the strong doses of Catholic, economically-protectionist Spanish nationalism which would mark the mentality of *primorriverismo* throughout the entire life of the regime. Primo's attempt to enter the political arena was also unsuccessful at first. He tried to win a seat as deputy in the districts of Torrijos and Écija, without being particularly concerned about whether he wished to represent the Liberal or the Conservative party. Yet the initiative proved fruitless and Primo ended up returning to Africa to continue his professional ascent in the army.[43]

Primo was a man of action, obsessed with prospering in the army and fairly unattached to his family. In 1908, when his wife Casilda died, the then lieutenant colonel left his six children in the care of his sister, María Jesús. A few months later, when he had already been named colonel, he went to France in a study trip designated by the Central General Staff. Once he was in Paris, however, he asked to be transferred to Melilla, where advancement by war merits accelerated the process of promotion through the military ranks. It is possible that the mediocrity of Primo's studies, coupled with his impetuous character, endowed him with a somewhat simplistic vision of reality which allowed him to attack his problems in a decisive, resolute manner. But we must not forget that Primo was a tremendously calculating person, who had learnt to manoeuvre effectively within the complex inner workings of the corrupt Restoration system and who had discovered how to claw his way up through the clientelist military network guided by his uncle Fernando.[44]

Primo's status as a calculating, and in many cases arriviste, man of action did not prevent him from having some fairly solid ideological ideas. In reality, the postulations on Primo de Rivera's ideology in the first decades of the twentieth century fit perfectly into what has become known as 'military nationalism'. This ideology, which emerged within a section of the Spanish officer corps after the loss of empire, proposed the modernization of the country through the fomenting of military industry, an increase in the number of schools and the reinforcement of the work of the state in Spanish society. Meanwhile, in the ambit of patriotic mythology, it considered the martial spirit of the Reconquest, the colonization of America, the struggle against the Protestants and the Peninsular War as the historic milestones which had forged the nation.[45]

As in the cases of many other military men, Primo's ideas were directly influenced by those of Joaquín Costa. Aside from his penchant for repeating

Costa's phrases in public, he displayed genuine interest in education as a way of indoctrinating the masses. Primo was convinced of the importance of creating a modern army. With this aim, he demanded a general plan of military training which would improve the education of recruits and officers alike.[46] But Primo went further than military instruction, proposing that the army itself should indoctrinate the population outside the barracks with Spanish nationalist ideals. As early as 1905, Primo complained that 'in Spain, neither the school nor the pulpit [had] believed that its principal mission was to make the national soul' of Spaniards. That is to say, the educational system and the Church were failing in their role of patriotic educators.[47] In 1916, our subject proposed openly that the army took responsibility for propagating nationalist ideas in schools and workers' groups, through the use of modern propaganda techniques like the film projector.[48] What underlies these proposals is the use of the nationalization of the masses as a barrier against the growing left-wing political activism of the popular classes. The nation became the bulwark against revolution.

Together with his use of the written and spoken word in the field of propaganda, Primo was gradually sharpening the 'sword' of military action. Although he initially displayed reluctance regarding the use of the army to maintain public order, the political and social upheaval provoked by the First World War caused him to change his mind. In 1912 he had maintained that the intervention of the army was an 'unfortunate factor', as the armed forces should dedicate themselves exclusively to 'ensuring success in war'. By 1916, however, he considered that the task of guaranteeing public order should be entrusted 'exceptionally' to the military.[49] And in 1919, after the victory of the Bolsheviks and amid revolutionary tremors across Europe, Primo arrived at the conclusion that, in those 'times of uncertainty', the foremost labour of the army was 'the defence of the Fatherland and of the flag', something which could be equated with 'the specific mission of defending social order'.[50] As was the case for so many other Europeans, the political and social cataclysm provoked by the First World War caused Primo to sharpen his militarist, nationalist and authoritarian tendencies. In 1919, Primo still did not consider himself to be the 'iron surgeon' who his much-admired Costa had called upon to regenerate the country, but the ideological bases which justified military intervention in order to save the fatherland appeared to be firmly consolidated.

The Forging of a Rebel, 1919–23

The years of the First World War were professionally excellent for Primo de Rivera. In July 1914 he was promoted to general of division and decorated with the Great Cross of Military Merit. In October of the same year, he was appointed military governor of Cadiz. In 1915 the Spanish government commissioned him to visit the French front, where he would meet the future marshal Philippe Petain. But these were also the years of his first significant political disappointments. According to José María Pemán, by 1914 Primo was already fantasizing about being the head of the Spanish government at the lunches he hosted for family members and friends at Cadiz's captaincy general.[51] However, in March 1917 he was dismissed from his post of military governor of Cadiz following a controversial speech given to celebrate his entry into the *Real Academia Hispano-Americana de las Ciencias y las Artes*. His address proposed the exchange of Gibraltar for Spain's possessions in Morocco, as the African campaign was consuming resources fundamental for the construction of schools in Spain.[52]

In October 1918, Primo's uncle Fernando was replaced as Minister of War in the government of Eduardo Dato, due to his incapacity to resolve the lawsuit of the *junteros* (members of the military *Juntas de Defensa*). Miguel Primo de Rivera, who had worked as advisor to his uncle and who had negotiated with *junteros*, also lost his job. But his experience with the Juntas marked the young Miguel politically: 'It is better that [the military] govern than bring parties into the government pushed forward by ourselves,' he wrote in his correspondence with the *junteros*.[53] This phrase is significant because it displays that Primo's ideas regarding military intervention supposed a clear rupture with the classic nineteenth-century coup d'états (*pronunciamientos*). In the previous century, when a military leader staged a coup d'état, he soon handed power to civilians. The army was an instrument to gain power, not to govern. In the twentieth century, according to Primo, if the military was to take power, the army should govern.

Our subject's dismissal by the Eduardo Dato government only served to exacerbate the disdain he felt for professional politicians. In February 1920, Fernando Primo de Rivera proposed the idea of establishing a dictatorial regime under military tutelage to Alfonso XIII. The old general proposed the temporary suspension of constitutional guarantees and the formation of a government of 'technicians' which, even if it had a civilian presence, would be based on 'military force' and be presided over by 'a man of fortitude and character'.[54] The dictatorial model implanted by Miguel Primo in 1923 was very similar to the one proposed in this missive by Fernando Primo. If one considers, furthermore, that the two men lived together in Madrid when Fernando sent the letter to the king, this similitude seems far from coincidental.

However, it was Primo's experience as Captain General of Valencia, from July 1920, which definitively convinced him of 'the need to intervene in Spanish politics through different procedures to the habitual ones'.[55] In a city marked by considerable levels of worker agitation, he learned two fundamental lessons for the future. The first was that the absence of the province's civil governor left a power vacuum which a captain general could easily fill. Years later, remembering the situation in Valencia, Primo wrote that 'the position of governor was vacant for quite some time, which was good fortune, because, the secretary of the Civil Government, the colonel of the Civil Guard and I agreed to take some measures which were like miracles for Valencia, because with them the terrorist attacks ended'.[56]

The second lesson was somewhat more brutal: the selective assassinations of syndicalists put into practice by the generals Milans del Bosch and Martínez Anido in Barcelona could be extended to the rest of Spain. From his arrival in Valencia, Primo applied a firm hand against anarchist activists, and one of the first things he did upon taking possession of the post was to go to Barcelona to meet with Martínez Anido.[57] The general from Jerez had no qualms about making criminal use of the Ley de Fugas – the infamous law that allowed security forces to shoot those prisoners who attempted to flee while in custody. Like Martínez Anido, Primo de Rivera used the cover of the law to facilitate the assassinations of those he considered to be terrorists. His tactics were simple: 'a raid, a transferral, an attempt to flee and some gunshots will begin to resolve the problem'.[58] Primo's actions not only reduced the activities of the anarchist movement; they also gained him the admiration of the 'hard men' Martínez Anido and Milans del Bosch.

Primo de Rivera's appointment to the post of Captain General of Catalonia in March 1922 placed our subject in a privileged position, from which the idea of leading a future military coup matured and developed. From the outset, the general from Jerez had a clear idea of the type of policy he would follow in the Catalan capital. Just 24 hours after his arrival in Barcelona he met with Martínez Anido, who occupied the post of civil governor of the province, presumably in order to plan his main lines of his action against the anarchists of the Sindicato Único.[59] The following day, Primo inspected the Somatén of Barcelona, the civic guard under military supervision created in January 1919 with the support of the regionalists of the Lliga, the Spanish nationalists of the Unión Monárquica Nacional and the Carlists, and financed by the Barcelona's financial elite.[60] From the captaincy general of Barcelona, assisted by Martínez Anido and General Miguel Arlegui, the police chief, and with the backing of a large proportion of the Catalan employer class, Primo promoted the Sindicatos Libres (gunmen hired by employers) and consolidated the parapolice networks devoted to assassinating trade unionist leaders.[61]

However, within a few months, Primo de Rivera's bid to follow his predecessors' path of militarized firm-handedness was under threat. In October 1922, General Miguel Arlegui was dismissed from the post of police chief of Barcelona and Martínez Anido resigned as civil governor in solidarity with

Figure 2.3 General Primo de Rivera with three army officers. Spanish military nationalism was the key ideological driving force of the Dictatorship's policies.

the man who had been his loyal companion in the coordination of the dirty war against organized labour. Arlegui's dismissal for misuse of the *Ley de Fugas*, that is to say, for orchestrating assassinations of syndicalists in police custody, constituted an attempt by the Madrid government to undermine the military network which had become an autonomous de facto power in Barcelona from 1919 onwards. Such an attempt to recover fractions of civil power was not viewed positively by the Catalan employers. These sectors, in spite of the political differences between Catalan regionalists and Spanish nationalists, concurred in their view of the Madrid government as incapable of stemming syndicalism, and were committed to the repression of the working classes.[62] According to Primo, Martínez Anido's resignation meant 'the loss of a great collaborator'.[63] Yet paradoxically, our subject benefitted from his friend's departure. When Martínez Anido was replaced in the Barcelona's civil government by a civilian, the Catalan employers realized that Primo de Rivera was the only figure whom they could trust. The Catalan employers encouraged Primo de Rivera to continue with the policies initiated by Martínez Anido, something which eventually turned the general from Jerez into the bulwark of the counter revolution in Catalonia. The military captaincy, rather than the civil government of Barcelona, became the place to go to deal with problems.

And these problems soon arrived. In the spring of 1923, the firing of some tram drivers affiliated to the *Conferación Nacional del Trabajo* (CNT) escalated into a general strike in the transport sector. By the beginning of May, Barcelona was completely paralyzed. Factories and shops had to close due to lack of supplies, while the streets filled with rubbish. Furthermore, the development of the strike was marked by violence. The anarchists soon began to assassinate employers and strike breakers. The employers' organizations, led by the *Fomento del Trabajo Nacional*, accused the civil governor, Salvador Reventós, of supporting the anarchists of the *Sindicato Único* and declared that Primo de Rivera was their only remaining hope.[64] The Carlist newspapers started a campaign against Raventós, criticizing his inaction and opposing his proposed negotiated solution to the strike.[65] The assassination of two members of the *Somatén* in the Les Corts sports ground as they watched a football match was the final straw.[66] The employers' organizations published a letter calling upon the government to take energetic measures. The government responded by firing Raventós and appointing Francisco Barber as the new civil governor.

During the strike, Primo played his cards perfectly, practically turning himself into the 'viceroy' of Catalonia. At the beginning of the conflict he declared that the army would not remain passive in the face of the events and he immediately mobilized the *Somatén*.[67] Furthermore, he organized military parades through the streets of Barcelona, something which constituted a clear show of force against the strikers and an attempt to mobilize the masses on the side of the employers.[68] Less than ten days into the strike, Primo had to deny that the garrison of Barcelona was preparing a coup d'état.[69] Astute, and with a great sense of political opportunity, Primo took advantage of the days following the departure of governor Raventós in order to meet with the dozens of employers and small businessmen who poured into the captaincy general to ask for protection.[70]

The arrival of the new civil governor, Francisco Barber, did not change things significantly. On 7 June, negotiations between the employers' organizations, the trade unions and the government broke down.[71] On 9 June, a crowd booed, insulted and jostled Barber at the funeral of José Franquesa Sardany, a Carlist and member of the *Somatén* and of the *Sindicato Libre* (the employers-controlled syndicate) who had been assassinated by anarchists. The Captain General had to intervene, escorting the civil governor to the car in which he escaped. Primo stayed put, amid cheers, applause and cries of 'long live!' for the Captain General, Spain and the army. If Primo's ego needed some kind of confirmation that he was a highly esteemed figure among

Barcelona's conservative groups, this was the definitive proof.[72] The general from Jerez felt then that he was the chosen man to lead not only Barcelona's crisis situation, but also a military coup which would change definitively the Restoration political system. Years later, he wrote the following about the situation created by the transport strike: 'What can be said about everybody's mood, that they had placed their trust in me alone and they urged me to do something, to proceed in any manner, as long as Catalonia was liberated from the hecatomb which so obviously threatened it?'[73]

Faced with the continual deterioration of the situation, Primo and Barber were called to Madrid for a consultation. The Spanish government, aware that Barcelona's employers' organizations and all of its conservative groups supported Primo, did not dare to relieve him of his post. However, it had no problem at all in firing Barber. By dismissing the civil governor, the government simply confirmed the victory of the military sector in Barcelona. Primo, always calculating, took advantage of his time in Madrid to meet with General Francisco Aguilera and the men of the 'quadrilateral' (the generals José Cavalcanti, Antonio Dabán, Federico Berenguer and Leopoldo Saro), who had been conspiring to put an end to the constitutional order for some time. When he returned to Barcelona, a crowd received him with a heroes' welcome in the train station. Primo then increased the army's intervention in order to guarantee transport for Barcelona, and on 28 June he ordered a raid on the CNT's headquarters which resulted in the detection of 18 anarchist leaders. On 12 July the anarchists announced the end of a strike which had left 22 people dead and 32 wounded, and which had affected more than 140,000 workers.[74]

The end of the strike did not mean the end of the social tension. The summer of 1923 was marked by a series of armed robberies of banks, hotels and various businesses orchestrated by the anarchists. Primo did not want to let his moment pass and continued to use the army and the *Somatén* to patrol the streets of Barcelona day and night.[75] What is more, throughout July and August 1923, the general from Jerez devoted himself to consolidating support for his coup d'état project. In a very intelligent manner, Primo told each political, business and military group exactly what it wanted to hear. On occasion, this has been seen as proof that Primo had no defined ideology, when what the Marques of Estella really did in the months preceding the coup was to gather support in diverse political sectors by promising each group a dictatorship which would resolve its particular problems.[76] In this way, Primo assured the most Spanish nationalist sectors of the employer class that he would put an end to trade unionism and Catalan separatism, while promising the *Lliga*'s regionalists greater autonomy for Catalonia together with much yearned-for 'social peace'.[77] Within the army, he saw fit to gain the support of the *junteros* of the Barcelona garrison. Meanwhile, he told General López

Ochoa, who had certain republican and Catalan regionalist tendencies, just before the coup that the military would only remain in power until a more efficient civil government could be formed. Primo also told the monarchist Ramón Mercader that the uprising was necessary to save the king.[78] On the other hand, Primo supported the colonial offensive planned by Martínez Anido in the summer of 1923, which served as a means of convincing the men of the 'quadrilateral', who wanted to retain the Spanish position in Africa, that his defeatism regarding Morocco was a thing of the past.[79]

On 7 September 1923, Primo met with the generals Berenguer, Saro, Dabán and Cavalcanti in Madrid and convinced them that he was the appropriate man to lead the rebellion from Barcelona.[80] The generals decided that the uprising would take place within the space of a week. By that time, Primo had already secured the support of General José Sanjurjo, the military governor of Zaragoza. When he returned to the Catalan capital on 9 September, Primo spoke with his loyalist officers from the Barcelona garrison, communicating his intentions to stage an uprising. They were delighted with the idea.[81] According to some authors, on the eve of the uprising, Primo also met with the president of the *Fomento del Trabajo Nacional*, the Viscount of Cussó, the Count of Güell and Milá i Camps to read them the manifesto which he had drawn up for the uprising.[82] Primo also allegedly informed the president of the Mancomunitat, the Catalan regional government, Josep Puig i Cadafalch, of his plans.[83] In the dawn of 12–13 September, Primo de Rivera declared a state of war in Catalonia, sent the gunmen of the *Sindicato Libre* and the Carlist *requetés* to patrol Barcelona, informed the king of the uprising, requested the support of the rest of the captains general, and made public his 'Manifesto to the Country and the Army'.

The Military Directory, 1923–5

Primo entered with force into the leadership of the Spanish government. During the first days of his regime, he created a junta to run the country (the *Directorio Militar*), chose Martínez Anido as Minister of the Interior and second in command, declared a state of war across Spain and dismissed all the civil governors, replacing them with high-ranking military men. Primo also created the *delegados gubernativos* – army officers assigned to all of the country's districts with the aim of controlling municipal politics and destroying the networks of *caciquismo*.[84] The state machinery of administration underwent a de facto militarization. Furthermore, the Military Directory soon took a series of measures which, as the Marques of Estella himself recognized, were of a 'radical' nature.[85] Four days after the coup, Primo de Rivera created the *Somatén Nacional*, extending the armed Catalan organization to the whole of Spain. This was a clear attempt to equip the regime with a civilian militia, in case of future public order problems.[86] Along the same lines, on 18 September the military junta passed a decree against separatism. This legislation gave a legal framework to the persecution which Catalan regionalists and nationalists suffered during the Dictatorship. Meanwhile, another royal decree subjected crimes against the security and the unity of the fatherland to military jurisdiction.[87]

Primo created a permanent state of emergency. With the 1876 constitution suspended as of 13 September 1923, the dictator established a system of pre-censorship for all publications. In January 1924, telephonic and telegraphic censorship also came into effect.[88] What was new about Primo's system of censorship was its unprecedented scope and duration. Censorship had frequently been imposed during the Restoration, in reality every time that the government had declared a state of war, but under Primo it assumed an indefinite character. The dictator created an Office of Information, which was later re-baptized as the Office of Information and Censorship, with the specific goal of prohibiting 'every manifestation of rebelliousness and opposition'.[89] Strongly centralized and under Primo's direct and exclusive control, the department of censorship enjoyed extraordinary powers. It had the legal authority to eliminate paragraphs from press articles, to insert official comments and corrections into the editorials of daily newspapers, to prohibit entire articles, to impose economic sanctions upon newspapers and even to close them down. The Office of Information and Censorship's authority covered all public demonstrations, including those of the King Alfonso XIII. To complement these actions, the military men appointed as civil governors were given instructions to use energetically the 'extraordinary faculties which the suspension of guarantees and the state of war confer on you' and to punish severely anybody who questioned the Directory's role, in the press and in private conversations.[90]

Alongside repression, the Marques of Estella nurtured propaganda with great care. From the first day, he was aware of the necessity to maintain an uninterrupted communication with the general public. In order to survive without the legitimacy of the Cortes, the regime needed to gain the backing of the masses and, with this aim, Primo followed the Italian example, using the weapons of political propaganda and popular mobilization.[91] In the field of propaganda, Primo initially attempted to transmit his ideas and governmental plans through press conferences, rallies, articles which he wrote in newspapers supportive of the regime, and, above all, with the so-called 'official notes'. These notes were press releases, which appeared frequently, sometimes even twice a week, and were obligatory content for all of the country's newspapers. Together, they represented the lengthy monologue which the dictator maintained with the population throughout his entire time in power.

As the regime consolidated itself, its propagandistic machinery became more effective. Primo's speeches and official notes were published in a diverse selection of books and pamphlets, the Office of Information and Censorship became the body which coordinated the regime's line of information both in Spain and overseas, and the government paid newspapers in different parts of the world to ensure that the international press presented a positive image of the Dictatorship.[92] More importantly, more than 60 provincial newspapers were placed under the regimes' control. Furthermore, on 19 October 1925, the daily newspaper *La Nación*, the regime's official mouthpiece, was founded. In 1925, *Unión Patriótica*, the official magazine of the regime's political party, was launched as a fortnightly publication. Soon afterwards, *La Nación* declared that it had a circulation of 55,000 copies, while *Unión Patriótica* asserted that it sold 15,000 copies every two weeks.[93]

During the years of the Military Directory, the Marques of Estella also set in motion the ambitious programmes of mass indoctrination which he had dreamed of after the First World War. The formation of a militarized and politically active 'new citizen' became a priority for Primo, who was sure that Spanish nationalism of an authoritarian nature was the best solution against left-wing ideas. The creation of the *delegados gubernativos*, the *Somatén Nacional* and the offical party, *Union Patriótica* (UP) responded to diverse necessities, but all of these institutions had a common role: they were 'educators'. The *delegados gubernativos* were assigned the task of creating a 'new citizenship' in villages and towns by propagating the military nationalism which had spread through Spain's military barracks during the final years of the Restoration.[94] With this goal, the *delegados* organized mass patriotic rallies and processions in support of the regime, simultaneously launching governmental campaigns aimed at fomenting patriotic morals and duties in multiple localities. In order to complete their educational mission, the *delegados* received direct orders from Primo entrusting them with the task of organizing patriotic conferences which would promote the virtues of the 'Spanish race'.[95]

The Military Directory also brought about significant transformations in the structure of the state. The Municipal Statute (1924) and the Provincial Statute (1925) had a centralist character: they gave civil governors the power to form, dissolve and renew both provincial councils and town councils as they wished throughout the Dictatorship.[96] What is more, in an attack upon democratic proportional representation, the Municipal Statute introduced corporate suffrage for the first time since the fall of the Ancien Régime, and presented the municipality as the 'natural base of the state'.[97] The Provincial Statute, in turn, presented the provinces as directly linked to the state, an action which eliminated the region as an intermediate connector. In fact, the new legislation explicitly prohibited the creation of any kind of association between provinces. This resulted in the abolition of the *Mancomunitat* on the same day that the Provincial Statue came into force.

With this conversion to 'provincialism', Primo was openly rejecting the apparent regionalism which he had initially expressed to *Lliga* members and Carlists in Barcelona. In an official communiqué which coincided with the promulgation of the Provincial Statute, the dictator recognized that in 1923 he himself had believed that regional decentralization was a good strategy for 'affirming the bonds of national unity in Spain', but that the functioning of the *Mancomunitat* had forced him to change his mind.[98] As he understood it, Catalan institutions spread 'anti-Spanishness' which in turn fed the independentist ambitions of the population. Following this logic, a regional administrative division of the state would lead to the glorification of regional peculiarities, thus functioning to 'undo the great work of national unity'.[99] The dissolution of the *Mancomunitat* was the culmination of a policy which, in reality, had begun during the early days of the Dictatorship, when people suspected of maintaining openly Catalan regionalist stances were arrested en masse. Among them were dozens of priests, who were imprisoned or sent into exile by the military authorities.[100]

It is hard to believe that there was any sincerity in the pro-regionalist comments which Primo made in private to *Lliga* members and Carlists in Barcelona before 13 September 1923. As we have seen, the Marques of Estella told each political group what it wanted to hear in order to obtain support for his coup d'état. Whatever the case, Primo de Rivera's vision of Spain anticipated, in many ways, the one which Francisco Franco would impose for 40 years. In the summer of 1926, when Primo set out his vision of a new state structure, he referred to the 'family, with its ancient virtues and its modern concept of citizenship' as the 'cells of the municipalities'. In turn, the municipalities constituted the basic unit of the nation, while the provinces were considered the 'nuclei' of the fatherland.[101] Above these, the state was 'the principal vertebra which directs all of the system'.[102] This was a concept of the nation as a hierarchical entity, composed of families, municipalities and provinces, with the state as the vertebral column – a concept which clearly foreshadowed the positions which the Falange would defend during the 1930s.

An analysis of the first years of the Primo de Rivera regime makes it clear that the Dictatorship imposed by the Marques of Estella cannot be identified with conservative liberalism, as has been asserted on occasions.[103] In reality, the actions of the general from Jerez kept the country in a state of war for more than two years following the military coup; suspended the 1876 Constitution; dissolved parliament; declared the political indoctrination of citizens to be a duty of the state; censored any type of criticism against the regime from day one (it is useful to take into account that censorship was not definitively established in Mussolini's Italy until 1926); unleashed a highly arbitrary political repression which led to the detention of hundreds of opponents; created a system of anonymous denunciations; formed networks to spy on citizens; left judicial authority in limbo due to his continual personal interference; and carried out an unprecedented purge of government employees. Primo de Rivera's political 'service record' placed Spain at the head of the European authoritarian systems in 1925.

The Civil Directory, 1926–30

It is difficult to establish if Primo intended to stay in power indefinitely from the beginning of the Dictatorship or if the idea developed as the Military Directory advanced. Despite having given himself 90 days to solve Spain's problems in his 'Manifesto to the Country and the Army' of 13 September 1923, it is probable that his statements concerning the Dictatorship's temporality were just another ruse within the string of promises which Primo made in order to garner support from different political sectors. After all, this idea of the temporary dictator who endowed himself with supreme powers in order to bring order to the constitutional disarray linked up perfectly with the well-known figure of Joaquín Costa's 'iron surgeon' held in such high esteem by middle class regenerationist sectors.[104] But it is beyond doubt that the break-up of the Restoration system began with the Military Directory. In spite of the comments which Primo repeated from time to the effect that he intended to return to the 1876 Constitution in an undetermined future, the truth is that the official dissolution of parliament, the destruction of the Restoration's dynastic parties and the creation of the Unión Patriótica indicated precisely the opposite. With the creation of the Civil Directory, the door to a return to the 'normality' of the Restoration closed definitively and the construction of a new authoritarian state began.

The new state was, to a large extent, designed by the dictator. The creation of the National Assembly, the development of a corporatist system, the attempts to prepare a new authoritarian-style constitution and the educational reform were the Civil Directory's key transformations, and Primo played a decisive role in all of them. The Marques of Estella tended to intervene personally in the projects which he entrusted to his ministers, and any moderately important piece of legislation needed the dictator's approval. Primo usually spent the first hours of the night amending royal decrees, before the secretary of the presidency of the government sent them to the Gaceta de Madrid for official publication. Controlling and somewhat obsessive, Primo did not want to delegate excessively. He used the ever faithful Martínez Anido to supervise directly the projects which he considered could cause problems, although the Marques of Estella always reserved the last word for himself.[105] Primo tried to create a new, authoritarian, modern Spain adapted to the post-First World War European stage, but he was also certain that his bid was a personal one.

Something that did not change during the Civil Directory was the regime's tactic of combining the indoctrination of the masses with repression of opponents. During this period, new reforms were introduced to improve patriotic education in prisons, army officers were ordered to organize thousands of patriotic conferences in towns across Spain, and a National Service of Physical, Citizenship and Pre-military Education was formed. Educational reforms were carried out in primary and secondary schools with the stated objective of 'nationalizing the school' and Unión Patriótica and the Somatén continued to be used as 'citizenship schools'. Furthermore, the regime placed special emphasis upon the promotion of patriotic fiestas, be they celebrations inherited from the Restoration (like the Day of the Race or the Fiesta of the Tree) or ones invented by the Dictatorship (like the Fiesta of the Book or the Fiesta of the Teacher). The idea was to present clear, simple and direct messages. As Primo would tell his old friend Françesc Cambó, the ideas of the crowds were 'simplistic', so it was necessary to adapt the message to their comprehension abilities.[106]

All of these ceremonies, together with anniversaries of 13 September and celebrations of the Spanish victories in Africa, were also used to extol the figure of Primo as 'national caudillo'. On a discursive level, the regime's press propagated the image of the dictator as a prophetic leader and saviour of the fatherland in religious terms.[107] Portraits of Primo were also frequently hung in the headquarters of the UP, while images of the dictator were paraded through the streets during the party's public ceremonies and official functions.[108] Still not satisfied with these actions, the government named dozens of streets in different towns across Spain after the dictator, and after 1926 the vast majority of new public primary schools bore Primo de Rivera's name.[109] It is true that Primo lacked the loquacity of Mussolini and that the UP did not have the propagandistic force of the Partito Nazionale Fascista, but this did not prevent the Spanish regime from attempting to create a personality cult around the dictator. For example, in Madrid the UP regularly coordinated parades in front of the Palace of Buenavista, where Primo's office was located, in order to show its support for the dictator. Upon witnessing this type of liturgy, the British ambassador in Madrid could not help but think of the fascist assemblies which were organized in Italy in front of the Palazzo Venezia.[110] On some occasions, the dictator's presence succeeded in assembling large crowds of people. In January 1926, the ceremonies celebrated during his visit to Barcelona included a colossal parade of 20,000 UP members.[111] In September 1928, all of the regime's propagandistic machinery swung into action for the celebrations of the fifth anniversary of the coup. For a week, members of the UP organized meetings, dinners and parades in hundreds of towns across the country.[112] Furthermore, activists from all over the country received train tickets and free sandwiches in order to travel to Madrid. According to the official press, 100,000 UP members participated in a procession in the Spanish capital to commemorate the coup.[113] Three days later, 40,000 regime supporters congregated in Barcelona.[114]

There is no doubt that these kinds of stage-managed mobilizations pleased Primo greatly. It is possible that they made him feel that he was truly loved by the people, but they also irritated Alfonso XIII, who observed that the personalized dictatorial project propounded by the Marques of Estella consigned him (the king) to the background. This royal distancing from the Primo regime became evident in 1927, when Alfonso XIII refused to sign off the project for the creation of the National Assembly on the grounds that it would mean the definitive liquidation of the Restoration regime. He was, however, eventually pressured by Primo into accepting the project.[115] By 1928, the differences between king and dictator had mounted. In September the monarch flew to Sweden in order to avoid being present at the celebrations of the coup which had brought Primo to power. The Marques of Estella, nevertheless, had a clear idea of who was running the country and declared that he would not allow himself to be 'Bourbonized' as others had done in the past.[116] Long gone were the days of 1923, in which Alfonso XIII could proudly call Primo 'my Mussolini' in the presence of the Italian king Vittorio Emanuele III. The relationship between king and dictator, which had been the key to setting the Primo regime in motion, cracked during the Civil Directory.

Continuity could be found, however, in the Dictatorship's repressive policies. The system of anonymous denunciations, networks of espionage among government employees, censorship and policies of mass imprisonment of opponents which had been established during the Military Directory remained in force during the second part of the Dictatorship. Moreover, when Primo saw that his regime was under threat, he made a move towards profoundly repressive policies. This was the case with the new legislation introduced following the attempted insurrections in Valencia and Ciudad Real of 1929. The legislation turned the Somatén and the UP into institutions of espionage with policing functions. The Royal Decree of 4 February 1929 gave the party and the militia 'complementary vigilance duties' and called for an increase in both organizations' participation in tasks of political repression.[117] Among the new measures taken were the creation of 'centres of civic investigation and information, set up to collaborate with the Authorities in whatever might affect the maintenance of public order'.

These centres, which were under the UP's control, processed denunciations presented by ordinary citizens. The centres also organized espionage
networks through which the corporals of the *Somatén* of 'each district, town
or neighbourhood' had the duty to accumulate information and establish
files on all of the regime's political opponents in the local headquarters of
the party and the militia. Likewise, paramilitaries and UP members were
given authority to carry out searches in the houses of the regime's alleged
opponents.[118] Furthermore, *Somatén* members were encouraged to use
violence against those who threatened 'public order', and they were given
authorization to close any association which conducted 'political debates'.[119]

Undoubtedly, these measures marked a qualitative shift towards semi-
totalitarian postures on the Dictatorship's part.[120] The party, the militia, the
security forces and the army overlapped in the service of the Primo regime's
repression in what constituted the creation of a de facto police state. The
distinction between the public and private spheres blurred as the paramilitaries started to invade political opponents' homes and premises. As was to
be expected, the 'blank cheque' which the regime had handed over to the
militia and the party increased the incidence of abuses of authority, unfounded
anonymous accusations and mass imprisonments of political opponents, who
were held without charge for months on end.[121] The consequences of the
regime's radicalization were catastrophic for the Dictatorship's public image.
At the end of December 1929, Primo publicly recognized something which
was already an open secret: many sectors of Spanish society were dissat-
isfied with the regime, including Catholic groups and government employees
– that is to say, the pillars of the UP.[122] At the end of January 1930, the
Dictatorship fell.

Yet Primo did not give up his power voluntarily, as his propagandists
maintained at the time, and as some historians still claim.[123] In fact, he was
very reluctant to let go of the reins of power. At the end of 1929, when
Alfonso XIII realized that that the only way he could maintain the monarchy
would be to rid himself of Primo, a series of problems arose. The king established contacts with some of the politicians of the Restoration, but they
refused to help him without the calling of a previous session of the Cortes.
This meant that the king had to make do with supporting, from behind the
scenes, a military conspiracy orchestrated by his cousin, Prince Carlos de
Borbón, and led by General Goded, the military governor of Cadiz. Primo then
played his final cards. Aware that the Goded conspiracy was being prepared
for mid-February 1930, the Marques of Estella acted quickly, denying publicly
on 25 January that the seditious activity was underway in order to foil it. On
26 January, Primo announced that he would refer the question of his continuity in power to all of the captains general. This was a kind of plebiscite
on the Dictatorship, which entailed an explicit recognition that the regime's

fundamental legitimacy lay in the army rather than in the monarchy. Crucially, it also revealed that the Marques of Estella was prepared to continue, even with the opposition of Alfonso XIII.[124] But Primo lost the bet. On 27 January, the only generals who gave the dictator their unconditional support were José Sanjurjo and Enrique Marzo Balaguer. The remainder of the captains general were ambiguous in their responses, something which was equivalent to not backing the Marques of Estella's proposal. Primo resigned in the afternoon of 27 January 1930.

Myths and Inheritances

Following Primo de Rivera's death on 16 March 1930, the men of the Dictatorship devoted themselves to perpetuating the image of the general from Jerez which the regime's propaganda had been constructing, and which, as we have noted, would have a long-lasting role in Spanish historiography.[125] This image was composed of three fundamental myths: that of the unpretentious man loved by the people; that of the religious patriot who was forced to intervene in order to save Spain from debacle; and that of the kind-hearted man who governed the country with great leniency and who never wished to shed blood. However, the writings and actions of the Marques of Estella display a radically different man: a military man who, far from being straightforward and unaffected, was populist and demagogical in his attempts to indoctrinate the masses who he considered to be simplistic; a dictator who, far from lacking ideology, or from sustaining vague patriotic principles, tried to impose a brand of authoritarian Spanish nationalism as a panacea against the reforms being proposed by the workers' movement; a man who used Catholicism as an ideological component in order to endow the nation with a sacred character, but who was not ashamed to persecute members of the clergy who supported Catalan autonomy. He was a general who promoted the assassinations of trade unionists, and who established a police state which transformed thousands of people into the victims of reprisals.

The caricatured image of Primo also does nothing to help us understand that our subject was an intelligent politician, capable of convincing very different groups in 1923 that he was the appropriate man to carry out their projects once he had ascended to power via a coup d'état. Primo, furthermore, knew perfectly how to read the profound social and political transformations which followed the First World War. He believed that the only way of controlling the masses without paying the toll of democracy was by means of a dictatorship which would 'educate' the people in the values of authoritarian nationalism. Like his contemporary Mussolini, Primo combined the use of repression and propaganda, conscious of the impossibility of constructing a new state merely over a base of coercive force. As in Italy, the construction of the new regime lay in the prior destruction of the liberal system. But, unlike the case of Mussolini, the level of opposition aroused by the initiation of the authoritarian project was able to put an end to the Dictatorship.

Primo was not a nineteenth-century-style brass hat. His authoritarian project has to be understood within the framework of the crisis of liberalism in interwar Europe. We must understand his ideological legacy, crucial to both the extreme right during the Second Republic and to Francoism, in the same context. There is no doubt that the Franco Dictatorship, much crueller and more bloodthirsty, both in its Civil War origins and in its development, was different to Primo's. Yet it is also beyond doubt that Francoism was constructed using many of the same ideological postulations which had previously been developed by *primorriverismo*.

Endnotes

* The author is grateful to the British Academy and Spanish *Ministerio de Ciencia e Innovación* for their financial assistance.

1 J. Cortés Cavanillas, *La dictadura y el dictador. Rasgos históricos, políticos y psicológicos* (Madrid: Talleres Tipográficos Velasco, 1929), pp. 303–10. Both quotations on page 310.

2 Ibid., p. 70.

3 Ibid., p. 71.

4 M. Gandarias, *Perfiles síquicos del dictador y bosquejo razonado de su obra* (Madrid: Escuelas profesionales salesianas, 1929), pp. 8–9.

5 For instance, E. R. Tarduchy, *Psicología del dictador. Caracteres más salientes morales, sociales y políticos de la Dictadura española* (Madrid: Sáez Hermanos, 1929), pp. 150–1; J. Pemartín y Sanjuán, *Los valores históricos en la dictadura española* (Madrid: Sáez Hermanos, 1928), p. 50; Cortés, *La dictadura*, pp. 316–17.

6 For the 'nervous sanguineous temperament', see Tarduchy, *Psicología*, pp. 74–7. The attribute of 'intuitionism' in Pemartín, *Los valores*, pp. 596–601. R. D. Desmond also highlighted that Primo had 'a constitution of iron and a capacity of work that [was] enormous' in his 1927 article 'Dictatorship in Spain', *Foreign Affairs*, V (2): 276–92. The quotation is on page 292. Much more critical with a man 'fond of rhetoric' and a 'weakness for wine, women and gambling' was Carleton Beals in his 10 July 1929 article for the American magazine *The Nation*. See also his articles on Primo de Rivera in *The Nation* dated 26 June 1929 and 3 July 1929.

7 F. Villanueva, *La dictadura militar: II tomo de 'Obstáculos tradicionales'. Crónica documentada de la oposicón y la represión bajo el Directorio (1923–1926)* (Madrid: Javier Morata, 1930); Q. Saldaña García-Rubio, *Al*

servicio de la justicia. La orgía áurea de la Dictadura (Madrid: Javier Morata, 1930); G. Maura Gamazo, *Al servicio de la historia. Bosquejo histórico de la Dictadura*, 2 vols (Madrid: Javier Morata, 1930); idem, *España bajo la Dictadura. Siete años sin ley* (Madrid: El Sol, 1930); R. Salazar Alonso, *La justicia bajo la Dictadura* (Madrid: Zeus, 1930).

8 For example, I. Fernández de Henestrosa y Moiño, *El Marqués de Estella, soldado, dictador, hombre de estado* (Madrid: Imp. de D. Antonio Marzo, 1930), p. 7.

9 C. González Ruano, *Miguel Primo de Rivera. La vida heroica y romántica de un general español* (Madrid: Nuestra Raza, 1940?), p. 174.

10 E. Aunós, *El general Primo de Rivera. Soldado y gobernante* (Madrid: Alhambra, 1944), pp. 12–20.

11 Ibid., pp. 238–40.

12 J. M. Cuenca Toribio, 'Miguel Primo de Rivera a escala histórica', *Historia y Vida*, 22 (1970): 50–8. The quotation is on page 50.

13 Ibid., 54.

14 Ibid., 54.

15 R. Salazar, *Historia y Vida*, 22 (1970): 58–65.

16 A. de Sagrera, *Miguel Primo de Rivera. El hombre, el soldado y el político* (Jerez de la Frontera: Ayuntamiento de Jerez de la Frontera, 1973).

17 The same 'anecdotal' approach was taken by Rocío Primo de Rivera in her book *Los Primo de Rivera* (Madrid: La Esfera de los Libros, 2003). According to the author, the book is 'like a movie based on real events', where one cannot differentiate between 'reality and fiction'. This is not a hyper-postmodern approach to writing biography but rather a biological-spiritual one. Rocío Primo de Rivera believes that her genetic connection to the subjects of the book helps her to reach a better understanding of the 'souls' of her forebears. The quotations are on pages 16–18.

18 R. Morodo Leoncio, 'El 18 de Brumario español: la dictadura de Primo de Rivera', *Triunfo*, 572 (1973): 22–7; M. Pastor, *Los orígenes del fascismo en España* (Madrid: Túcar, 1975); M. Tuñón de Lara, 'En torno a la Dictadura de Primo de Rivera', *Cuadernos Económicos del I.C.E.*, 10 (1978): 9–35; Colectivo de Historia, 'La Dictadura de Primo de Rivera y el bloque de poder en España', *Cuadernos Económicos de I.C.E.*, 6 (1978): 178–216.

19 J. Tusell Gómez, *La crisis del caciquismo andaluz (1923–1931)* (Madrid: Cupsa, 1977); J. Tusell Gómez and G. García Queipo de Llano, 'La Dictadura de Primo de Rivera como régimen político. Un intento de interpretación', *Cuadernos Económicos de I.C.E.*, 10 (1979): 38–63. For an updated account of the same thesis see C. Seco Serrano and J. Tusell Gómez, 'La España de Alfonso XIII. El Estado y la política (1902–1931). Vol. II: Del plano inclinado hacia la Dictadura al final de la Monarquía, 1922–1931', in J. M. Jover Zamora ed., *Historia de España de Menéndez Pidal* (Madrid: Espasa-Calpe, 1995), Vol. XXXVIII, pp. 11–51.

20 For the idea of 'fascism from above' see S. Ben-Ami, *Fascism from above: the Dictatorship of Primo de Rivera in Spain 1923–1930* (Oxford: Clarendon

Press, 1983). The interpretation of *primorriverismo* as a regime similar to the dictatorships which emerged in Central and Eastern Europe in J. L. Gómez-Navarro, *El régimen de Primo de Rivera. Reyes, dictadura y dictadores* (Madrid: Cátedra, 1991).

21 S. Ben-Ami, *La Dictadura de Primo de Rivera (1923–1930)* (Barcelona: Planeta, 1984), pp. 9–10.

22 Gómez-Navarro, *El régimen*, pp. 530–1; Ben-Ami, *La Dictadura de Primo de Rivera*, pp. 257, 261. The idea of the Dictatorship of Primo de Rivera as a precursor of Francoism had been put forward for the first time in a serious academic study in D. F. Ratcliff, *Prelude to Franco. Political Aspects of the Dictatorship of General Primo de Rivera* (New York: Las Americas Publishing Company, 1957).

23 X. Casals Masseguer, 'Miguel Primo de Rivera, l'architetto del franchismo', *Passato e presente*, 82 (2011): 39–65; idem, *Miguel Primo de Rivera. El espejo de Franco* (Barcelona: Ediciones B, 2004); ídem, 'Primo de Rivera. El espejo de Franco', *Clío,* September, 38 (2005). In the same line, J. L. Gómez-Navarro, 'Primo de Rivera. ¿Un modelo para Franco?', *Clío,* September, 14 (2003).

24 E. González Calleja, *La España de Primo de Rivera. La modernización autoritaria* (Madrid: Alianza, 2005), p. 391.

25 'Don Miguel Primo de Rivera: el dictador que no derramó sangre', *ABC,* 26 May 2006.

26 R. Tamames, *Miguel Primo de Rivera* (Barcelona: Ediciones B, 2004); ídem, *Miguel Primo de Rivera. Ni Mussolini ni Franco* (Barcelona: Planeta).

27 S. Hillers de Luque, 'El pensamiento social del General Primo de Rivera', *Revista de la Facultad de Derecho de la Universidad Complutense*, 69 (1983): 113–38.

28 J. Escribano Hernández,, 'Formación y defensa del Directorio Militar', *Cuadernos de Investigación Histórica*, 22 (2005): 373–99. The quotations are on pages 375–6 and 378.

29 Ibid., 376.

30 Ibid., 379.

31 Sagrera, *Primo de Rivera*, pp. 3–23.

32 Casals, *Miguel Primo de Rivera. El espejo de Franco*, pp. 134–5.

33 M. Primo de Rivera, *Yunque y Martillo* (Madrid: Rafael Caro Raggio, 1930), pp. 11–30.

34 Casals, *Miguel Primo de Rivera. El espejo de Franco*, pp. 20–2.

35 Ibid., pp. 142–3.

36 Aunós, *Primo de Rivera*, p. 28.

37 J. Tusell Gómez, *Radiografía de un golpe de estado: el ascenso al poder del general Primo de Rivera* (Madrid: Alianza Editorial, 1987), p.30.

38 Sagrera, *Primo de Rivera*, p. 114.

39 The manifesto is in J. Casassas Ymbert, *La Dictadura de Primo de Rivera (textos)* (Barcelona: Anthropos, 1983), pp. 81–5.

40 S. Balfour, *The End of the Spanish Empire, 1898–1923* (Oxford: Clarendon Press, 1997), pp. 230–1.

41 As he later acknowledged in M. Primo de Rivera, *El Pensamiento de Primo de Rivera. Sus notas, artículos y discursos* (Madrid: Sáez Hermanos/Junta de Propaganda Patriótica y Ciudadana, 1929), p. 169.

42 Ibid., p. 169.

43 Tusell, *Radiografía*, pp. 32–3.

44 Casals, *Miguel Primo de Rivera. El espejo de Franco*, pp. 138, 143.

45 S. Balfour, 'The Lion and the Pig: Nationalism and National Identity in Fin-de-Siècle Spain', in C. Mar-Molinero and A. Smith (eds), *Nationalism and the Nation in the Iberian Peninsula* (Washington/Oxford: Berg, 1996), pp. 107–17; G. Jensen, 'Military Nationalism and the State. The case of Fin-de-Siècle Spain', *Nations and Nationalism*, 6 (2) (2000): 257–74.

46 M. Primo de Rivera, *Los nuevos moldes de organización militar* (Madrid: R. Velasco, 1919).

47 *Revista Técnica de Infantería y Caballería*, 2 (10), 15 November 1905, 445–50.

48 M. Primo de Rivera, 'Prólogo', in T. García Figueras and J. de la Matta y Ortigosa, *Elementos de educación moral del soldado* (Sevilla: F. Díaz, 1916), pp. xi–xiv.

49 C. Navajas Zubeldia, 'La ideología corporativa de Miguel Primo de Rivera (1905–1919)', *Hispania*, LIII (184) (1993): 644.

50 Ibid., 644–5.

51 J. M. Pemán, *Mis almuerzos con gente importante* (Barcelona: Dopesa, 1970), p. 19.

52 M. Primo de Rivera, *La cuestión del día. Gibraltar y África. Discurso del General PR. Una carta íntima. Un prólogo. Dos apéndices* (Cadiz: Imp. De M. Álvarez, 1917), p. 34.

53 Tusell, *Radiografía*, p. 38.

54 Casals, *Miguel Primo de Rivera. El espejo de Franco*, pp. 163–4.

55 M. Primo de Rivera, *La obra de la Dictadura. Sus cuatro últimos artículos* (Madrid: Sáez Hermanos, 1930), p. 8.

56 Ibid., p. 8.

57 F. Romero Salvadó, *The Foundations of Civil War. Revolution Social Conflict and Reaction in Liberal Spain, 1916–1923* (London: Routledge, 2008), p. 231.

58 Tusell, *Radiografía*, p. 44.

59 *El Correo Catalán*, 24 March 1922.

60 *El Correo Catalán*, 25 March 1922.

61 E. González Calleja, *El Máuser y el sufragio. Orden público, subversión y violencia política en la crisis de la Restauración (1917–1931)* (Madrid: CSIC, 1999), pp. 116–216; P. Foix, *Los archivos del terrorismo blanco. El fichero Lasarte: 1910–1930* (Madrid : Ediciones la Piqueta, 1978).

62 Romero, *Foundations*, p. 285.

63 Primo de Rivera, *La obra*, p. 10.

64 Romero, *Foundations*, p. 286.

65 The Carlist campaign in *El Correo Catalán*, 4 May 1923, 8 May 1923, 10 May 1923, 12 May 1923, 16 May 1923 and 19 May 1923.

66 *La Vanguardia*, 29 May 1923.

67 *El Correo Catalán*, 8 May 1923.

68 *El Correo Catalán*, 17 May 1923 and 18 May 1923.

69 *La Vanguardia*, 13 May 1923 and *El Correo Catalán*, 15 May 1923.

70 *El Correo Catalán*, 31 May 1923, 1 June 1923, 2 June 1923, 3 June 1923; *La Veu de Catalunya*, 2 June 1923.

71 *La Vanguardia*, 8 June 23.

72 *La Vanguardia*, 10 June 23.

73 Primo de Rivera, *La obra*, p. 10.

74 Romero, *Foundations*, pp. 287–8.

75 Ibid., p. 288.

76 For the lack of a sound ideology, see, for example, D. Dionisio Pérez, *La Dictadura a través de sus notas oficiosas* (Madrid: Compañía Ibero-Americana de Publicaciones, 1930), p. 17.

77 F. del Rey and S. Bengoechea, 'El capitalismo catalán y Primo de Rivera: en torno a un golpe de Estado', *Hispania*, XLVIII (168) (1988): 289–307; J. Jacob, and M. Jordá, 'Hacia la Dictadura Primo de Rivera en la Capitanía General de Cataluña', *Profesor Nazario González. Una Historia Abierta* (Barcelona: Universitat Autònoma-Publicacions de la Universitat de Barcelona, 1998), pp.438–49.

78 C. Boyd, *La política pretoriana en el reinado de Alfonso XIII* (Madrid: Alianza, 1990), p. 311.

79 Ben-Ami, *La dictadura*, pp. 32–3.

80 Primo de Rivera, *La obra*, pp. 12–13; Boyd, *La política pretoriana*, p. 310.

81 Romero, *Foundations*, p. 288.

82 Primo's alleged meeting with the president of the *Fomento del Trabajo Nacional*, the Viscount of Cussó, the Count of Güell and Milá i Camps in A. Perucho, *Catalunya sota al Dictadura* (Barcelona: Proa, 1930), pp. 18–19.

83 The presumed leak to Puig i Cadafalch, in ibid., p. 19.

84 The Royal Decree creating the *delegados gubernativos* in *La Gaceta*, 21 October 1923.

85 Primo de Rivera, *La obra*, p. 18.

86 The Royal Decree creating the Somatén, in *La Gaceta*, 18 September 1923.

87 The Royal Decree against separatism, in *La Gaceta*, 18 September1923, and the Royal Decree placing crimes against the unity and the security of the patria under military jusrisdiction, in *La Gaceta*, 19 September 1923.

88 M. Rubio Cabeza, *Crónica de la Dictadura* (Madrid: Sarpe, 1986), p. 124.

89 C. de la Iglesia, *La censura por dentro* (Madrid: CIAP, 1930). The quotation is on pages 75–6.

90 See the circulars sent by Martínez Anido to all civil governors, dated 10 October 1923 and 27 October 1923, Archivo Histórico Nacional (AHN), Gobernación Serie A, Bundle 18 A.

91 R. Martínez Segarra, 'La Unión Patriótica', in J. Tusell, F. Montero and J. M. Marín (eds), *Las derechas en la España contemporánea* (Madrid: UNED, 1993), p. 169.

92 For the compilations of the dictator's speeches and notes, see M. Primo de Rivera, *España: Honor, patria, Justicia* (prologue by Benito Mussolini) (Madrid: Imprenta y Encuadernación de Julián Espinosa, 1923); idem, *Discursos del Excmo. Sr. D. Francisco Bergamín, Presidente de la Academia [de Jurisprudencia] sobre Tribunales de Comercio, y del Excmo. Sr. D. Miguel Primo de Rivera* (Madrid: Talleres de la Editorial Reus, 1924); idem, *Discurso leído por el Excmo. Señor D. Miguel Primo de Rivera y Obraneja en la Solemne Apertura de los Tribunales* (Madrid: Talleres de la Editorial Reus, 1924); Marqués de Casa Ramos, *Dos años de Directorio Militar* (Madrid: Renacimiento, 1926?); M. Primo de Rivera, *Disertación ciudadana. Destinada a mantener la comunicación entre el gobierno y los ciudadanos sobre algunos aspectos de la vida pública* (Madrid: Sanz Calleja, no date, but 1926); idem, *Actuación ciudadana que corresponde al Ejército* (Madrid: Juan Pérez Torres, 1927); idem, *Del General Primo de Rivera: documentos originales y artículos inspirados por él* (Madrid: Junta de Propaganda Patriótica y Ciudadana, 1928); idem, *El pensamiento de Primo de Rivera. Sus notas, artículos y discursos* (Madrid: Sáez Hermanos/Junta de Propaganda Patriótica y Ciudadana, 1929); idem, 'Prólogo', in E. Pérez Agudo et al., *Curso de ciudadanía. Conferencias pronunciadas en el Alcázar de Toledo. Marzo 1929* (Madrid: Junta de Propaganda Patriótica y Ciudadana, 1929), pp. ix–xi; idem, *Mirando al futuro* (Madrid: Junta de Propaganda Patriótica y Ciudadana, 1929). For the *primorriverista* propaganda machine abroad, see R. Cal, 'La agencia *Plus Ultra*: un instrumento de propaganda de Primo de Rivera', *Mélanges de la Casa de Valázquez*, XXXI (3) (1995): 177–95.

93 J. L. Gómez-Navarro Navarrete, 'Unión Patriótica: análisis de un partido del poder', *Estudios de Historia Social* (32–3) (1985): 156.

94 *La Gaceta*, 21 October 1923.

95 The instructions to the *delegados* in the Royal Decrees of 20 October 1923 and 20 March 1924 and the Royal Order of 9 December 1923. Primo's orders to the *delegados*, in his letters of 10 December 1923; 5 April 1924; 24 April 1924. Martínez Anido's order in his circular of 7 December 1923. All documents in Archivo General de la Administración del Estado (AGA), Subsecretaría Sección de Orden Público, Interior, box 149.

96 M. T. González Calbet, *La Dictadura de Primo de Rivera. El Directorio Militar* (Madrid: El Arquero, 1987), pp. 244–5.

97 See the 'Preamble' to the Statute in *La Gaceta*, 9 March 1924.

98 Official note, 21 March 1925 in Primo de Rivera, *El Pensamiento*, pp. 102–5.

99 Ibid., p. 103.

100 For the *primorriverista* repression in Catalonia, see E. Ucelay Da-Cal, 'La repressió de la Dictadura de Primo de Rivera', in *Iles. Jornades de debat. El poder de l'Estat: evolució, força o raó* (Reus: Centre de Lectura de Reus, 1993), pp. 153–210; J. M. Roig Rosich, *La Dictadura de Primo de Rivera a Catalunya. Un assaig de repressió cultural* (Barcelona: Publicacions de l'Abadia de Montserrat, 1992); González Calleja, *El Máuser y el sufragio*, pp. 344–87.

101 'Manifiesto a la nación', 5 September 1926, in Primo de Rivera, *El Pensamiento*, pp. 35–8.

102 Ibid., p. 36.

103 This was the case of C. Beadman, 'Official nationalism of the Primo de Rivera Regime: Some findings from the pages of *Unión Patriótica* and *Somatén*', *International Journal of Iberian Studies*, 11 (2) (1998): 74; J. Tusell Gómez and G. García Queipo de Llano, 'La Dictadura de Primo de Rivera como régimen político. Un intento de interpretación', *Cuadernos Económicos de I.C.E.*, 10 (1979): 56; and Tusell, *Radiografía*, p. 270.

104 González Calbet, *La Dictadura*, pp. 50–1, 265.

105 This was also the case in the elaboration of both the Municipal and the Provincial Statutes. Primo ordered Martínez Anido to supervise personally the works of the committees created to draft the statutes. See A. Quiroga, *Making Spaniards. Primo de Rivera and the Nationalization of the Masses, 1923–30* (Basingstoke: Palgrave-Macmillan, 2007), p. 46.

106 Primo de Rivera, *El pensamiento*, p. 30.

107 See, for example, *La Nación*, 11 December 1925; *El Somatén*, August 1924; Mask (pseudonym of Enrique Díaz Retg), *Páginas para la Historia. Hacia la España nueva: pasado, presente y porvenir del Directorio Militar* (Madrid: Sucesores de Rivadeneyra, 1925), p. 189.

108 See, for instance, *El Somatén*, August 1924; *Unión Patriótica*, 1 November 1926; 1 April 1927; *La Nación*, 13 September 1927.

109 See the reports by the *delegados gubernativos* in Archivo Histórico Nacional, Presidencia del Gobierno, Bundle 358.

110 Ben-Ami, *La dictadura*, p. 100.

111 *Unión Patriótica*, 15 April 1927.

112 *La Nación*, 10 September 1928; 11 September 1928; 12 September 1928.

113 *La Nación*, 13 September 1928.

114 *La Nación*, 17 September 1928.

115 González Calleja, *La modernización*, p. 141.

116 Ben-Ami, *La dictadura*, p. 121.

117 Royal Decree 4 February 1929, in *El Somatén*, February 1929.

118 Article 3, Royal Decree, 4 February 1929, and Article 5, Royal Circular Order, 8 February 1929, in *El Somatén*, February 1929; Royal Circular Order, 16 April 1929, in *Colección Legislativa del Ejército*, 147 (1929): 86–7.

119 Royal Circular Order, 8 February 1929, in *El Somatén*, February 1929; and Royal Circular Order, 16 April 1929, in *Colección Legislativa del Ejército*, 147 (1929): 86–7.

120 E. González Calleja, 'La defensa armada del "orden social" durante la Dictadura de Primo de Rivera (1923–1930)', in J. L. García Delgado ed., *España entre dos siglos (1875–1931). Continuidad y cambio* (Madrid: Siglo XXI, 1991), p. 104.

121 For cases of anonymous accusations and mass imprisonments of political opponents held without charges, see the correspondance of Martínez Anido in the Archivo Histórico Nacional, Gobernación (Estado), Bundle 59, Box 2.

122 Official note, 31 December 1929, in *El Sol*, 1 January 1930.

123 For example, C. Seco Serrano, 'Don Miguel Primo de Rivera: el dictador que no derramó sangre', *ABC*, 26 May 2006.

124 González Calleja, *La dictadura*, pp. 323–4.

125 In April 1930, *Unión Patriótica* devoted an entire issue to praise the dictator. In 1932, *Acción Española*, the far-right magazine in which most of the *primorriverista* ideologues wrote during the Second Republic, also dedicated a monographic number to the dictator.

3

José María Gil Robles: The Catholic Challenge to Democracy

EDUARDO GONZÁLEZ CALLEJA

On 4 October 1935, *Who Am I?*, a comedy by Juan Ignacio Luca de Tena, premiered at Madrid's Alcázar theatre. The play's protagonist is Mario Colomer, a young professor turned Minister of Saldaria (an imaginary country whose name was inspired by the Greek populist Panagis Tsaldaris who, having won the elections of March 1933, had become dictator two years later, leading the abolition of the democratic constitution of 1927) who finds his exact double and a willing accomplice in Juan Brandel. The two switch places, whereupon Brandel's warm personality wins the favour of the people and of Claudina, a representation of the national spirit and the lover of the authentic and taciturn leader. The substitute exceeds his authority, however, and puts the personal and political situation of Colomer in danger at a time when rumours of a coup d'état are becoming more insistent. The jealous confrontation between the two protagonists ends with the death of one without the spectator knowing for certain which. After the crime, the General Barclano, to whom Colomer had made manifest his legalist scruples, cedes unlimited and unconditional power to the enigmatic protagonist and makes of him 'the symbol, the flag that must be of service to make the revolution'.[1]

This fable by a mediocre playwright condenses to perfection the image that conservative sectors forged of a leader of the Spanish right at the height of his power: José María Gil Robles made ambiguity the essence of his strategy for the conquest of power and faced on several occasions the temptation of authoritarianism, but a confluence of adverse circumstances brought him to premature failure.

Born in 1898 into the bosom of a deeply traditionalist family, the young José María was a brilliant student of Law in Salamanca, his native city. He became chair of Political Law in the University of La Laguna on 29 May 1922, whereupon he immediately became involved in the activities of *Acción Católica* (Catholic Action), joining the editorial team of *El Debate*, the daily newspaper where he would attain the post of deputy editor. Hand in hand with his mentor, Ángel Herrera, with whom he maintained tortuous relations, he joined the propaganda campaigns of social Catholicism on platforms such as those provided by the Asociación Católica Nacional de Propagandistas (ACNP), *Acción Social Popular* (People's Social Action) and the *Partido Social Popular* (PSP – People's Social Party), in whose presentation rally at the Comedy theatre of 15 April 1923 he spoke with disdain of the 'rotten, unburied corpse of liberal democracy'.[2].

The arrival of Primo de Rivera's dictatorship in September gave him the opportunity to participate in the design of the longed for authoritarian policy, aiding in the creation of the *Unión Patriótica Castellana* (Castilian Patriotic Union) and forming part of the team of specialists that, headed by José Calvo Sotelo, drew up the project of the Municipal Statute. In those years of apprenticeship he laid the foundations of his political influence in the Castilian agricultural world, establishing a dense network of relations through his position as Secretary General of the Catholic-Agrarian National Confederation. True political recognition would come, however, during the crisis and fall of the monarchy. In the campaign of 'civic reaction' for the municipal elections of April 1931, Gil Robles unveiled a catastrophist discourse in which he alternated between basic anti-republicanism and an accidentalist thesis on forms of government. This was the path he had signalled in the editorial he wrote for *El Debate* the day following the proclamation of the Republic, lyrically described by one of his hagiographers: 'When the Crown collapsed, between the mud of multiple passions and buffeted by the urges of many Pharisees, he tried to save what he could, and what he arrived at was the Cross, which he would serve utterly.'[3]

In May of 1931, the foundational manifesto of *Acción Nacional* (AN – National Action) described itself, not as a political party, but as an organization of 'social defence' charged with the preservation of conservative principles and institutions untied to any specific form of government. The theretofore stunted representation of the Catholic-agrarian right catapulted it immediately to the forefront of political activity, above all during discussion of the controversial Article 24 (later 26) of the Constitution, which withdrew state support for the Church along with its special legal status. Gil Robles announced his non-violent hostility to the constitutional project on 8 October 1931 and, having done so, the vote on this article prompted the withdrawal of the Catholic deputies and acted as a clarion call that triggered an intense campaign of mobilization for a revision of the constitution. This would be the great unifying cause of rightist political action in the months that followed.

While in the final moments of Franco's dictatorship Gil Robles asserted that 'one of my principal objectives in those years was to convert the Spanish right into a moderate element of conciliation, in order to save it from shipwreck when that was still possible from our point of view',[4] in his previous book of memoirs he had brought less seraphic intentions to light. The revisionist campaign had as its end: 'First: to vigorously externalise the protest against the sectarian policy. Second: to give back to the right, by means of great concentrations of the masses, the lost consciousness of their strength. Third: to make them accustomed to confronting leftist violence and to struggling, when necessary, for possession of the streets. Fourth: to disseminate ideas and make converts through the exposition of the doctrine.'[5] During the campaign, the leader spurred the Catholic multitudes to defend their rights in the street, arousing the ferment of civil war through permanent attacks on the government. The well-known conservative Miguel Maura warned that the language he was employing was a call to religious war that could do irreparable damage to the Republic.[6] The great error, which Gil Robles would finally recognize during Francoism, was that the obsession of the confessional right with safeguarding its own identity took precedence over concern for the extension of civil rights appropriate to secularism, which was itself considered to be an attack on their rights.

When Ángel Herrera resigned from the leadership of AN at the end of 1931, Gil Robles became the leader of a group virtually split into monarchist and accidentalist tendencies. While the former supported the coup that was being prepared by General Sanjurjo, Gil Robles was more circumspect, using the theoretical resources of Christian public law and even Maurrasian rhetoric to postpone the decision to participate in an adventure that, like that of Primo de Rivera, could by its failure smooth the way of the revolution. In spite of having participated in conspiratorial meetings such as that which took place in Biarritz on 7 August,[7] the failure of the 'Sanjurjada' ensured that AN (which from April had had to change its name to Acción Popular [People's Action] by order of the government) would reaffirm its collaborationist tendency, precipitating the defection of the monarchists in January 1933, although Gil Robles confided at the time to the leader of the Alfonsists, Antonio Goicoechea, that their differences were merely due to questions of tactics, not of principles or programme.[8] The convergence of the Catholic and agrarian right culminated, on 4 March 1933, in the birth of the Confederación Española de Derechas Autónomas (CEDA – Spanish Confederation of the Autonomous Right). Gil Robles continued to criticize the 'revolutionary' work of the government, the atmosphere of 'sectarian violence' against the right under-represented in parliament, and the tactic of annihilation of the adversary based on the 'brutal criteria of majorities' throughout 1933.[9] He aspired to the forging of a great anti-Marxist coalition that would include monarchists and republicans but which would be united by the CEDA, for whom the union represented, first and foremost, 'the clear recognition on the part of all parties of the right of the urgency of a counterrevolution and the inflexible subordination of the episodic to that end'.[10] This was of the essence: for the traditionalist Lamamié, the parties resulting from AN (CEDA, *Renovación Española* [Spanish Renewal] and *Comunión Tradicionalista* [Traditionalist Communion]) were 'three corps of the same army', three conclusive tactics in a one common counter-revolutionary strategy.[11]

Gil Robles, Republican and Democrat? On Accidentalism and the CEDA Strategy

From a doctrinal point of view, Gil Robles scarcely moved from the theological-political principles defended by his father; in *Peace was not Possible* he would continue to affirm that 'power has its origin in God'. During the stage of opposition to the Republican–Socialist government, and even many years later, a clear definition of democracy is difficult to find in his writings and speeches. It is far simpler to collate his critiques of parliamentarism, which go far beyond ideological opposition, and approach an ontological rejection of a moral character. He related

> ... the almost physical repugnance it caused me to work in an environment whose defects were so palpable to me. My doctrinal education, my family ancestry and my sensibility brought me into daily conflict with the system in which I was obliged to operate. The more I intervened in Parliament, the firmer became my conviction of how difficult it would be to remedy the ills of the Fatherland in this way; but it was the only terrain on which I could struggle. Although I had not contributed to the implantation of the system, I considered myself obliged to use it.

Gil Robles asserted that 'parliamentarism, that is to say, the concentration of sovereignty in Parliament, has brought as a consequence the instability of governments, the weakness of public power and, as an inevitable reaction, coups d'état and situations beyond control'.[12] His critique of the deliberative process was not accompanied by advocacy of democratic forms of government; instead, he extolled the virtues of corporatism as a sociopolitical system of organization superior to inorganic democracy, which he considered degenerate. In his opinion, the Salazarist regime in Portugal had provided the most complete attempt at a political system based on integralist nationalism, with a strong but not omnipotent state, respectful of the privileges of the human person, a mid-point between liberal individualism and the absorbing, anti-individualist and pantheist statism of fascist and communist totalitarianisms.[13] His organicist conception of political society as a moral entity, in accordance with the postulations of Christian public law, made him conceive of parliamentary constitutionalism as something foreign to the Hispanic historical tradition, alien to the spirit of the people and incompatible with its social structure.[14] His most well known and bloody invective against democracy was made during the act of presentation of the candidates of the anti-Marxist coalition on 15 October 1933:

> We have to found a new state, to clean the country of Judaic Masons ... We must found a new state and that imposes duties and sacrifices. What does it matter if we have to spill blood ...! Our need is for complete power and that is what we ask for ... To accomplish this ideal we are not going to waste time with archaic forms. Democracy is not an end but a means for the conquest of the new state. When the moment arrives, either Parliament will submit or we will make it disappear. Democracy is not for us an end but a means to launch the conquest of the new state. We are going to liquidate the revolution ... We have endured for two years, now the moment has arrived at which we will not cede one more step. If they want the law, law; if they want violence, violence.[15]

Unsurprisingly, the left-wing newspaper *El Socialista* would brand this aggressive speech a 'fascist oration'. At the close of the electoral campaign, his belligerent rhetoric continued to be condensed into affirmations of the intrinsically perverse nature of the parliamentary regime, whose imminent fall was leaving the way clear for the right to carry out experiments of an authoritarian hue. The accidentalist right did not conceive of its famous 'strategy' as a simple operation of reliving the governmental experiences of the centre-right but as a superior alternative to the democratic regime. After the triumph at the urns and the opening of a period of pre-revolutionary expectation on the part of the workers' organizations, the CEDA leadership began to protest their adherence to the constituted power. *El Debate* propounded the possibilist theses, summarized by Gil Robles with customary savagery: 'Today I will facilitate the formation of Governments of the Centre; tomorrow, when the moment arrives, I will demand power, carrying out the constitutional reform. If we do not enter into power, and the facts demonstrate that the Republic will not allow of an internal rightist evolution, it will pay the consequences.'[16] Gil Robles began the operation through external support for the Lerroux government, which would allow it to pass the first measures to rectify the reformist policies of the Republic's first two years, and later bring his entrance into a Cabinet of coalition that would affirm the presence of the CEDA in certain decisive departments, proceeding later to demand the presidency of the Council of Ministers and approaching constitutional reform from there. This positioning ('that they cannot govern against us' and 'that they cannot govern without us') culminated in a final stage ('that it is we who govern') when, nevertheless, the power of veto would be held by others, particularly the head of state, who would enforce it at the end of 1935. In any case, during those years of commitment to the governance of the state, the CEDA attempted to keep open the possibility of constitutional reform without scuppering it through excessive demands that would have obliged the Radical party to abandon the counter-reformist policy that it wanted to pursue at a more cautious pace, without giving the impression that the Republic had been handed on a plate to the monarchists, with whom Gil Robles had truly ambiguous relations.

Gil Robles; Monarchist? Conversations with the Ex-King Alfonso

In his memoirs, Gil Robles recognized his personal adherence to the monarchy, which 'in terms of its power of arbitration and as an element of stability and continuity, is advisable in a country such as Spain'. Nevertheless, he considered it a means and not an end, as 'I had in front of me a reality that, as a politician, it would have been unjustifiable to ignore. The Monarchy could not be restored in Spain. At least for several years. If the right remained obstinate in linking their political activity to the business of restoration they would remain totally outside of the tasks and responsibilities of government'.[17]

In the second fortnight of June 1933, Gil Robles met the old monarch in Paris on two occasions to explain his intentions to him. The leader of the CEDA asked for a ceasefire in the hostility professed by the Alfonsists to his high-risk strategy of exhausting all possibilities for political action within the legal bounds of the Republic. He argued that if all such attempts failed it would be proven beyond doubt that the right could not operate under the Republic, and the monarchy would thus recover all of its force and authority for the future.[18] According to Gil Robles, Don Alfonso replied:

> ... if you can save Spain through the Republic you are obliged to attempt it. Neither your tranquillity nor my crown overrides the interests of the Fatherland. I cannot publicly disavow those who defend the cause of the Monarchy, but nor will I create difficulties for you. For the good of Spain, I would be the first Republican.[19]

Figure 3.1 Gil Robles with some of his followers in the years of the Second Republic.

At the second meeting, which took place a week later, the points of view propounded at the first were ratified, and the 'obligatory consequences deduced in practical order'; that is, the 'strategy' of the progressive conquest of power was put into effect. With the adoption of this commitment to not head any political offensive against the CEDA, Don Alfonso 'bourboned'[20] his own supporters and significantly reduced the possibilities for a political growth of monarchism. At that time he thought that the chances of a return to Spain were greater through the triumph of the accidentalist strategy than through trusting his luck to the 'salon monarchists' of *Removaeión Española*.[21] Gil Robles even suggested to certain Alfonsists that he represented the ex-king,[22] but the emphasis placed on the coincidental nature of forms of government led to the permanent loss of authority of Gil Robles and of CEDA, due either to his 'embarrassed monarchism' (according to the extreme right) or his disloyalty to the Republican regime (according to the left).

Whatever the truth of this account of displays of mutual political disinterest, the transformation of the CEDA into the most numerous parliamentary minority created counter-revolutionary expectations that the monarchists confused with the immediate unleashing of the process of restoration, inspired by what was happening in Greece in those years. However, after the ratification of the accidentalist thesis and the parliamentary support for the Radical governments that caused the destruction of the right wing alliance, the CEDA had to suffer the redoubled attacks of some Alfonsists who, in spite of everything, did not succeed in having the ex-king proclaim the incompatibility of activity in the CEDA with the defence of monarchic ideals. The president of the *Juventud de Acción Popular* (JAP – People's Action Youth Wing), José M.ª Valiente, met with Alfonso XIII in Fontainebleau on 3 June 1934 with the intention of prolonging the non-aggression agreement of the previous year: Gil Robles asked of the old monarch that he accede to a final period of six months of political collaboration between the monarchists and AP, in exchange for maintaining the hope of restoration. More explicitly, he asked that 'monarchists not be prohibited from belonging to the CEDA and that they wait and have confidence in it, because the way of legality was the only one possible to arrive at the restoration of the Monarchy'.[23] Valiente received the tacit assent of the ex-king, and he communicated this to Gil Robles. In practice, the nebulous agreements between Gil Robles and Don Alfonso did not go beyond a non-aggression pact by which the CEDA saw the extreme right reduce the pressure to trigger the longed for counter-revolution. The plan of the CEDA to conquer power did not politically compromise the old monarch, and increased the expectations of a process of gradual restoration that would have to encompass the stages of a new constituent process, concluding or not with a consultative plebiscite.

Gil Robles, Fascist? The Nature of his Charismatic Leadership

Gil Robles was attracted to the corporatism, anti-Marxism, anti-liberalism, anti-parliamentarism and the guaranteed social order of the fascist regimes, but, faithful to the traditional doctrine of the Church, he loathed their pan-statism and lack of religious spirit. In the political debate of confidence in the new Lerroux government which took place on 19 December 1933, he rejected the ideology of the Falange as pantheist;[24] on 12 January 1934 he claimed to respect but not to share totalitarian conceptions; five days later he proclaimed that 'our programme is contrary to fascist postulates';[25] and on 18 February he referred mockingly in Pamplona to those who waste time 'intoning lyrical cantos to the light of a beautiful dawn'.[26] Gil Robles proposed a traditional authoritarian state modified by social-Catholic corporatism as against the national-syndicalist totalitarian state of political corporatism advocated by the Falange. His supposed totalitarianism was reducible to the Christian ideal of a 'strong and energetic government' above party politics. After attending the Nazi Nuremburg congress, he reiterated his reservations as a Catholic about a violent and pantheist movement, although 'violence in order to rebuff aggression in legitimate defence is quite another thing, something which I do not only admit and proclaim, but which I have been the first to put into practice'. He also declared, however:

> ... in fascism there is much to approve of: its eminently popular roots and work; its exaltation of patriotic values; its clear anti-Marxist significance; its enmity to liberal and parliamentary democracy; its labour to coordinate all social classes and energies; its youthful air, soaked with optimism ... All of this provides a guideline for a new order of things, that we are duty bound to pick up, in order to harmonise it with the postulates of the Catholic doctrine.

He considered, however, that it would be difficult for fascism to take root in Spain, as it lacked propitious circumstances, particularly a sufficiently serious socialist threat. And yet, 'who knows if in the inscrutable plans of providence it is not written that the young rightists who today are in formation will take on the arduous task of harmonising the new political currents with the immortal principles of our Catholic tradition!'.[27] His initial opposition to encouraging a process of radicalization of the JAP gave way, after his visit to Germany, to a mimesis of fascism modified by the CEDA 'strategy':

> ... we find ourselves before a new reality. First Italy and then Germany, the two nations that today weigh most decisively on world politics,

march with a firm step on the path of anti-democracy. Against corrosive parliamentarism, destroyer of the internal unity of power, strong authority concentrated in a single hand. Against the ideological disintegration of the parties, a single national force ... Against corrosive liberalism, germ of all anarchies, a totalitarian concept of the state channelling the maximum energies of a race.[28]

One of the most controversial aspects in the biography of Gil Robles is his aspiration to charismatic leadership that must be situated in the context of the 'fascistization' of the party's youth. A personality cult was erected around Gil Robles that placed him at the level of other historical heroes of the right (Cánovas, Maura, Vázquez de Mella, Primo de Rivera) and far above contemporary politicians by the virtues ascribed to him (authority, courage, foresight, eloquence, altruism, sacrifice, serenity, capacity to work ...); as such, he was converted into a symbol of the 'true Spain' in the same way that Azaña was that of the Anti-Spain. José María Hueso, a Madrid deputy, proposed at the rally of Uclés the slogan 'Leader and glory be to Spain!', a ridiculous attempt at mythmaking around a leadership that justified blind obedience and which was taken to its most comical extreme by Cándido Casanueva when he affirmed in Albacete that 'with a leader like Gil Robles, even cleaning out latrines is a pleasant task'.[29] The total identification of the CEDA with their great leader derived from their unconditional acceptance of his messianic mission: 'The CEDA is Gil Robles' and 'God providentially places the destinies of Spain in the hands of Gil Robles'.[30] The leader of the JAP, José María Pérez Laborda, affirmed in September 1935 that 'the Leader' par excellence was 'a gift of providence for Spain'.[31] His photograph was hung in houses next to images of the Sacred Heart, an element in the sacralization of his counter-revolutionary labour, although on other occasions the monumental exhibition of his image was linked to secular political symbols of a totalitarian hue, such as the exhibition of uniformed masses who provide the background to the grand electoral poster put up at the Puerta del Sol on 13 February 1936 which stated: 'These are my powers. Give me an absolute majority and I will give you a great Spain'. On the charismatic exaltation of Gil Robles, Valiente affirmed with habitual ambiguity that the attitude of the JAP was 'messianism, no; cult of the leader, yes'.[32]

This charismatic leadership had a particular effect on the youth of the CEDA. Gil Robles recognized decades later that 'from October 1934, and especially during the year 1935, the JAP, increasingly estranged from democratic tendencies, vigorously stamped their characteristics on the rest of the party, creating no little difficulties for myself'.[33] What is certain is that, as had occurred in previous epochs with unique figures of populism, such as the pretender Carlos VII, Lerroux or Maura, this type of leadership was efficient in reducing the generational distance that existed between the mature and younger activists, as the charisma of Gil Robles acted as a symbolic mediator between the traditional doctrine of Catholic conservatism and the fascistic radicalization of the less mature bases. Adhesion to the 'Leader' guaranteed the cohesion of the movement as long as his leadership was backed up by the success of the 'strategy'. When the entrance into power was delayed and frustrated by the end of 1935, however, the CEDA entered a phase of confusion during which the star of Gil Robles faded at the same pace at which political gradualism was ceding ground to violent rupture.

Gil Robles, Partisan of Violence? The Putschist Temptations of 1934–6

The attitude of Gil Robles to violence was also somewhat ambiguous. During a constituent debate he asserted that 'neither as a citizen nor as a Catholic do I believe that it would be justifiable to use violence against the constituted power, as that would mean violence or rebellion against a regime that, as it is today of all Spaniards, we should all respect, and for that reason I would always raise my voice in condemnation and protest against it. I do not believe, in any way, that violence and force should ever be the manner in which to resolve conflicts between civilised people.'[34] This orthodox declaration of compliance with constituted power was to give way to more nuanced positions: in a speech given on 15 June 1932 he ruled out a solution based on force not on principle, but for tactical reasons, as it 'would leave the two tendencies which are grappling for hegemony in Spain profoundly divided, and would harvest acute problems that could not in the moment be resolved, and whose unravelling would drive Spain towards chaos, as well as being totally inopportune'. He rejected the militarist alternative except in cases of extreme necessity. He doubted the viability of civil elements of Catholic origin bringing about a state of emergency, and yet, in harmony with the pontifical doctrine of opposition to a regime considered illegitimate either in origin or practice, defended the viability of rebellion in extreme circumstances, albeit extolling passive resistance and the mobilization of the masses as ideal methods for a powerful, organized and modern right to initiate the reconquest of power:

> We who proclaim the legal struggle, we who do not want to turn to the terrain of violence, know how to turn to this terrain when the struggle places us on it, because we would not then proceed on the offensive but in legitimate defence, and would be obliged to meet violence with violence to bring about the triumph of our ideals ... This procedure of legal struggle

has extraordinary advantages. In the first place it accustoms us to the civic struggle, which has the characteristic of perseverance ... A forceful solution would resolve this situation for us, and the Spanish right, which is on a war footing, would return to their houses and would allow the fruit of an easy victory to be lost within a short time ... The long struggle purifies and configures man with a spirit of sacrifice.[35]

The pastoral letter of 17 May 1933, signed by the bishops, which prescribed to the faithful passive resistance to the secular policy of the government, and which was ratified by the encyclical *Dilectissima Nobis*, hardened the Gil Robles discourse; that became evident at the moment of the change in the parliamentary majority. On 19 November he threatened: 'We have endured for two years, now the moment has arrived at which we will not cede one more step. If they want the law, law; if they want violence, violence'; and on 5 February in Seville he warned that 'if they do not give us power, we will have to think of taking it';[36] although two days later he affirmed in the Cortes that 'we have never, either before or now, positioned ourselves nor have we had to position ourselves on any violent terrain ... Our duty ... has been to enable the bringing of all the forces of the right on to the terrain of legality, because we aspire – I want to make it very clear – to realising our programme within the current regime.'[37]

These contradictory declarations formed part of the rhetorical arsenal of pressure and conciliatory attitudes wielded before friends and enemies in the process of approximation to power. In practice, the strategies of street confrontation sponsored by the CEDA did not amount to much more than a vain attempt to instrumentalize patriotic-sporting institutions such as the ancient *Tiro Nacional* (National Shooting Club) or a threat of 'social defence' against the revolution such as the creation at the end of 1933 of a Section of Civil Mobilization in the headquarters of the JAP that would take charge of attending to essential public services in the event of a general strike. It was clear that the CEDA did not have the intention of recruiting an army of 'political soldiers' in the image of the fascists, but of mobilizing the 'good citizens' in an echo of the movement of 'civic unions' that had been adopted successfully among conservative European sectors in the post-war period.[38] This calculated distancing from party political violence did not prevent him from foreseeing the possibility of it being applied rigorously from the vantage-point of legitimacy offered by the control of governmental power. He recognized having precipitated the eruption of the revolutionary movement of October, challenging it to emerge through provocative manoeuvres:

I asked myself the following question; if I do not enter government I would grant Spain three months of tranquillity. If I enter, would the revolution break out? Better that it does so before it is well prepared, before it might defeat us. This is what we did; we obliged the movement to speed up its rhythm, confronted it and destroyed it from within the government.[39]

After the failure of the revolution, Gil Robles was the most enthusiastic partisan of the application of extremely rigorous measures. On 9 October he proposed the suspension of parliamentary sessions in order to grant impunity to a repression that acquired extremely bloody characteristics; and on 5 and 15 November he proposed that the declaration of 'moral incompatibility' with the Socialist deputies requested by Goicoechea be extended to the left Republicans, opening the possibility of controlling the activity of the unions and the professional associations. The energetic use of governmental power was not only a way of re-establishing threatened legality but also an effective instrument to eliminate obstacles in the way of the counter-revolutionary advance orchestrated by the CEDA.

Gil Robles did not discount the use of violence in the process of the conquest of power and understood that this would attain greater or lesser intensity depending on the conditions in which the struggle developed. In any case, the armed forces would assume, as in Portugal and Greece, the role of protagonist, although he believed that the positive labour of institutional replacement would not be a military mission but the work of a cold man who, like Salazar, would become the executor of the national interest.[40] At that time, Gil Robles did not propose an armed solution carried out by civil elements, but a military coup d'état of which he could be the beneficiary. The dramatic circumstances through which the country passed following the revolutionary commotion of October seemed to lend weight to this expectation. After the reprieve of Pérez Fárras in mid-November, generals Fanjul and Goded urged Gil Robles to adopt a firmer policy with the support of the army. To this he let them know that 'it was impossible for us to take the initiative in provoking an exceptional situation, although in no way would we oppose the army letting the President know of their firm desire to impede that which endangers the fundamental code of the nation'.[41] According to certain testimonies, Gil Robles had convinced them that the movement would be unnecessary given the policy being developed by the new government. In this way he could appear as the saviour of the political situation, asserting that 'the CEDA is not going to permit the end of the parliamentary regime',[42] but also as the foremost interest in improving the situation of the armed forces in order to bolster their anti-revolutionary predisposition from the Ministry of War, the department he entered on 6 May 1935.[43] From there he initiated a policy of partial dismantling of the reformist measures of Azaña, nominating leaders relegated for their lack of sympathy for the regime, purging others of markedly republican character and giving carte blanche to the destabilizing activity of the secret association *Unión Militar Española* (UME – Spanish Military Union).

In the autumn of 1935, the extreme right still contemplated the possibility that Gil Robles would assume the role of Tsaldaris, and from the Ministry of War, or better yet the Presidency of the Council, deal the legal blow that would open the way to a monarchic dictatorship and the foreseeable restoration of the Bourbons. During the days in which *Who Am I?* premiered, Gil Robles continued to deny any intention of bringing about a coup d'état, affirming that, as the Primo de Rivera dictatorship had triggered a democratic political revolution, a second dictatorship could prove the prelude to a soviet revolution. He opined that 'the army must not intervene in politics nor promote a coup d'état. It is the guarantor of independence and of security abroad and also the guarantor of internal order, when power finds itself in the street against any type of subversive movement.'[44] In contrast to the unconditional militarism of Calvo Sotelo, Gil Robles did not believe that the army was the backbone of the nation, but the armed wing of the fatherland, charged with its internal and external defence. It was not an end in itself, but a means to arrive at his political ambitions.

At the moment of truth, however, the Spanish populists did not take advantage, as did their Greek equivalents, of the failure of the insurrectionary movement of the left to annul the parliamentary opposition and establish a

Figure 3.2 José María Gil Robles in his office.

de facto dictatorship. When, after the fall of Chapaprieta, Gil Robles claimed power on 14 December, Alcalá Zamora aborted the manoeuvre at the price of dissolving parliament. After a violent argument with the President, the outgoing Minister of War received the visit of the generals Fanjul and Varela, who suggested that he give the order of a declaration of war throughout Spain. According to his version, elaborated three decades after the fact, Gil Robles replied to them:

> I will not attempt any *pronunciamiento* in my favour, as I am impeded by the firmness of my democratic convictions and my unconquerable revulsion at the placing of the armed forces at the service of a political faction. However, if the army, grouped around its natural command, is of the opinion that it must occupy transitional power with the intention of saving the spirit of the Constitution and thereby avoiding a gigantic revolutionary fraud, I will not provide the least obstacle and will do what is necessary so that it does not break the continuity of action of public power.[45]

Everything seems to indicate that, in his capacity as Chief of Staff, Franco warned them that the military body did not have the necessary unity to trigger an insurrection, so that on 15 December, the leader of the CEDA abandoned the ministry after having suffered the insults and sarcasm of Calvo Sotelo for his 'betrayal of the generals', who would have seconded his putschist proposal if he had been more energetic and unequivocal. Certainly, Gil Robles did not react with the decision his supporters would have expected of him, and he was disqualified by the extreme right as a future dictator. He had, however, in his seven months as minister, left the army with the moral and material disposition to bring about the much desired coup.

On 20 December he made new protestations of legalism in a speech at the cinema Madrid:

> I have left the Ministry of War for three reasons: because I, in conformity with my doctrine, will not depart from the path of the law, rather I suspect that it will be the others who leave that path; because to launch the army on a coup d'état would be to destroy it and to attach it to a party, and I believe that the army is of Spain, by Spain and for Spain; and because although I have left, I will return very soon, but I will return not by way of a rebellion and conspiracy that would prejudice my supporters, I will return with Spanish opinion, by the mandate of a triumphant democracy.[46]

The electoral result sealed the failure of this procedure, and the progressive eclipse of the public star of Gil Robles.

Was Peace Not Possible? The Responsibility of Gil Robles and the CEDA for the Outbreak of the Civil War

The leader of the CEDA attempted during the early hours of 17 February 1936 to persuade Prime Minister Portela to declare a state of war, and remained with his office staff in the hope of being put in charge of a possible extra-constitutional government that would depose Alcalá Zamora.[47] He tried again at eight o clock in the morning of the 19th, pressuring Portela to remain in power until the results of the second electoral round were known. The entrance to power of Azaña that same night precipitated the failure of the third serious coup attempt in 15 months. Gil Robles left hurriedly to situate his family in Biarritz, and although he returned the following day, having verified with relief that a government of republicans had been formed, he spent numerous weekends in the Franco-Basque resort, a fact that would save his life when the vengeful group headed by Captain Condés appeared at his home on the night of 13 July.

In the first weeks after the elections, *El Debate* proposed as minimum conditions of agreement the observance of the law, the dissolution of the party militias, a reasonable economic programme and respect for Catholic education. In spite of the denials of People's Action of organizing armed groups with a view to an uprising,[48] *El Socialista* accused the CEDA of forming bands of gunmen with rapid trucks to carry out destabilizing activity that would lead to a coup in the space of three months.[49] Gil Robles then sent a note to the Ministry of Governance in which he branded the affirmations of the socialists an 'unspeakable falsehood', and reiterated his intention to operate within the bounds of legality, although he attempted to avoid responsibility for the violent drift of the rightist masses should the 'current state of subversion' not end.[50] This would be his dominant discourse during the spring: denunciation in the darkest, catastrophist tones of the situation of the country as an exculpatory alibi as much for the radicalization of the rightist grassroots as for the incapacity of their leaders to canalize this political frustration. Alluding to the violent regional election campaign in Cuenca, he distinguished between 'good' and 'bad' terrorists: 'there are those that follow the path of violence, believing honourably that national problems might in this way be resolved and those that do so because today the party cannot give out positions and privileges. The first, absolutely respectable, may constitute magnificent auxiliaries on that day in the future when, with eyes opened, they return to the common house.'[51]

In an interview in April 1936 with the acting president Martínez Barrio, Gil Robles 'was plainly looking for the disappearance of the Popular Front and the abandonment of legislative and governmental commitments accepted by the republican groups. Spanish society, according to him, could not be reconciled if the dragon be not slain (this abominable monster was Marxism).'[52] He entrusted to Giménez Fernández the task of sounding out the possibilities of constituting a centrist parliamentary force with other republicans and moderate socialists (followers of Prieto). The politician from Seville pointed out that 'at the end of May Gil Robles confronted Lucia and me with the impossibility of continuing to prepare for occupying the centre-ground, which in reality very few people wanted, as the mysticism of civil war had sadly overcome the majority of Spaniards'.[53] On 2 June he vetoed any participation of CEDA representatives in these negotiations and at the same time declared in an interview with *Diario Español* of Buenos Aires·that one could be fascist and a fervent Catholic, when on the 19 May he had rejected both the essence of fascism and state socialism as their strategy 'serves uniquely and exclusively the conquest of power by violent means'.[54]

After the painful events that befell Madrid during the commemorative parade of the 5th Anniversary of the Republic, Gil Robles recognized, dispirited, the crisis of political representation of the CEDA exemplified by the loss of control of its youth: 'The parties that operate within the bounds of legality are starting to lose control of our masses; we are starting to appear to them as failures; the idea of violence to struggle against persecution is starting to germinate in our people.' Rightist violence was justified as a defensive response to provocations and the ineffectiveness of the government:

A considerable body of opinion, incorporating at least half of the nation, will not resign itself implacably to die, I assure you. If it cannot defend itself one way, it will in another. Against the violence advocated from there will arise violence from the other side, and public power will have the sad role of being merely spectators in a civic confrontation which will ruin the nation materially and spiritually … If the way is not rapidly rectified, no other solution will remain in Spain save that of violence; either the red dictatorship advocated by those gentlemen, or an energetic defence of the citizens who will not permit themselves to be run down.[55]

His later parliamentary interventions of 19 May, 16 June and 15 July regarding the successive extensions to the state of alarm followed a similar pattern to those of Calvo Sotelo: catastrophist denunciation of the 'state of subversion' of public order through a biased account of violent deeds, demanding the government be held to account for tolerating and even protecting the 'revolutionary' excesses, exoneration of the permanently abused right and justification of the future rebellion due to the state of necessity generated by the vacuum of authority.[56]

On 15 July, after a tense exchange by telephone with the President of the Cortes, Martínez Barrio, whom he accused of complicity in the murder of Calvo Sotelo, Gil Robles intervened for the last time before the Permanent Council of Parliament, again accusing the government of responsibility for the state of pre-insurrectionary tension that, in his judgement, had caused the death of the monarchist leader. After recalling the declaration of anti-fascist belligerence made by Casares on 19 May, he made an analysis of fascism as a self-preservation reflex of the rightist masses fearful of revolution that coincided partially with that made by politicians of such diverse origins as Calvo Sotelo, Maura and Prieto:

> What is growing and developing is that which in generic terms you denominate fascism, but which is nothing more than the anxiety, very often highly noble, of liberating oneself from a yolk and from an oppression ... a movement of healthy and even holy rebellion that beats in the heart of the Spanish and against which we, who day after day and hour after hour have taken refuge in democratic principles, in legal norms and normal behaviour, are totally impotent. Just as you ... are totally and absolutely overtaken by the working masses that you no longer control, we are also now overwhelmed by a sense of violence that you have created and are disseminating throughout all Spain.[57]

That same afternoon he left for Biarritz, where he arrived in the early hours of the 16th. Three days later, El Socialista denounced his cowardice, 'for fleeing after lighting the fuse'. In spite of his subsequent declarations of reticence about the conspiracy,[58] Gil Robles recognized in a letter written in Lisbon on 27 February 1942 for the drawing up of the Causa General (which was conveniently exhumed by the Francoist government to discredit him for his participation in the 'Contubernio de Munich') the failure of the legalist strategy of the CEDA and his support for a 'military solution' that then seemed to him to be justified:

> No solution other than military was in sight and the CEDA was disposed to give it all possible support ... I co-operated with advice, moral stimulus, with secret orders of collaboration and even with economic help, taken in not insignificant quantity from the electoral funds of the party ... In direct relation to the Alzamiento, I could do little or nothing save for secondary tasks, such as attempting to cover general Franco with parliamentary immunity through his election with general Fanjul to the province of Cuenca; a procedure carried out in San Juan de Luz, close to señor Fal Conde, commissioned by general Mola; the drawing up of a manifesto printed in Biarritz and sent to Pamplona on 16th July; and the procedures

carried out in France, in union with other elements, to send a plane to the Canary Isles to general Franco.[59]

During the months of June and July a series of directives had been circulated directed to the provincial organizations of the CEDA so that affiliates might join the military as soon as the rebellion began. The youth would have to present themselves at the barracks to place themselves under the command of the corresponding military, refraining from forming their own militias. The renunciation of all acts of reprisal was ordered, with operations against responsible leftists to be carried out through ordinary and extraordinary military tribunals, and it was decided that the party and its affiliates would lend the maximum financial support to the rebels. The CEDA hoped for the implantation of a traditional authoritarian regime, corporatist and respectful of individual rights.[60] Their cooperation with the conspiracy was not limited to the handing to Mola of half a million pesetas from the electoral funds of the party through the intermediaries Francisco Herrera Oria and Rafael Aizpún,[61] but also included tasks of 'moral stimulus' such as the mediation between Mola and Fal Conde, with whom Gil Robles was interviewed on the afternoon of 5 July, although he showed such a lack of tact in expressing his own political ambitions (prominent participation in a government of concentration of the rightist forces that would proceed, in case of triumph, to share out civil governments) that the conversation drifted towards more violent expressions.[62] It would seem that Ángel Herrera Oria, on the recommendation of General Mola, had invited Gil Robles to a meeting of deputies of the right that would have had to meet in Burgos on 17 July, with the intention of declaring the government and parliament to be seditious, launching the people and the army against them. According to the CEDA leader, 'I refused to collaborate in this project, with which I could not believe that general Mola was in agreement.'[63]

After being expelled from France by the Popular Front government, he installed himself in Lisbon, where he continued to work for the rebels in the headquarters of an officious junta formed by the marquises of Aledo and Vega de Anzó, Joaquín Bau, Alfonso Tuero and the diplomats Amoedo, Saro, Erice and Villaurrutia, who were in close contact with Salazar and with Franco, through his brother Nicolás. Gil Robles managed to arrive in Pamplona on 28 July to be interviewed by Mola with a guard composed of militants of the JAP, but he was received with hostility by the large number of old CEDA members who, disappointed by their old 'leader', joined the *Requeté* or the forces of citizens' protection.[64] After an attempted aggression prepared by the Falangists of Burgos, he had to hurriedly return to Portugal, but returned on other occasions to his Salamancan fief to make repeated proclamations of compliance with the military power that 'has to be, after its triumph, the Axis of national politics for no short period'.[65] Gil Robles ordered his militants to be disciplined before the military authority and loyal to the new 'Caudillo', and did not miss an occasion to justify his previous political activity and to prohibit the entrance of CEDA members in other political militia, particularly those of the Falange.[66] Later, in declarations made to the British newspaper *The Universe* on 22 January 1937, he denied any identification with fascism, and reiterated that after 16 February 1936, AP 'refused recourse to illegal procedures and tried again to apply the principle of cooperation, working loyally with the opposition to try to resolve national problems'. He recognized his adhesion to the uprising against the Republic, however, from the moment in which it was produced: 'from the first instant of the military patriotic movement, People's Action has joined with it with all its soul ... has given thousands and thousands of soldiers that with their shoulders are ready to carry the national cause with all our energies, with all our resources and with life itself'. The military uprising 'cannot be called rebellion, but perfectly legitimate resistance to oppression, to tyranny'.[67]

The process of political unification gave occasion for a final act of authority to Gil Robles, who at the beginning of November 1936 had met in Lisbon with his representative Luciano de la Calzada to demonstrate the necessity of threatening Franco with a prior takeover of AP on the part of the Carlists, with the intention of averting any attempt at unification with the Falange, which maintained in its press and at the front its traditional hostility to the JAP and their leader.[68] In the first months of 1937 he seems to have been resigned to keeping the party free from harm until the more than foreseeable unification of the militias. After the acceptance of the process by a general assembly of the JAP celebrated in Burgos on 19 March, Gil Robles made manifest his unconditional support for the unification decision, as it avoided the primacy of a single political group and facilitated the prosperity of the CEDA in the ranks of the new state. On 22 April he put an end to his public activity by handing over to Franco the party as well as the militias.[69] Immediately after, he decreed the dissolution of AP, after 'contemplating with joy the splendid crop that we are harvesting'.[70]

His hostility to the hierarchies of the single party caused increasingly serious conflicts to befall him: after spending some days in May of 1938 at the Rábida farm at Ciudad Rodrigo, the Falangist newspaper of Valladolid, *Libertad*, attacked him on 4 July for the assumed conspiratorial manoeuvres of the 'resuscitated leader'. The campaign, which included veiled death threats, may have been orchestrated by his former subordinate Ramón Serrano Suñer, who controlled the Francoist censorship and brought about the opening of a military indictment against him for the crime of conspiracy.[71] Obliged to reside permanently in Lisbon, Gil Robles was made to understand that he held no place in the power structure of the new regime and that, from then on, his public life would remain limited and subordinate, like so many other Spaniards of his time, to the trauma of exile.

Gil Robles, Restorer of the Monarchy? His last Public Activities

His years of political and personal maturity were spent in exile. Between the summers of 1938 and 1941, his image faded in the no-man's land between accidentalism and monarchism, authoritariansism and democracy, collaboration and opposition. In June of 1941 he was required by General Orgaz to collaborate in a monarchic movement against the 'Caudillo', an offer he rejected because he thought that a conspiracy allegedly directed from London could precipitate German intervention in the peninsula.[72] The internal crisis of summer 1942 and that of the Russian front that winter induced Gil Robles to communicate again with the new pretender, Don Juan de Borbón, his opinion that Germany had lost the war, although he thought that this must not cause a rupture with Franco because he had 'a de facto legitimacy that cannot be fought with', while the monarchy must construct itself as a regime of law. In sum: 'Franco is the winner of a civil war. The king must be a peace maker. Neither hinder nor defend him; remain in your place in expectation of the moment when the nation demands you.'[73]

Gil Robles officially joined the monarchic cause by means of an article which appeared in the Buenos Aires daily *La Nación* on 18 May 1943.[74] At that time he opted for a 'national solution' based on the implacable principles of the traditional Catholic monarchy. He did not suggest an armed uprising against Franco, but rather awaited the unfavourable unfolding of the World War and pressure from military high command (something similar to the internal consultation that caused the fall of Primo de Rivera in January 1930, although the sycophantic document that the lieutenant generals sent to the 'Caudillo' on 8 September 1943 did not have such an effect) to bring him down as a shameful ally of Germany. The indecision of Don Juan who, in spite of everything, remained in contact with the dictator, induced Gil Robles to demand a more energetic attitude at the end of 1943, based on a plan of cohesion of the monarchic forces, the spreading of political bases and the naming of a delegate to coordinate civil, military and diplomatic action. Persuaded that the key to this operation was Gil Robles himself, to whom Don Juan conceded full powers on 17 April 1944, the Francoist press began on 5 May a new campaign to discredit him, branding him a 'prop of the Republic' and demanding that his Spanish nationality be withdrawn.[75] Although Gil Robles demanded directly of Franco that he be guaranteed the right of a court appearance before a judge or an impartial tribunal to respond to said accusations,[76] he could not avoid the Salazar regime moving him away from his residence in Estoril until the end of 1945.

The Lausanne Manifesto of 19 March 1945, which marked the point of rupture with Falangist totalitarianism and which extolled the traditional

Figure 3.3 Gil Robles at a CEDA rally.

monarchy as the only regime capable of reconciling the Spanish people, seemed to Gil Robles to be 'noble, firm, categorical, opportune; to my mind, politically perfect'.[77] It was the occasion of his greatest influence; with the World War over, he put into action a project of restoration on the basis of a search for greater consensus among the anti-Francoist forces. Having managed to install Don Juan in Portugal, he actively participated in drawing up the Bases of Estoril on 28 February 1946: a constituent plan with an archaic, anti-democratic tone. At that time, certain North American circles looked favourably on the eventuality of a crypto-liberal government brought together around the ex-leader of the CEDA, who nevertheless criticized the sanctions adopted by the powers against the Spanish regime in March of 1946 and resisted any understanding with leftists that would not make explicit their recognition of the monarchy.

The Law of Succession, adopted unilaterally by Franco and replicated in the Manifesto of Estoril on 7 April 1947, accelerated the rupture between the Pretender and the 'Caudillo' and smoothed understanding between the monarchists and other anti-regime forces. Declarations of Don Juan to *The Observer* on 13 April against the regime and in favour of democratic liberties led to a threat of resignation from the Committee of Monarchic Action that worked in the interior. Gil Robles, who identified a radical difference between the monarchists 'abroad' and those 'inside', always ready to make a pact with Franco, threatened to resign, and was disposed that summer and autumn to give exterior support to their policy of reconciliation: at the beginning of August he went to the Vatican to explain the attitude of Don Juan, of acceptance of the essence of the Movement, but without uniting his fate to that of Franco. On 15 and 18 October he met with Indalecio Prieto, interspersed by a visit to the British Foreign Secretary Ernest Bevin, to whom he requested that the 'Spanish case' be seized from the jurisdiction of the United Nations and that papal mediation be sought. After several vicissitudes, the Confederation of Monarchic Forces (CEDA, Spanish Renewal, *Lliga* and Spanish Action, created on 14 February 1947) signed the Pact of San Juan de Luz with the Socialists on 30 August 1948, a minimum programme of national conciliation that was communicated to diplomatic representatives on 6 October. At that very moment, however, the meeting between Franco and Don Juan, which had been hidden from Gil Robles, inaugurated a new stage of conciliation on the basis of which Prince Juan Carlos was sent to Spain without a clear policy of compensation. The *Azor* talks put paid to the plans of the CEDA leader and accentuated the discrepancies between the monarchists in exile and in the interior.

A new press campaign orchestrated against him, and continued pressure from the monarchists for him to be dismissed from Estoril, caused him to abandon that 'clique of idiots' in mid-October and depart once again from active politics.[78] Certain declarations of Don Juan made to *ABC* on 24 June 1955, in which he supported the ideological principles of 18 July, caused him to definitively resign as private counsel. Recovering his freedom of action, he again declared himself to be an accidentalist and created the group Christian Social Democracy in the middle of 1960. He still had time to play the leading role in a new political scandal when, after participating in the IV Congress of the European Movement in Munich from 5 to 8 June 1962, he found himself subject to an intense campaign to discredit him which drove him into exile for a further two years.[79] After this, the monarchist sector that was more conciliatory to the regime obtained from Don Juan the disavowal of those members of his Private Counsel that had participated in the said meeting; at the beginning of the summer, Gil Robles cut off all political and personal relations with the voluble pretender.[80]

In March of 1975, under the protection of the Law of Political Associations, he created the People's Democratic Federation as an entity of public debate, and in 1977 merged with the Democratic Left of Joaquín Ruiz Giménez to create the Democratic Christian Federation, which obtained mediocre results (200,613 votes and no deputies) in the elections to the Constituent Cortes on 15 June of that year.[81] He then abandoned political life forever, and died in Madrid in 1980.

At the end of his life, like Brandel in Luca de Tena's comedy, Gil Robles unconditionally accepted and cultivated, not without a certain narcissism, his image as a failed politician, a 'beaten fighter, who has what those who have beaten me do not: a clear conscience'.[82] Beyond the complacent picture of the hardened old anti-Francoist there remained, however, the memory of a young politician who, in the first half of the 1930s, was a tireless battler in the campaign for constitutional revision and an energetic polemicist in parliament, who, in the words of Burgos y Mazo, 'had in his hands the regeneration and salvation of the Republic and lost everything, everything he squandered through a lack of astuteness, skill, of ability to take charge, of aplomb and maturity, of a true understanding of men, of clear judgement, of a spirit of self-abasement and sacrifice, of loyalty, and through a surfeit of impatience, ambition and pride'.[83]

Mediocre statist and perfect party man, he transformed the CEDA into an instrument of battle in complete harmony with his verbal incontinence, far from the moderation that should have presided over his theoretical position on the centre-right. This made the contrast with his lack of resolve in the crucial moments still more dramatic. Of him Cambó said that 'as with all men of verbal audacity, he was extraordinarily timid in action. To that his failure was owed. His verbal audacity brought him the maximum hatred of the left. His incapacity for action, governmental or revolutionary, ensured that this hatred was not counterbalanced by either terror or respect.'[84] This discrepancy between word and deed blurred his role in the tragedy that unfolded on the stage of Spanish history. As with Colomer/Brandel, we will never know which character, the authoritarian or the conciliator, would have survived if the gigantic crime of passion that was the Civil War had not taken place.

Endnotes

1   Juan Ignacio Luca de Tena, *¿Quién soy yo?* y *¡Yo soy Brandel!* (Madrid: Escelicer, 1970), p. 57. The sequel to this work, *I am Brandel!*, which premiered in the Infanta Isabel theatre on 19 December 1969, uncovers the enigma, and in a farcical tone describes the political downfall of the imposter who does not know how to govern energetically. The moral is clear in its unrefined anti-parliamentarism: 'Nations are like women: the more men there are to look after them, the more they are lost' (ibid., p. 119).

2   Juan Arrabal, *José María Gil Robles. Su vida, su actuación, sus ideas* (Madrid: Lib. Internacional de Romo, 1933), p. 66.

3   'El poder constituido', *El Debate*, 15 April 1931, 1. Cited in José María Gil Robles, *No fue posible la paz* (Barcelona: Ariel, 1968), p. 34.

4   José María Gil Robles, *La fe a través de mi vida* (Bilbao: Desclée de Brouwer, 1975), p. 119.

5   Gil Robles, *No fue posible la paz*, p. 64.

6   *El Sol*, 15 October 1931.

7   Julián Cortés-Cavanillas, *Gil Robles ¿monárquico? Misterios de una política* (Madrid: San Martín, 1935), pp. 145–6.

8   *ABC*, 11 January 1933.

9   In the Prologue of Gil Robles to José de Medina y Togores, *Un año de Cortes Constituyentes (Impresiones Parlamentarias)* (Madrid: Ibérica, 1933), p. VIII.

10 'Unidad en el fin, diversidad en los medios', *CEDA*, No. 10, 20 September 1933, 1.

11 *ABC*, 7 February 1933.

12 Gil Robles, *No fue posible la paz*, pp. 48–9.

13 Prologue of Gil Robles (Estoril, XII-1937) to Antonio de Oliveira Salazar, *El pensamiento de la Revolución Nacional* (Buenos Aires: Poblet, 1938), p. 20.

14 Preface of Gil Robles, 'Su problema en España' to André Tardieu, *La reforma del Estado* (Madrid: Lib. Int. de Romo, 1935), pp. 24–5.

15 Speech at the Monumental Cinema in Madrid, 15 October 1933, in 'Gil Robles habla de la posición de las derechas', *El Debate*, 17 October 1933, 1, cited in José María Gil Robles, *Discursos parlamentarios* (Madrid: Taurus, 1971), p. 270 and José Gutiérrez-Ravé, *Gil Robles, caudillo frustrado* (Madrid: Prensa Española, 1967), p. 85.

16 Editorial 'Los católicos y la República', *El Debate*, 15 December 1933 and interview with Gil Robles, *El Debate*, 22 December 1933.

17 Gil Robles, *No fue posible la paz*, pp. 79–80.

18 Cited by Gutiérres-Ravé, *Gil Robles, caudillo frustrado*, 77.

19 Gil Robles, *No fue posible la paz*, pp. 87–9.

20 Translator's note: 'to bourbon', deriving from the royal name, means to make use of someone until such a point as he has outlived his usefulness, whereupon he is discarded.

21 Julián Cortés-Cavanillas, *Vida, confesiones y muerte de Alfonso XIII* (Madrid: Prensa Española, 1956), p. 426.

22 Cortés-Cavanillas, *Gil Robles ¿monárquico?*, p. 148.

23 Gil Robles, *No fue posible la paz*, p. 89, note 14, where he denies giving explicit notes to Valiente and setting a time limit to the collaboration between Alfonsists and the CEDA.

24 Gil Robles, *Discursos parlamentarios*, pp. 285–6.

25 *Luz*, 17 January 1934.

26 *El Debate*, 20 February 1934.

27 José María Gil Robles, 'Antidemocracia', *La Gaceta Regional*, 8 September 1933, 1, collected declarations in *El Debate*, 15 September 1933, 3–4 and *No fue posible la paz*, p. 208.

28 *Claridad* (Jerez), 2 October 1933, cited by Diego Caro Cancela, *Violencia política y luchas sociales: La Segunda República en Jerez de la Frontera (1931–1936)* (Jerez: Ayuntamiento, 2001), p. 325.

29 José Ramón Montero Gibert, *La CEDA. El catolicismo social y político en la II República* (Madrid: Revista de Trabajo, 1977), Vol. II, p. 25.

30 Francisco Casares, *La CEDA va gobernar (Notas y glosas de un año de vida pública nacional)* (Madrid: Gráfica Administrativa, 1934), p. 293.

31 *El Debate*, 17 September 1935, 2.

32 Francisco Casares, 'Reportajes de la actualidad nacional: ¿Son o no son fascistas las Juventudes de Acción Popular?', *Blanco y Negro*, 11 February 1934, 1–2 and *CEDA*, no.19, 15 February 1934, 18.

33 Gil Robles, *No fue posible la paz*, 202.

34 Francisco Casares, 'Reportajes de la actualidad nacional: ¿Son o no son fascistas las Juventudes de Acción Popular?', *Blanco y Negro*, 11 February 1934, 1–2 and *CEDA*, No. 19, 15 February 1934, 18.

35 Speech in Madrid (16 June 1932), in Gil Robles, *Discursos parlamentarios*, p. 126, and Juan Arrabal, *José María Gil Robles. Su vida. Su actuación. Sus ideas*, 2nd edition (Ávila: Tip. y Enc. de Senén Martín Díaz, 1935), pp. 322–6.

36 *El Debate*, 6 February 1934.

37 Speech of 7 February 1934, in Gil Robles, *Discursos parlamentarios*, pp. 302–3.

38 On the phenomenon of the 'civic unions', their impact in Spain and their recuperation on the part of the CEDA, see Eduardo González Calleja and Fernando del Rey Reguillo, *La defensa armada contra la revolución. Una*

historia de las 'guardias cívicas' en la España del siglo XX (Madrid: CSIC, 1995), pp. 237–43.

39 Declarations of Gil Robles at an act of the AP in Madrid (15 December 1934), CEDA, Nos 36–7, December 1934, 5.

40 Prologue of José María Gil Robles (Estoril, XII-1937) to Antonio de Oliveira Salazar, El pensamiento de la Revolución Nacional (Buenos Aires: Poblet, 1938), p. 9.

41 Gil Robles, No fue posible la paz, pp. 145–8. A new account of the interview with the generals, dated 18 November 1934, in a testimony of Gil Robles collected by Carlos Seco Serrano, España Contemporánea (Barcelona: Gallach, 1971), p. 125, note.

42 Henry Buckley, Vida y muerte de la República española (Madrid: Espasa-Calpe, 2004), p. 136.

43 Paul Preston, 'El 'accidentalismo' de la CEDA: ¿Aceptación o sabotaje de la República?', Cuadernos de Ruedo Ibérico, 42 (February–May 1973): 72.

44 El Debate, 10 November 1935, 5–6; CEDA, No. 54, 30 November 1935, 12, and Gil Robles, Discursos parlamentarios, p. 524.

45 Gil Robles, No fue posible la paz, p. 365.

46 Cited by Miguel Ardid Pellón and Javier Castro Villacañas, José María Gil Robles (Madrid: Eds. B, 2004), p. 104.

47 Juan Simeón Vidarte, Todos fuimos culpables (México: FCE, 1973), p. 49.

48 El Debate, 27 February 1936.

49 El Socialista, 14 March 1936, 1.

50 El Socialista and El Sol, 15 March 1936, 1, cited in Gil Robles, No fue posible la paz, p. 575.

51 Mundo Obrero, 11 May 1936, and Stanley G. Payne, Falange. Historia del fascismo español (Paris: Ruedo Ibérico, 1965), p. 88.

52 Diego Martínez Barrio, Memorias (Barcelona: Planeta, 1983), p. 321.

53 Giménez Fernández in the prologue of Carlos Seco to Javier Tusell, Las elecciones del Frente Popular en España (Madrid: EDICUSA, 1971), Vol. I, p. XVIII.

54 Gil Robles, Discursos parlamentarios, p. 571.

55 Speech in the Cortes of 15 April 1936, Gil Robles, Discursos parlamentarios, pp. 560–1.

56 Speech of 19 May 1936, in Gil Robles, Discursos parlamentarios, pp. 573 and 575.

57 Gil Robles, Discursos parlamentarios, pp. 626–7.

58 Gil Robles, No fue posible la paz, p. 802.

59 Declaration of Gil Robles in Lisbon (27 February 1942), in the Institute of Military History and Culture, leg. 273bis, carp. 18, arm. 4, reproduced in ABC and Ya, 1 May 1968, and cited by Ricardo de la Cierva, Historia de la Guerra Civil Española, I: Perspectivas y antecedentes, 1898–1936 (Madrid: San Martín, 1969), pp. 742–3.

60 Ricardo de la Cierva, *Los documentos de la primavera trágica. Análisis documental de los antecedentes inmediatos del 18 de Julio de 1936* (Madrid: Ministerio de Información y Turismo, 1967), pp. 742–3.

61 Gil Robles, *No fue posible la paz*, p. 798, note 50, and Joaquín Arrarás et al., *Historia de la Cruzada Española* (Madrid: Ediciones Españolas, 1939–1944), Vol. III, p. 411.

62 *ABC*, 3 May 1968, and Melchor Ferrer, Domingo Tejera and José F. Acedo, *Historia del Tradicionalismo Español* (Madrid–Sevilla, Ed. Trajano-Ed. Tradicionalista-Ed. Católica, 1941–79), Vol. XXX, pp. 162–3, 327–9.

63 Manuel Rubio Cabeza, *Diccionario de la Guerra Civil* (Barcelona: Planeta, 1987), Vol. I, p. 376.

64 Jaime del Urgo, *Conspiración y Guerra Civil* (Madrid–Barcelona: Alfaguara, 1970), p. 208.

65 *El Adelanto*, 8 September 1936, 5–6.

66 Letter from Gil Robles to Luciano de la Calzada (7 October 1936), cited by Ricardo de la Cierva, *Francisco Franco, un siglo de España* (Madrid: Editora Nacional, 1973), Vol. I, pp. 534–5.

67 Declarations of Gil Robles to *The Universe*, compiled by *Diario de Navarra*, 17 February 1937 and *El Noticiero* de Zaragoza, 18 February 1937, and cited in *Documentos inéditos para la Historia del Generalísimo Franco* (Madrid: Fundación Nacional Francisco Franco, 1992), Vol. I, pp. 106–9. The arguments are identical to those employed in his propagandistic pamphlet *Spain in Chains* (New York: America Press, 1937), pp. 7–8.

68 On the vicissitudes of the CEDA in the political atmosphere of Francoist Spain prior to the unification, see Francisco Torres García, 'Actuación de Gil Robles en la guerra civil', *Historia* 16, 186 (October 1991): 26–8.

69 *Heraldo de la Rioja*, 24 April 1937, cited by Ardid Pellón and Castro-Villacañas, *José María Gil Robles*, pp. 261–2, and Maximiano García Venero, *Historia de la Unificación (Falange y Requeté en 1937)* (Madrid: Agesa, 1970), p. 218.

70 'Gil Robles cancela sus actividades políticas' (letter to the national leader of the militias of AP Luciano de la Calzada), *Diario de Navarra*, 28 April 1937, 1.

71 Gil Robles, *La fe a través de mi vida*, pp. 141–2.

72 Gil Robles, *José María, La Monarquía por la que yo luché. Páginas de un diario (1941–1954)* (Madrid: Taurus, 1976), p. 17.

73 José María Toquero, *Franco y Don Juan: La oposición monárquica al franquismo* (Barcelona: Plaza & Janés, 1989), p. 57.

74 Gil Robles, *La Monarquía por la que yo luché*, pp. 339–40.

75 The article of *ABC* and the exoneration of Juan Ignacio Luca de Tena in Gil Robles, *La Monarquía por la que yo luché*, pp. 88, note 34, and 378–9, and Javier Tusell, *La oposición democrática al franquismo, 1939–1962* (Barcelona: Planeta, 1977), pp. 84–7.

76 Gil Robles, *La Monarquía por la que yo luché*, pp. 379–80.

77 Ibid., p. 118.

78 Ibid., p. 279.

79 His speech of 8 June 1962, in José María Gil Robles, *Marginalia política* (Barcelona: Ariel, 1975), pp. 63–4.

80 The acid letter of resignation to Don Juan of July 1962 can be found in Tusell, *La oposición democrática al franquismo*, p. 428.

81 For his analysis of the defeat, see 'Mis culpas y responsabilidades', in José María Gil Robles, *Un final de jornada (1975–1977)* (Madrid: 1977), pp. 589–96.

82 Declarations to Tomás Fernández in *Ya*, 15 October 1976, 16. Another recognition of his failure can be found in Gil Robles, *La fe a través de mi vida*, p. 135.

83 Cited by José María García Escudero, 'Gil Robles, la tentación totalitaria', in *Vista a la derecha. Cánovas, Maura, Cambó, Gil Robles, López Rodó, Fraga* (Madrid: Rialp, 1988), p. 214.

84 Francesc Cambó, *Memorias, 1876–1936* (Barcelona: Alpha, 1981), p. 476.

4

José Antonio Primo de Rivera: Catholic Fascism

CHRIS BANNISTER

During the Franco regime, José Antonio Primo de Rivera was, apart from the dictator himself, the most celebrated and revered individual in Spain. The name José Antonio Primo de Rivera was carved into the sides of churches as every Spaniard knew of this 'martyr' of the Civil War. The post-war years saw the creation of the myth of José Antonio: he was portrayed as brave, pious and patriotic, an embodiment of the values of the 'New Spain'.[1] Critically to the regime, José Antonio was the *fundador* (founder) of the Falange, Franco's ruling party. This connection allowed Franco to be portrayed as the successor to José Antonio, the new *jefe* (leader), justifying his actions as the completion of the work that the young Primo de Rivera had begun.[2] Furthermore, José Antonio was Franco's link to fascism. It was Jose Antonio's party and ideology that had hispanified the Italian doctrine and permitted Franco to be recognized as fascist leader and stand, in his eyes, shoulder to shoulder with the Axis powers.

Francoist historiography went a long way to reinforcing this myth, with hagiographies of José Antonio portraying him as a martyr, prescient ideologue and harbouring a profound respect for Franco.[3] Recent historiography has gone some way to redefining our understanding of José Antonio, stating that on a personal and political level his being the subject of a cult of personality did not suit his character and, ultimately, that he was a martyr for a reactionary regime that represented an ideology that he had little support for while alive.[4] However, while it is true that José Antonio was not a supporter of Franco, work on José Antonio somehow fails to address his contribution to the doctrinal foundations of the Franco regime's ideology. The accepted belief is that José Antonio was a fascist and Franco a reactionary, the latter using the 'ideological paraphernalia' of the Falange to dress his traditionalist regime up as a fascist one.[5] While this is not wholly untrue, it ignores the groundwork provided by José Antonio in 'hispanifying' fascism and allowing for a synthesis between fascist ideas, mainly drawn from its Italian guise, and the beliefs of traditionalist Spain.

While alive, José Antonio Primo de Rivera y Sáenz de Heredia, was, according to some sympathetic accounts, an amiable character. In his private life he was the witty, urbane man-about-town, charming Madrid high society, interested in riding, hunting and poetry; it was even rumoured that he enjoyed an affair with his close friend Elizabeth Asquith, daughter of the former British Prime Minister, Herbert.[6] Born on 24 April 1903, the first child of military officer Miguel Primo de Rivera and his wife Casilda Saénz de Heredia, José Antonio's childhood would be dominated by the military and nationalist beliefs of his father and the piety of his aunts, especially María Jesús, who would care for José Antonio and his siblings following the death of their mother in 1909. Mass was attended daily and interaction with his father Miguel would almost always involve a soliloquy on duty and the patria.[7] Franco would later describe the upbringing of José Antonio as one borne 'in the severe discipline of a military household, which tempered his character in the cult of patria, attaining the serenity and strength of a soldier'.[8] After childhood, José Antonio would go on to study and practice law in Madrid, and became known for his eloquence in the courtroom. In short, in upbringing and social stature, José Antonio was every inch the traditional Spanish *señorito* – well educated and with a strong understanding of nation and tradition.[9]

José Antonio's political awakening came when his father, now General Primo de Rivera, dictator from 1923 to 1930, fell from power in January 1930 and six weeks later died in exile in Paris. José Antonio was now head of the family and, following a brief flirtation with monarchist politics that culminated in his standing as an unsuccessful parliamentary candidate for Unión Monárquica in October 1931, he became enamoured with the ideology of Mussolini's Italy.[10] His admiration for Italy and the Duce were great, yet his reasons for adopting fascism as his political credo are not made explicit in his own works. The arguments put forward in historiography are varied, ranging from the assertion that its authoritarian nature and strong nationalism were reminiscent of his father's regime, to a belief that, in light of its success in Italy and Germany, it was a political doctrine that held the greatest potential to allow Spain to once again flourish.[11] Regardless of his motivation, upon the creation of *Falange Española* in the summer of 1933, José Antonio was an avowed fascist, a commitment that was to only deepen over the course of his political career. He was dedicated to the immediate and violent overthrow of the liberal state, he preached social revolution, land reform and staunch anti-capitalism, and his blue-shirted fascist foot soldiers were often found brawling in the streets with socialists and communists throughout the remaining years of the Second Republic. To José Antonio, the *jefe* of the Falange, 'there [was] no more admissible dialect than the dialect of fists and pistols'.[12]

Before José Antonio's creation of the *Falange Española*, there had been previous attempts to introduce fascism to Spain. Of these attempts, the most prominent were those led by philosophy student Ramiro Ledesma Ramos and extremist Catholic Onésimo Redondo. The two were far from ideologically identical, Ledesma was a studious man and his conception of fascism was concerned with the role of the state and the economic revolution as a means of national rebirth. Redondo, on the other hand, was more interested in a Catholic interpretation of the nation, tempered with virulent anti-Semitism.[13] Yet despite their differences, through a shared lack of means and support, the two would ultimately pool their resources, leading to the creation of the *Juntas de Ofensiva Nacional Sindicalista* (JONS) in October 1931. The JONS would have little success as a political organization and would ultimately join with José Antonio's Falange in February 1934 to create the *Falange Española y de las JONS*. The new organization would initially be led by an 'executive committee' composed of José Antonio, Ledesma and former soldier Julio Ruiz de Alda, but by September 1934 this was disbanded with José Antonio assuming sole leadership.[14]

José Antonio's role as *jefe* would ultimately lead to his death as, at the outbreak of war, he found himself imprisoned. He was arrested in February 1936, linked, albeit dubiously, to a failed Falangist assassination attempt on Socialist professor of law Luís Jiménez Asúa, an attempt that resulted in the death of Asúa's police bodyguard, Jesús Gisbert.[15] He was sent to the *Cárcel Modelo* in Madrid, yet, due to fear of his escape, was later transferred to a more secure prison in Alicante in early June 1936. He spent four months of the Civil War in Alicante until he was tried and found guilty on 17 November 1936. His execution by Republican firing squad occurred three days later, in the early morning of 20 November 1936.[16]

The focus of this chapter will be on José Antonio as *jefe* and ideologue of the Falange and his role in transferring the ideas of fascism to the Spanish nation, in adapting its fundaments to a different economic system, a different polity and, most importantly for fascism, a different *patria*. The chapter will consequently look at how he fitted the key tenets of traditional Spanish rightist ideals, those that Franco subscribed to, namely Catholicism, anti-Separatism, anti-Marxism and the glorification of the past, into a fascist framework.[17]

Figure 4.1 Onésimo Redondo and José Antonio Primo de Rivera, side by side, wearing the uniform of the *Falange Española y de las JONS*.

The aim is to show that the *falangismo*, as defined by José Antonio, was an ideology that was both influenced by the Italian and, to a lesser extent, German ideas of fascism, but also rooted firmly in the right-wing Spanish traditionalism that the Franco regime is often seen as embodying.

Catholic Fascism

As this chapter deals with the introduction of a foreign ideology to Spain, an understanding of this ideology, Italian fascism, is patently necessary. However, defining fascism is a difficult practice and for the purposes of this chapter it is best understood in classic terms as an ultra-nationalist, authoritarian, vehemently anti-Marxist and often violent ideology that understood the nation as an organic and indivisible entity. Fascists entertained romantic ideas of palingenesis, seeing the nation in decline, and fostered ideas of mass mobilization and the transformation of class structures through a corporatist and syndicalist economic policy.[18] It shared some similarities with the traditionalist Spanish right, but not enough for them to be comfortable bedfellows.

At its root, the unifying ideal of José Antonio's Falange, as with all fascism, was the belief that the nation would be the champion of history and that the current travails of the country were to be attributed to a national failure to value the patria. To support this, he drew particularly on the Italian and German Romantic conception of the nation and some Spanish philosophical influences, namely the famed 'Generation of 1898' and, from the subsequent 'Generation of 1914', José Ortega y Gasset – the then professor of metaphysics at the Central University of Madrid and author of the book *España Invertebrada*.[19] From reading Ortega and following the Italian and German fascist Romantic tradition, José Antonio came to understand the patria as 'a unity of destiny in the Universal', a people that through a shared culture and history transcended the confines of state and territory, becoming more than 'a physical entity, individualized by accident of terrain, ethnicity or language, but an historical entity, distinct from others in the universal by its own unity of destiny'.[20] This unity of destiny was the key to both national prosperity and the individual happiness of those who composed the nation as, in José Antonio's Ortegan interpretation, the life of the individual was only truly meaningful if it was in pursuit of a higher cause.[21] Therefore, all José Antonio's rhetoric would have, at its root, the fundamental assertion that for the people of Spain to prosper, both individually and as a nation, the patria needed to be unified in its aims and without division (whether that division be based along party political or class lines or borne from regional separatism).[22] Upon the foundation of the *Falange Española* in 1933, José Antonio would in his first speech to Madrid's *Teatro de la Comedia* outline exactly the fundamental importance of the patria to his plans for Spain:

> The patria is a total unity, which integrates all individuals and classes; the patria cannot be in the hands of the strongest class or the best organized party. The patria is a transcendent synthesis, an indivisible synthesis, with

its own ends to accomplish; and what we want is for the movement of this day, and the State that it will create, to be the effective, authoritarian, instrument in the service of an undisputed union, of a permanent union, of an irrevocable union that is called the patria.[23]

This was the belief that would inform all of José Antonio's political ideas, that the patria was irrevocable, supreme, and that subservience to its interests was the only means for the entire Spanish people to be truly happy. All Falange policy and rhetoric would evoke the patria and from this José Antonio would forge a fascist political programme. However, the patria, despite being the crux of *falangismo,* was a fundamentally vague notion – difficult to define, not merely the people or geographical territory of Spain, but also an understanding of the nation, its culture and its history. In the Italian case that definition was the imperial ideal of *Romanità,* in the German, it was the sanctification of the race, the *Volk.*

In order to create a distinctly Spanish fascism, an equivalent of the *Romanità* or the *Volk* needed to be found – an all encompassing ideal that united shared history, race and culture and also enthused its constituents. In José Antonio's search for such an equivalent he would come to share the beliefs of revered nationalist intellectual Marcelino Menéndez y Pelayo, that the patria and religion were deeply linked; as such, Catholicism 'profound and elemental' would come to be the spiritual basis of *falangismo.*[24] For José Antonio, Catholicism was part of the patria, it was part of the Spanish character and could not be, nor was it desired to be, sidelined: 'the Catholic interpretation of life is in first place, the truthful one, but furthermore, it is the Spanish one'.[25] Yet to turn to an idea as traditional as National Catholicism, José Antonio appeared to be reverting to a traditional, reactionary position, that of a confessional state.[26] This was, however, not the case; Catholicism came to represent not only Spain's religion, but its history and its people, responsible for its greatest achievements. Despite not being exclusively Spanish, Catholicism, to José Antonio, was 'a glorious tradition and predominant in Spain', it was the fundamental driving force behind all of Spain's great endeavours. The fifteenth-century Catholic kings (*Reyes Católicos*) received their name for their piety and their enthusiasm to both spread the faith to the New World and defend it in Europe, while the *Reconquista* was a crusade undertaken to expel the Muslim Moors from the peninsula.[27] It was Spain's existential aphorism – in the Falange's *Puntos Iniciales,* published in December 1933, José Antonio made the fundamentality of Catholicism to the Spanish national character clear:

Falange Española cannot consider life as a mere set of economic factors. It does not accept the materialist interpretation of history. The spiritual has been and remains instrumental in the roots and lives and men and peoples. No man can stop formulating the eternal questions of life and death, about the creation and beyond. To these questions ... Spain always answered with the Catholic claim.[28]

Needless to say that the reverence for Catholicism was not something exclusive to the Falange; in fact, those of more explicitly conservative persuasion, such as José María Gil Robles of the the explicitly Catholic CEDA (*Confederación Española de Derechas Autónomas*) and Royo Villanova of the monarchist paper *ABC*, criticized the movement for being anti-Catholic, arguing that the Church had suffered persecution under its Italian equivalent.[29] This criticism was fuelled further as the Falange advocated a secular policy forbidding the Church to interfere in state affairs and closed the door to the return of a confessional state. Yet to state that the Falange was anti-Catholic was a nonsense; the party's *Puntos Iniciales* and 1934's *Norma Programática* outlined the relationship as follows:

Any reconstruction of Spain has to have a Catholic expression [*sentido*]. This does not mean they will revive the persecution of those who are not. The times of religious persecution are over. Nor does it mean that the State will assume religious functions that correspond directly to the Church. Not unless you plan to tolerate interference or machinations of the Church, with possible damage to the dignity of the state or national integrity.[30]

The Church and the State will agree their respective powers, without interference or support any activity that undermines the dignity of the state or national integrity.[31]

Clearly this did not mean that José Antonio and the Falange were opposed to Catholicism – they felt quite the opposite – only that Catholic feeling as opposed to institution was to be the basis of the Spanish patria. This transcended the necessity for a formal confessional state, as Catholicism constituted the national character and would inform decisions 'organically'. The Church, as the guardian of the Catholic faith, was fundamental to the national milieu, yet would not dictate to the patria – just as Ancient Rome did not dictate policy to Mussolini. By integrating the national and the religious on a spiritual and metaphysical level, as opposed to an official one, José Antonio avoided the conservatism of a confessional state yet also adopted a suitably profound basis for the patria, one that encompassed the history of the nation and integrated the desirable elements of the population.

The embrace of religion continued a theme that existed within Italian fascism and its German equivalent. Neither of these ideologies themselves placed Catholicism or Christianity in such an explicitly important position to the nation, but both adopted Christian liturgy and rituals into their practices.

Furthermore, both adopted sympathetic approaches towards the ideals of the Church. In Germany staunch anti-communism, anti-Semitism and the idealization of agriculture and the countryside were close to the Lutheran ideal. In Italy, Mussolini signed the Lateran agreement, allowing for peaceful coexistence between Church and state, and returned the crucifix to schools.[32]

Furthermore, Catholicism in terms of its spirituality fit well with José Antonio's fascist-Ortegan idea of the nation: each promulgated a shared destiny of those who believed and a transcendental belief in something greater than the individual. There was a Manichean understanding of morality and mutual reverence for sacrifice which was to be embraced by José Antonio and the Falange as a link between religion and the patria: a fundamentally Christian idea, yet also supported by fascist thought. Giovanni Gentile, the self-described 'philosopher of fascism', would in his *Origini e dottrina del fascismo* argue that, 'Those who understand existence as a service, as a path to a higher goal, have always made an offering of his life, with the sacrifice of life to serve the fulfilment of a higher end.'[33] As a dual fascist and Catholic duty, 'self-denial and sacrifice [would] save Spain' and a life in the Falange was one of 'service and sacrifice'; it required the ultimate show of commitment and was mutually rewarded by lay and divine martyrdom. The linguistic manifestation of this was witnessed at the funeral services of *falangistas* killed in violent clashes.[34] Here, the religious and Falangist came together to honour sacrifice in the name of the nation and all those who died became 'the glorious fallen', 'martyrs' who 'offered [their] life and blood on the altar of immortal Spain'. Moreover, as with all martyrs, their sacrifice was to be emulated rather than dreaded:

We are all prepared ... to make the supreme sacrifice to fulfil our mission. Mission in the clear sense, in the religious sense of the word ... Let us always remember that Spain is 'a unity of destiny' and know how to demonstrate ... with Spanish pride, that [we are willing] to live and die for Spain in fulfilment of a sacred duty.[35]

The religious-nationalist mission that José Antonio forged for the Falange glorified the death of *falangistas*; their sacrifice was to be emulated rather than dreaded: bound the 'unity of destiny in the universal' with blood.

Religion, therefore, served as the basis for a strong nationalist sentiment. It was the guide for the 'unity of destiny in the universal' as it had been responsible for Spain's greatest achievements and was the spiritual, historical and cultural basis of the patria. Furthermore, it was an idea that was both key to fascism and *españolidad* (Spanishness) as, by making Catholicism the Spanish *Romanità*, José Antonio brought the two concepts ideologically closer, but avoided a return to a traditional confessional state.

Figure 4.2 José Antonio Primo de Rivera based his Spanish fascism in Catholicism. In the picture, José Antonio presides over a Falange meeting during the Second Republic.

History, Empire and Anti-Marxism

Fascism's belief in palingenesis, that the current polity was corrupt, decadent, that a 'rebirth' was necessary and that this rebirth would set the nation on a new course, often resulted in a fetishization of the past.[36] For José Antonio this was no different and once again his inspiration came from the Catholic faith – venerating those eras of Spanish and European history when he believed religion and the nation were closest. In his interpretation, history began its apotheosis in the thirteenth century, the century of St Thomas Aquinas:

> In this epoch the idea of all is metaphysical 'unity', the unity in God; when one has these truths everything is explained, the entire world, in this case Europe, operates according to the centuries' most perfect economy ... The world has found itself. Soon the Spanish Empire will be realized, which is historical, physical, spiritual and theological unity.[37]

This 'metaphysical unity' allowed for the Spanish people to prosper, and, ideally, would permit them to do so again. The Catholic kings of the fifteenth century were the shining example of the Spanish right; uncorrupted by the decadent ideas of liberalism and Protestantism, they were the perfect marriage of the autocratic and the pious. Moreover, history had vindicated them: the Catholic kings united the nation, expelled the heathen Jews and Muslims from the peninsular, discovered new continents and forged a huge Empire. José Antonio shared this belief and argued that the Empire had been a time of contentment for the Spanish people:

> ... from here, from this Castile, that had never seen the sea, the ocean routes were traced and laws enacted on distant continents. And precisely when this happened, when all Spain was a single yearning in this universal enterprise, the Spanish people lived better and were freer and happier.[38]

Empire united people, it gave the people a national mission that the 'unity of destiny' called for and superseded the conflict of classes. Ernesto Giménez Caballero, the eccentric fascist intellectual, placed this in simple terms in his work *Genio de España*:

> There has been only one means in the world to overcome the eternal rancour of classes and it is to transfer the social struggle to a different plane ... To transfer it from the national plane to the international. A nation's poor and rich can only come to agreement when they both decide to attack other peoples or lands.[39]

However, since the era of the Catholic kings the nation had been in decline, and the year 1898 saw the issue of Empire become one of national crisis as Spain lost its final vestiges of imperial prestige in Cuba and the Philippines. For many on the right, the 'crisis of 1898' had seen the patria enter a terminal malaise.[40] For José Antonio, the creation of an empire was therefore fundamental to restore national honour, as natural in the twentieth century as it had been in the fifteenth. José Antonio stated that the Falange, the party most in tune with the Catholic kings, would 'seek the traditions of our Empire'. Point three of the Falange's *Norma Programática* began by stating, 'We have the will of Empire. We affirm that the historical fulfilment of Spain is the Empire.'[41] The notion of empire, therefore, was a means to show Spanish supremacy over other, lesser peoples, satisfying the fascist palingenetic ideas of rebirth of the nation as a strong unified entity while linking the Falange with Spain's glorious past.

This glorification of the past often dictated a glorification of Castile, the traditional imperial seat of power. The 'Generation of 1898' were keen exponents of this belief, with notable works by Azorín and Miguel de Unamuno dedicated to its plains and villages.[42] José Antonio, too, would revere Castile as it embodied the timeless virtues that he wished to recapture. To him the region was:

... the land without finery of particulars, the absolute land ... the land that is not the aggregate of a few farms, nor the support of a few agricultural interests to be haggled over in assemblies, but is the earth, the earth as a repository of eternal values, austerity in conduct, religious feeling in lime, the speech of silence, solidarity between ancestors and descendants.[43]

Castile embodied and led the Spanish 'unity of destiny', and the region's historical importance was that of a centralizing power, one that united peoples across the Empire under the rule of one Catholic monarch. To stray from this understanding was to undermine the national 'common enterprise', as Spain only prospered when its people came together, and united in the 'universal historical justification of their existence'.[44] This sentiment was transferred to the modern era, and consequently manifested itself as anti-separatism. One of the strongest beliefs of the right, territorial unity was fundamental to the nation's fortunes – monarchist José Calvo Sotelo famously proclaimed in 1933 that 'I prefer a red Spain to a broken Spain.'[45] José Antonio, therefore, criticized Spain's peripheral nationalist groups for their spiritual redundancy: they were the sign of a national malaise, a return to 'a primitive state'.[46] The 'unity of destiny' was a triumph of the historical over the primitive; Spain represented a national mission; separatism was 'barbarian at heart' for with the absence of 'faith in a common destiny, everything dissolves into native regions, into local colours and flavours. There is no reason, for example, not to subordinate economic status to each valley, from one to the next.'[47]

A further key belief shared by the Spanish right and the Falange was anti-communism. However, there existed problems in the creation of a suitably fascist, yet also Spanish, anti-Marxism. Criticism of Marx in classical fascism took on a Social Darwinist tendency, arguing that simple weight in numbers was not an acceptable means of deciding the value of peoples and disregarded the innate discrepancies of nature. Yet the pseudo-scientific assumptions of Social Darwinism did not suit José Antonio's more spiritual and metaphysical understanding of the Spanish patria. Falangism's reasons needed to be based in something more Spanish. In addition to this, the constitution of the traditional anti-Marxists in Spain, namely the bourgeoisie, big business or the landed gentry, offered little common ground in their conservative and capitalist opposition. In this situation, Catholicism as Romanità enabled the creation of an authentically Spanish basis for anti-Marxism, as through the definition of the national group along the relatively well-defined lines of faith, political opponents could be easily identified. This definition made a simple distinction: those without faith became enemies of the patria, and Marxists lacked faith: 'We are anti-communists, but not because we draw back from the transformation of an economic order in which there are so many destitute, but because communism is the negation of the Western, Christian and Spanish sense of existence.'[48]

This created the ideological situation where the mutual enemies of fascism and other groups of the Spanish right could be victimized for the same reasons – a spiritual poverty and lack of nationalist sentiment. Through this the Falange reiterated its Spanish nationalist commitment while not resorting to economic criticisms of Marx, thereby maintaining the movement's anti-capitalist, corporatist credentials. Fundamentally this conceit functioned as a simple means to strip Marxists of their Spanish nationality: Marxism was 'the anti-patria, lacking in faith in God' and communists were 'ignorant of all that might hold significant historical or spiritual value'. Its sponsorship of 'the monstrous Dogma of the struggle of the classes' served only to show further its lack of patriotism as it was willing to undermine the whole people's 'unity of destiny' for a single class.[49] By presenting Marxism as both irreligious and anti-patriotic, José Antonio portrayed it as a foreign doctrine. Thus Karl Marx was reduced to a 'German Jew' who wrote about workers in Manchester, and communism itself was in the thrall of Moscow, unconcerned with Spain or the Spanish people.[50] To José Antonio, Marxists were Muscovite, and 'the triumph of communism would not be the triumph of the social revolution of Spain: it would be the triumph of Russia'.[51] Here we see a Falangist root of Francoism's vilification of its Civil War enemies, the 'reds', who, according to Nationalist propaganda, lacked faith, were commanded by foreigners and had no regard for the patria.[52]

A *Jefe* to Save Spain

The political programme of the Falange followed the fascist ideal of the unity of the patria and the subordination of all other interests in the pursuit of the national mission. There was to be a firm rejection of the liberal state, by which José Antonio meant the liberal democracy of the Second Republic, in favour of an authoritarian regime. The liberal polity was fundamentally flawed, it rejected eternal truths in favour of 'that which has the highest number of votes', it 'believed in nothing, not even itself'.[53] This resulted in a polity that was wrought with division as political parties came to hate each other and under-mined the nation; to José Antonio it made a mockery of the vaunted concept of fraternity as 'there never was a collective living situation where insulted men, enemies of one another, feel less like brothers than in the turbulent and objectionable liberal state'.[54] The solution was the immediate overthrow of the parliamentary democracy. The party's *Norma Programática* promised that the Falange would 'ruthlessly abolish the system of political parties with all their consequences: inorganic suffrage, representation by warring factions and Parliament in its current guise'.[55] The new regime would not, however, be a complete retreat into the old tradition of Spanish autocracy, introverted and in support of vested interests, but instead a totalitarian dictatorship that would foster the concept of national unity:

> The remedy that I see is in an authoritarian state, not in the service of a class, nor the victorious party in a free competition of political parties. In a strong state, at the service of the historical idea of the patria. In the subordination of individual interests to the national interest.

In José Antonio's rhetoric, if this new state was to provide support to any strata of society it would, in fact, be for the proletariat as 'it is precisely the one that needs protection, the others are strong and can defend themselves'.[56] That is not to say that those in power would lose their positions of privilege – the Italian and German systems were testament to the fostering of national business and the reduction of workers' rights – only that the ultimate aim would be national, not private, prosperity.

The economic basis of José Antonio's revolution was his understanding of corporatism known as national syndicalism. To José Antonio, the free-market capitalist system favoured by liberal-bourgeois democracy fostered discord, divided the patria and served only those who constituted the financial system itself, 'dealers, brokers, managers, bankers, owners, stockholders [and] directors of large companies'.[57] Opposition to it was enshrined in point 10 of the *Norma Programática*: 'we reject the capitalist system, which ignores the needs of the people, dehumanizes private property and workers, agglomerates the workers into shapeless masses, conducive to misery and despair'.[58] The dehumanization of private property that José Antonio spoke of was capitalism's greatest crime, as it complicated 'the elemental relationship between men and things' and reduced individuals and individual ownership to 'an abstraction represented by pieces of paper'; the result was strife as the system permitted for 'workers and employers to fight bitterly ... and express a cruelty beyond repair'.[59] His solution came in the realization that labour and capital were part of an economic struggle, in which 'the two are on the same side [and], on the opposite side, against employers and workers, there is the power of capitalism, the technique of financial capitalism'.[60] This was originally Ramiro Ledesma's conception of national syndicalism, adopted enthusiastically by José Antonio. The Falangist aim was the creation of large quasi-autonomous syndicates that included both labour and employers. The idea was to use the Italian corporatist system as a 'starting point, not an arrival point'.[61] It was to be a system that was, at heart, the economic expression of the 'unity of destiny in the universal', a national undertaking that needed all classes. The ultimate aim of the system was to 'make the class struggle radically impossible, because all those cooperating in the struggle are an organic whole', as it would include Spain's leading agitators of class war, the syndicates.[62] What José Antonio failed to address was the fascist tendency to rob workers of collective bargaining rights and to create a rigid relationship between capital and labour, free of debate or renegotiation of terms.[63]

As fascism dictated, in order for this system to function there needed to be an authoritarian regime, one that was free of the infighting of the democratic system and understood the national mission. The authoritarian regime was embodied in a single individual, the great man as saviour of the nation. In his introduction to the Spanish translation of Mussolini's *Il Fascismo*, José Antonio outlined why a single leader was the ideal:

> The man is the system, this is one of the profound human truths that has returned to give value to fascism. All the nineteenth century was spent devising machinery for good government ... Nothing real, eternal and difficult, as governing is, has been done by machine, it has always had to recourse, at the last minute, to that which, from the origin of the world, has been the only device capable of leading men: man. That is to say, the *jefe*. The hero.[64]

Spain itself had a long history of autocracy, and many on the right, including, as we have seen, José Antonio, believed that the reign of the Catholic kings was the apotheosis of national achievement. There was also a rich vein of right-wing thought on the topic of strong leaders, namely intellectual Joaquín Costa's idea of the 'Iron Surgeon'.[65] The 'Iron Surgeon', with its invasive and violent connotations, was part of the organicist conception of the patria: Spain was a body stricken with disease and needed to be 'cured'.[66] The diseases that affected the patria were the usual rightist bêtes noires of liberalism, Bolshevism, atheism, Protestantism and feminism. Fascism and Spanish tradition therefore dictated that some sort of authoritarian individualism was a prerequisite for a Spanish fascist movement, and there even existed prêt-à-porter linguistic equivalents of *Führer* and *Duce* in *caudillo* and *jefe*. Yet on a personal level, José Antonio would have his own reservations about his suitability for the role. He would repeatedly cite to friends that his calling was elsewhere, on one occasion stating, 'I wasn't born for this, I was meant to be an eighteenth century mathematician.' Moreover, in a letter to *ABC* in 1933, he noted that his attributes were 'the worst fit with those of a *caudillo*'.[67] In his private correspondence he would go further. A letter to his friend Julián Pemartín highlighted that José Antonio understood that his background was a far cry from that expected from a fascist:

> Being a *caudillo* requires something of the prophet; he needs a dose of faith, health, enthusiasm and anger which is not compatible with

refinement. I, for one, would serve as anything except a fascist *caudillo*. The attitude of doubt and sense of irony, that never leave those of us that have had, more or less, some form of intellectual curiosity, disables us from launching the robust claims that are required without hesitation by the leaders of the masses.[68]

José Antonio therefore saw himself as apart from the fascist ideal, and this sense of incongruity, of his 'refinement' undermining his fascism, would define him as a *jefe*. The philosopher Miguel de Unamuno would provide an astute summary of this apparent contradiction:

He [José Antonio] is a lad who has adopted a role that does not suit him, he is too refined, too much of a *señorito*, and basically too timid to be a leader, much less a dictator ... to which should be added that one of the basic attributes to lead a fascist party is to be an epileptic.[69]

Ultimately, however, fascism required an authoritarian system under the direction of one man and Spanish tradition called for a strong leader, and despite José Antonio's apparent personal limitations he, with his family name,

Figure 4.3 The 'señorito' that became *Jefe* of Spanish Fascism. José Antonio, addressing Falange members at a rally.

charisma and charm was far better suited to the task than either Onésimo Redondo or Ramiro Ledesma. That was, of course, until his death, when Franco would take on the mantle of the Iron Surgeon and *caudillo*.

José Antonio and Violence

Fascism remains a topic that is rarely discussed without the mention of the violence. This is unsurprising, as it fostered a fundamentally violent under-standing of politics and rarely manifested itself without the use of violent action. In doctrinal terms, fascism saw violence as a necessity for the elimination of its enemies in order for the nation to realize its palingenetic destiny.[70] There was no alternative; parliamentarism was decadent and debate was immaterial, and when it failed to hand power to the fascist movement, violence became the political vehicle, José Antonio's 'dialectic of fists and pistols'. Furthermore, violence, in the Sorelian 'creative' sense, was more than a means of gaining power but a part of fascist morality. To Mussolini this was evident, as to him 'the struggle is even more important than the triumph', and acts of violence provided a moral education on sacrifice for the people en masse.[71] José Antonio himself felt that violence also served a moral purpose, as we have seen in his own diktats on sacrifice, for it strengthened the commitment to the national mission.

José Antonio was not a man of peace by any stretch of the imagination; he was quick to throw punches when suitably provoked, especially when he perceived sleights against his father.[72] Examples of this were even witnessed in the Cortes: one incident saw José Antonio punch an opponent to the floor while on a separate occasion he sparked a mass brawl as he reacted angrily to a criticism of his father.[73] This 'proud violence' was mirrored in his rhetoric; in his inaugural speech at the Teatro de la Comedia he asked, 'Who has ever said that the supreme hierarchy of moral values lies in kindness? When our feelings are insulted, rather than react like men, we must be courteous?'[74] On a political level, José Antonio oversaw the inclusion of violence within Falange ideology. The 'El Escorial pact', an agreement between the Falange and the Monarchists of *Renovación Española*, had as its tenth and final point that 'violence is permissible in the service of reason and justice'.[75] Violence as a means of action was enshrined in the Falange's *Norma Programática*, which, in its 26th point, stated that the means of realizing the national revolution would preferably be 'direct, fiery and combative [for] life is military and has to be lived with an unblemished spirit of service and sacrifice'.[76] José Antonio would regularly this use martial language in his rhetoric, likening the Falange to the army and portraying the task of the movement as a military struggle:

'Life is military, the Falange is military', 'We must fight for Spain to regain her life', 'Militancy is a necessity, an unavoidable necessity of men and people who want to save themselves'.[77]

As we have seen, José Antonio himself did not feel that he was suited to the role of the fascist *jefe*, and historiography has painted him as a man who, despite being the head of a fascist organization, fostered a distaste for violence.[78] Examples proposed by historians are his vetoing of assassination attempts on socialists Indalecio Prieto and Francisco Largo Caballero, his reluctance to call for reprisals after the deaths of several Falangists in 1934, and his eventual, and arguably genuine, horror at the scale of violence that the outbreak of the Civil War brought.[79] However, these isolated cases distract from the larger issue: that he actively encouraged his party to commit violent acts to serve political and moral ends. The Second Republic was marred by political violence committed by both sides and throughout the period of 1933–6 the Falange was responsible for the deaths of several leftists.[80] Following the election of the Popular Front, the Falange took on a role as the leading provocateurs against Republican authority, engaging in a violent campaign against left-wing targets in the hope of inciting reprisals. One such event occurred in Granada in March 1936 when a squad of Falangist gunmen fired on a group of workers and their families, wounding women and children, and inciting the hoped for reprisals. [81] During this period, as the political situation became more and more polarized and the means of discourse between rival factions became reliant on violence, José Antonio's own rhetoric only served to fan the flames of discord.[82] This dispatch from early June 1936 is a typical example:

THERE IS NO PEACEFUL SOLUTION, war has been declared and the government has been the first to proclaim itself belligerent ... there is this violence, this war, in which not only do we defend the existence of the Falange, gained at the price of better lives, but the very existence of Spain ... Tomorrow when the brighter days dawn, the Falange will wear fresh laurels of primacy of this holy crusade of violence'[83]

This martial language placed the entire party on a war footing; their enemies, defined as the anti-patria, were the enemies of the nation and in order to save 'the very existence of Spain' needed to be defeated in a 'holy crusade'.[84] These ideas would not only serve to heighten tension within the Republic but the dichotomy of patria and anti-patria and the rhetorical use of the crusade were to be key tenets of wartime and early Francoism. Ultimately this commitment to violent language and deed would land José Antonio in prison, as he was linked, albeit dubiously, to the assassination attempt on Jiménez Asúa.

Following his incarceration and the outbreak of war, José Antonio would appear to show considerable anguish over the fate of his fellow Spaniards, yet before the hostilities he was one of the keenest exponents of a military coup d'état . Privately, he would write to Franco as early as 1934 warning him of the dangers of the left and the necessity of a prepared military (Franco never replied). In May 1936, from his prison cell in Madrid, José Antonio would write his *Carta a los militares de España* ('Letter to the Military of Spain').[85] In the letter, José Antonio called upon the military to intervene in the violent situation, for they were the only ones who could prevent the Popular Front's determination to permit 'the invasion of barbarians':

> The time has come when your arms come into play to save fundamental values ... It has always been so, the final game has always been the game of arms. As Spengler said, there has always been a platoon of soldiers that has saved civilisation.[86]

His support for a military coup could be construed as a wish to see an end to the cycle of violence that had gripped Spain in the 'hot' spring of 1936, an argument also put forward by Francoist historiography to legitimize the military uprising. Yet in reality any scholar of the political and social milieu of the Second Republic, as José Antonio was, knew that the industrial working class of Spain would not merely hand the country over without a struggle. The Asturias Revolution of October 1934 had shown that the workers could, at the very least, orchestrate a resistance.[87] José Antonio's support for the uprising was rooted in no more than a desire for the overthrow of the Popular Front, regardless of the violence it caused.

The ultimate result of the military uprising was the deaths of countless Spaniards, and José Antonio was to be one of them. His brother and cellmate Miguel, as well as one of the firing squad, would later recount that he went to his death with dignity and courage; it was a violent death for a man who preached violence.[88] For he did preach it; the use of violence was ingrained in the programme, the rhetoric and action of the Falange and it is certain that this contributed to the atmosphere of violence that characterized the polarized political atmosphere of the late Second Republic. He fostered a Sorelian under-standing of violence and death as a transcendental act and prized sacrifice as a nationalist idea. The outbreak of Civil War saw this morality taken to its logical conclusion as the Falange took to the repression of the 'enemies of the patria' with relish, its followers becoming responsible for the deaths of countless communists, leftists and other social 'undesirables', including the famous playwright and acquaintance of José Antonio, Federico García Lorca.[89] As much as José Antonio would in his trial decry these 'criminal acts' that had 'nothing to do with [his] status as founder of the Falange', it was his doctrine and rhetoric that encouraged them and this ideology would continue well into the Franco regime, with state-sponsored violence being a part of everyday life.[90]

Conclusion

The Francoist myth of José Antonio the martyr was most explicitly witnessed at his funeral, conducted on the third anniversary of his death, 20 November 1939. The proceedings were a highly choreographed affair lasting a whole week, beginning with his exhumation from his grave at Alicante. He was eventually interned at El Escorial some 500 kilometres away, having been carried from Alicante by pallbearers from the various regional Falangist authorities.[91] The procession marched day and night, the route being lit by torches and bonfires, and Mass was celebrated at every town the cortege passed through.[92] It was an ostentatious show of power by the regime, simultaneously beatifying José Antonio as a national martyr and highlighting the hierarchy of the new regime and the prominence of both the Church and the Falange within it. Yet it would seem that José Antonio would not have approved, either of its pomp or the political programme of the regime with which he was being linked. In his final weeks, José Antonio would come to denounce the Civil War and the groups with which his followers had sided. He would forlornly tell American journalist Jay Allen in October 1936 that if he discovered the Falange was to win and 'the result was nothing more than reaction, then I'll withdraw the Falange and I ... will return to this or another prison within the next few months'.[93] However, despite him having no say in the use of his legacy by the regime, José Antonio, as ideologue of the Falange, was far from an innocent man. It was his Spanish interpretation of fascism that imported the central tenets of the doctrine, namely authoritarianism, palingenesis, corporatism, anti-Marxism and extreme nationalism, and linked them to Catholicism, centralism and the myth of the 'Iron Surgeon'. This would ultimately make Franco's co-opting of the Falange a relatively simple task as they shared a mutual political heritage in Spanish tradition.[94] Furthermore, his positive attitude to violence and sacrifice created a situation where falangistas were willing to commit violent acts in the name of patria and see their enemies as an 'anti-patria', arguably the most pernicious and powerful concepts of Francoism. Ultimately, José Antonio's tenure as *jefe* and ideologue of the Falange created an ideological bridge between the old traditions of the right in Spain and the new ideals of European fascism, a bridge that Francoism traversed. He cannot be viewed as separate from the Falange of Franco merely because he did not live to see it become Spain's ruling party. José Antonio was the party's creator, its main ideologue and ultimately responsible for the ideology that was so easily co-opted by Francoism.

Endnotes

1 *Arriba*, 21 November 1939; *Proa*, 19 November 1939.

2 For more on Franco's political use of Civil War martyrs, see Zira Box, *España, Año Cero – La construcción simbólica del franquismo* (Madrid: Alianza Editorial, 2010), pp. 119–96.

3 Felipe Ximénez de Sandoval, *José Antonio: biografía apasionada* (Barcelona: Juventud, 1941); Francisco Bravo Martínez, *José Antonio: el hombre, el jefe, el camarada* (Madrid: Ediciones Españolas, 1939); José María Amado, *Via crucis* (Málaga: Editorial Dado, 1938).

4 Paul Preston, *Comrades! Portraits from the Spanish Civil War* (London: Harper Perennial, 1999), pp. 75–108, debunks the myth of José Antonio and Franco being personally close; Stanley G. Payne, 'Franco and the Institutionalisation of Mission', in António Costa Pinto, Roger Eatwell and Stein Ugelvik Larsen, (eds), *Charisma and Fascism in Interwar Europe* (London: Routledge, 2007), pp. 54–5; Julio Gil Pecharromán, *José Antonio Primo de Rivera – Retrato de un visionario* (Madrid: Temas de Hoy, 1996), pp. 523–38.

5 Javier Tusell, *Franco en la guerra civil – Una biografía política* (Barcelona: Tusquets, 1992), pp. 103–10; Ismael Saz, *España contra España – los nacionalismos franquistas* (Madrid: Marcial Pons, 2003), pp. 267–308. The phrase 'ideological paraphernalia' comes from Paul Preston, *The Politics of Revenge: fascism and the military in twentieth century Spain* (London: Routledge, 2005), pp. 107–10.

6 Elizabeth, under her married name Bibescu, would go on to write a novel in honour of José Antonio. Elizabeth Bibescu, *The Romantic* (London: William Heinemann, 1940).

7 Gil Pecharromán, *José Antonio*, p. 18; Preston *Comrades!*, p. 113; Pilar Primo de Rivera, *Recuerdos de una vida* (Madrid: Dyrsa, 1983), p. 17.

8 Francisco Franco, *Pensamiento politico de Franco – Tomo I* (Madrid: Ediciones del Movimiento, 1975), p. 51.

9 Accounts of José Antonio's early life can be found in Gil Pecharromán, *José Antonio*, pp. 1–85, Ximénez de Sandoval, *José Antonio*, pp. 1–56; Antonio Gibello, *José Antonio, ese desconocido* (Madrid: Dyrsa, 1985), pp. 1–85.

10 *La Nación*, 25 September 1931.

11 Payne, 'Franco', p. 54; Preston, *Comrades!*, p. 82; Gil Pecharromán, José Antonio, pp. 161–9.

12 Extract from a speech at the *Teatro de la Comedia*, Madrid, 29 October 1933, in José Antonio Primo de Rivera, *Obras Completas* (Madrid: Ediciones de la Vicesecretaria de Educación Popular de F.E.T y de las J. O. N. S., 1945), p. 24.

13 Stanley G. Payne, *Fascism in Spain 1923–1977* (Wisconsin: Wisconsin University Press, 1999), pp. 57–62; José Luis Mínguez Goyanes, *Onésimo Redondo (1905–1936): precursor sindicalista* (Madrid: San Martin, 1990).

14 Sheelagh M. Elwood, 'Spain: The Falange', in Aristotle A. Kallis, ed., *The Fascism Reader* (London: Routledge, 2003), p. 225; Preston, *Comrades!*, p. 89.

15 *Ibid*, p. 97.

16 Francisco Bravo Martínez, *José Antonio ante la justicia roja* (Madrid: Vicesecretaría de Educación Popular, 1941), passim.

17 See, for instance, his speech at the *Círculo Mercantil*, Madrid, 9 April 1935, in Primo de Rivera, *Obras Completas*, p. 67.

18 Robert O. Paxton, *The Anatomy of Fascism* (New York: Knopf, 2004), 218; Michael Mann, *Fascists* (Cambridge: Cambridge University Press, 2004), pp. 1–30; Alejandro Quiroga, *Making Spaniards – Primo de Rivera and the nationalization of the masses, 1923–1930* (London: Palgrave Macmillan, 2007), pp. 71–2.

19 José Ortega y Gasset, *España Invertebrada: bosquejos de algunos pensamientos históricos*, revised edn (Madrid: Espasa Calpe, 2006). Interestingly, the lack of support that the Falange was to receive from Ortega, previously a critic of José Antonio's father's regime, led to a fractious relationship. José Antonio would chide 'Don José' as a political 'flirt' who lacked the stomach for the practice of, rather than rumination on, politics, *Haz*, 5 December, 1935.

20 Point 2 of the *Norma Programática de la Falange* in Primo de Rivera, *Obras Completas*, p. 519; *F.E.*, 19 July 1934.

21 *F.E.*, 1 March 1934.

22 Extract from a speech at the *Teatro Calderón,* Valladolid, 4 March 1934, in Primo de Rivera, *Obras Completas*, p. 28.

23 Extract from a speech made in Madrid, 29 October 1933, in Primo de Rivera, *Obras Completas*, p. 22.

24 Saz, *España*, p. 67; Carolyn Boyd, *Historia patria: politics, history and national identity in Spain, 1875–1975* (Princeton: Princeton University Press, 1997), p. 189; *F.E.*, 7 December 1933.

25 *F.E.*, 7 December, 1933.

26 In any case, National Catholicism and fascism, especially its Italian form, were not ideologically dissimilar and *falangismo* itself could be argued to be a crystallization of thought first conceived during the Dictatorship of General Miguel Primo de Rivera. Alejandro Quiroga, *Making Spaniards*, pp. 70–6. For the concept of National Catholicism, see Alfonso Botti, *El cielo y el dinero. El nacionalcatolicismo en España, 1881–1975* (Madrid: Alianza, 2008).

27 Primo de Rivera, *Obras Completas*, p. 520.

28 *F.E.*, 7 December 1933.

29 *La Nación*, 23 October 1933.

30 *F.E.*, 7 December 1933.

31 Point 25 of the *Norma Programática de la Falange* in Primo de Rivera, *Obras Completas*, p. 520.

32 Quiroga, Alejandro, 'Miedo de clase y dolor de patria. Las dictaduras contrarrevolucionarias en la Guerra Civil Europea, 1917–1945', in Carlos

Navajas, ed., *II Congreso Internacional de Historia de Nuestro Tiempo* (Logroño: Universidad de La Rioja, 2010), pp. 24–6.

33 Giovanni Gentile, *Origini e dottrina del fascismo* (Rome: Quaderni dell'Istituto Nazionale Fascista di Cultura, 1929), p. 58; *Libertad*, 20 May 1935.

34 *Arriba*, 30 January 1936; *No Importa*, 6 June 1936 (italics in original).

35 *Arriba*, 11 April 1935 (italics in original).

36 'The arrow of time thus points not backwards but forwards, even when the archer looks backward over his shoulder to aim', Roger Griffin, *The Nature of Fascism* (London: Routledge, 1991), p. 36.

37 Extract from a speech made at the *Teatro Calderón*, Valladolid, 3 March 1935, in Primo de Rivera, *Obras Completas*, pp. 38–9.

38 Extract from a speech made in Toledo, 25 February 1934, in Primo de Rivera, *Obras Completas*, p. 139.

39 Cited in Douglas W. Foard, 'The Forgotten Falangist: Ernest Giménez Caballero', *The Journal of Contemporary History*, 10 (1) (1975): 12.

40 The 'Generation of 1898' would take their name from the moral, political and social crisis that would follow the loss of the colonies.

41 Point 3 of the *Norma Programática de la Falange*, in José Antonio, *Obras Completas*, pp. 519–20.

42 Azorín, *Castilla* (Madrid: Renacimento, 1912), passim; Miguel de Unamuno, *En torno al casticismo*, revised edn (Madrid: Espasa-Calpe, 1972), passim.

43 Primo de Rivera, *Obras Completas*, p. 27.

44 *F.E.*, 19 July 1934.

45 Gerald Brenan, *The Spanish Labyrinth – the social and political background of the Spanish Civil War*, revised edn (Cambridge, Cambridge University Press, 1990), p. 311.

46 Primo de Rivera, *Obras Completas*, p. 28.

47 *F.E.*, 12 July 1934; *F.E.*, 19 July 1934.

48 *Arriba*, 16 January 1936.

49 Primo de Rivera, *Obras Completas*, p. 27.

50 Ibid., p. 31.

51 *Arriba*, 20 November 1935.

52 For more on the Francoist conception of the enemy, see Eduardo González Calleja and Fredes Limón Nevado, *La Hispanidad como instrumento de combate – raza e imperio en la guerra franquista durante la guerra civil española* (Madrid: Centro de Estudios Históricos, 1988); Francisco Sevillano, *Rojos: La representación del enemigo en la Guerra Civil* (Madrid: Alianza, 2007).

53 *ABC*, 22 March 1933; Primo de Rivera, *Obras Completas*, p. 497.

54 Ibid., p. 19.

55 Point 6 of the *Norma Programática de la Falange*, in ibid., pp. 520–1.

56 *La Nación*, 26 August 1933.

57 *La Nación*, 29 November 1934; Point 15 of the *Norma Programática de la Falange* in Primo de Rivera, *Obras Completas*, p. 523.

58 Point 10 of the *Norma Programática de la Falange* in Primo de Rivera, *Obras Completas*, pp. 521–2.

59 Primo de Rivera, *Obras Completas*, p. 54.

60 Ibid., p. 55; *Arriba*, 1 March 1935.

61 Payne, *Fascism*, p. 151.

62 Point 11 of the *Norma Programática de la Falange* in Primo de Rivera, *Obras Completas*, p. 522.

63 Richard J. Overy, *The Nazi Economic Recovery 1932–1938 – Second Edition* (Cambridge: Cambridge University Press, 1996), p. 58; Adrian Lyttelton, *The Seizure of Power: Fascism in Italy 1919–29* (New York: Routledge, 2004), p. 187.

64 Primo de Rivera, *Obras Completas*, p. 457.

65 Joaquín Costa, *Oligarquía y caciquismo como la forma actual de gobierno en España: Urgencia y modo de cambiarla*, revised edn (Madrid: Revista de Trabajo, 1975), p. 16.

66 Manuel Vázquez Montalbán, *Los demonios familiares de Franco* (Barcelona: Dopesa, 1978), pp. 10–11.

67 Cited in Preston, *Comrades!*, p. 87. *ABC*, 22 March 1933.

68 Cited in Sancho Dávila, *Hacia la historia de la Falange: primera contribución de Sevilla* (Jerez: Jerez Industrial, 1938), p. 24.

69 Cited in Carlos Rojas, *¡Muera la inteligencia! ¡Viva la muerte! Salamanca, 1936. Unamuno y Millán Astray, frente a frente* (Barcelona: Planeta, 1995), p. 25.

70 Mann, *Fascists*, p. 13.

71 Benito Mussolini, *El Espíritu de la revolución fascista* (Buenos Aires: Temas Contemporáneos, 1984), p. 80.

72 Ximénez de Sandoval, *José Antonio*, p. 33.

73 The incidents in question are recounted by Paul Preston in *Comrades!*, p. 78; the opponent in question was Radical party deputy José María Alvarez Mendizábal who earned the cheap reproach, as he fell towards the government benches, of 'Thank me, because I've helped you get to the front bench for once in your life, albeit rolling on the floor.'

74 Primo de Rivera, *Obras Completas*, p. 24.

75 José María Gil Robles, *No fue posible la paz* (Madrid: Ediciones Ariel, 1968), p. 442.

76 Primo de Rivera, *Obras Completas*, p. 526.

77 *F.E.*, 18 January 1934; Speech in Cáceres, 4 February 1934, Primo de Rivera, *Obras Completas*, p. 133; *Haz*, 15 June 1935.

78 Payne, *Fascism*, pp. 113–14; Heleno Saña, 'La Falange: intento de un diagnóstico', *Índices de las letras y de las artes*, 259 (1969): 22–8, cited in ibid., p. 113.

79 Ibid., p. 112; Ximénez de Sandoval, José Antonio, p. 144; José María Mancisidor, *Frente a Frente: José Antonio frente al Tribunal Popular. Alicante – noviembre 1936* (Madrid: Editorial Almena, 1975), p. 195.

80 The first, but certainly not the last, death from a direct Falange hit came on 10 June 1934, a young socialist woman named Juanita Rico. Stanley G. Payne, *Spain's First Democracy: the Second Republic, 1931–36* (Wisconsin: University of Wisconsin Press, 1993), p. 200.

81 Paul Preston, *The Coming of the Spanish Civil War* (London: Palgrave Macmillan, 1994), pp. 255–6.

82 A more nuanced and detailed account of the political violence in the Second Republic can be found in Eduardo González Calleja, 'The Symbolism of Violence During the Second Republic in Spain, 1931–36', in Chris Ealham and Michael Richards, eds, *The Splintering of Spain – Cultural History and the Spanish Civil War 1936–39* (Cambridge: Cambridge University Press, 2005), pp. 23–44.

83 *No Importa*, 6 June 1936.

84 For more on the ideas of *la cruzada*, the patria and anti-patria, see Giuliana Di Febo, *La Santa de la Raza – un culto barroco en la España Franquista* (Barcelona: Icaria, 1988), passim; Michael Richards, *A Time of Silence – civil war and culture of repression in Franco's Spain, 1936–45* (Cambridge: Cambridge University Press, 1998), passim.

85 *Carta al General Franco*, 24 September 1934, in Primo de Rivera, *Obras Completas*, pp. 623–6.

86 *Carta a los militares de España*, 4 May 1936, in Primo de Rivera, *Obras Completas*, pp. 669–74.

87 Emilio García Gómez, *Asturias 1934 – Historia de una tragedia* (Zaragoza, Libros Pórtico, 2010), passim.

88 *Arriba*, 21 November 1939, 1; Preston, *Comrades!*, p. 350, n. 131.

89 There are myriad works on the role of the Falange in the repression of the Civil War; notable ones include Richards, *A Time of Silence*; Joan María Thomas, *La Falange de Franco: El proyecto Fascista del Régimen* (Barcelona: Plaza Janés, 2001); Alberto Reig Tapia, *Ideología e historia – sobre la represión franquista y la guerra civil* (Madrid: Akal, 1986). With regard to José Antonio and Lorca's friendship, the latter was to tell poet Gabriel Celaya that he and José Antonio 'dine together every Friday. We go out in a taxi with the shades drawn because it is not convenient for him to be seen with me, nor for me to be seen with him', Gabriel Celaya and José Yglesias, 'Last Encounter with Lorca', *The Massachusetts Review*, 5 (4), (1964): 639.

90 Mancisidor, Frente a Frente, p. 195. The ultimate number killed in post-war executions is hotly debated, estimates placing the number of executed between anything from 22,000 to 50,000. Gabriel Jackson, *La República España y la Guerra Civil, 1931–1939* (Barcelona: Crítica, 1976), p. 13; Ramón Salas Larrazábal, *Pérdidas de la guerra* (Barcelona: Planeta, 1977), *passim*; Richards, *A Time of Silence*, p. 30.

91 Twenty years later he was moved again to the Valley of the Fallen, Franco's monument to the dead of the Civil War, built by Republican prisoners of war in the post-war period.

92 *Y: Revista de la mujer nacional sindicalista*, Number 23, December 1939; *ABC*, Seville, 21 November 1939; *Proa*, 19 November 1939.

93 Payne, *Fascism*, p. 225. For a full transcript of the interview, see Ian Gibson, *En busca de José Antonio* (Madrid: Planeta, 1980), pp. 300–13.

94 For a more detailed insight into the reactionary politics of the Spanish military, see Geoffrey Jensen, *Irrational Triumph – Cultural Despair, Military Nationalism and the Ideological Origins of Franco's Spain* (Reno: University of Nevada Press, 2002).

5

Francisco Franco: The Soldier who became *Caudillo*

ENRIQUE MORADIELLOS

'**F**rancisco Franco, Caudillo of Spain by the Grace of God.' So read the inscription on the reverse of all coins minted in Spain from December 1946 by the unanimous decision of the Plenary of the Spanish Cortes. This was just one of the many official honours held by the general who had achieved unconditional victory in the Civil War of 1936–9 and who until his death, on 20 November 1975, had enjoyed the titles of Head of State, Head of Government, Generalissimo of the Armed Forces, *Homo missus a Deo* (a man sent by Divine Providence) and National Head of the Falange (the single national state party) 'only responsible before God and history'. He was, in short, the *Caudillo* of Spain, the 'Supreme Master of the Race', the 'Caesar undefeated', the 'Saviour of the Fatherland', the 'Guardian Angel of the Spanish Empire' and the 'Sentinel of the West': an omnipotent dictator with arbitral powers, deeply reactionary, ultra-nationalist and hardline Catholic, who had assumed on 1 October 1936 'all powers of the New State' and whose rule would be 'for life and providential'.[1] Of course, he was no mere and simple 'dictator' as the hyperbole of the Cádiz writer José María Pemán explained:

> Francisco Franco: the calm courage, the clear ideas, the strong will and the smile. Franco is not a 'dictator' who presides over the triumph of a single

party or one section of the nation. He is the father who brings under his control, like one big family, all national forces in Spain ... Franco smiles and welcomes. Because under his command are not only soldiers or the Falange or *requetés*. Under his leadership is all of Spain.[2]

A man who performed all these offices and received all this lavish praise for nearly 40 years was bound to be ever present at the centre of public and social life in Spain. In fact, for the writer Antonio Muñoz Molina, as he remembered the 25th anniversary of Franco's death, he was 'the face he saw everywhere'.[3] His image was present, of course, on the coins. But it was also on stamps, in the classroom next to the crucifix, displayed on the walls of government agencies, on the NO-DO newsreel, then again on the television news, as well as in impressive equestrian statues (in Madrid, Barcelona, Valencia, Ferrol, Santander ...). Also ever present was his name, pronounced both in official speeches that ended with the threefold invocation ('Franco, Franco, Franco!') and also in the homilies seeking divine protection for 'our head of state, Francisco'. His peculiar voice, high-pitched and monotonous, was also heard on radio or television on many solemn occasions: on 1 October, during the national holiday of 'the Exaltation of the Caudillo', on 18 July in commemoration of the start of the 'Glorious National Uprising', and, above all, on 31 December in the traditional 'Message of His Excellency, the Head of State, to the Spaniards'.

As a significant historical figure, Franco has been the subject of an extensive biographical literature. However, until recently, few biographies were historically balanced or of sufficient academic rigour. Of course, 40 years of personal dictatorship had resulted in a vast body of almost hagiographic work of an apologetic character. In this category must be included the works of the journalist Joaquín Arrarás, Franco's first official biographer during the Civil War; those of Luis de Galinsoga and Francisco Franco Salgado-Araujo, whose own titles and publication dates reveal the importance of their Cold War context; the text and screenplay by José María Sánchez Silva and José Luis Sáenz de Heredia, to commemorate '25 years of Franco's peace'; the penultimate biography of the prolific Ricardo de la Cierva; and the more recent, and bulkier, but also apologetic portrait by Luis Suárez Fernández.[4]

In response to the aforementioned literature, the anti-Franco opposition also produced its own biographies on the *Caudillo*, where demonological overtones and political denunciation in various degrees and forms dominated. Among them all, the work published in Paris by Luciano Rincón under the pseudonym of Luis Ramírez stands out for its insightfulness and influence. Less pretentious and more satirical in character were the two hostile portraits of Franco by Salvador de Madariaga and Amando de Miguel. Perhaps in this same category can be added, with appropriate qualifications, the most recent and well-known literary fiction of Francisco Umbral and Manuel Vázquez Montalbán.[5]

The historiographical re-evaluation of Franco began after his death with the restoration of democracy in Spain. In fact, it was not until 1985 that a biographical essay by Juan Pablo Fusi denoted a sharp break from previous biographies, for both its fairness and his use of the new documentation available. Further reconsideration came in 1992 with Javier Tusell's study on the figure of Franco during the Civil War; his analysis was based on new and revealing information (the diaries of three of the *Caudillo*'s close collaborators and ministers and a wealth of documents from the Spanish and Italian archives). However, despite this advance, a general biography on Franco and his role, that took into account the enormous amount of archival material and testimony that had appeared in recent years, was missing. This omission was rectified in the autumn of 1993 with the publication in England (and its translation into Spanish the following year) of the biography by Paul Preston. Not surprisingly, this work, the fruit of more than a decade's work, was monumental both in scope and in its use of primary sources.[6]

The efforts initiated by Fusi, extended by Tusell and completed by Preston have since been supplemented by a long list of relevant authors: Alberto Reig Tapia, Bartolomé Bennassar, Fernando García de Cortázar, Andrée Bachoud, José Luis Rodríguez Jiménez, and so on.[7] This body of biographical studies has made it possible to unravel many of the enigmas surrounding the private and public life of General Franco. Due to these efforts and the partial contributions of other authors, many myths developed by Franco's apologists have been shattered, particularly the three held most dear by the *Caudillo* himself: his persona of crusader who saved Spain from communism in the Civil War; his masterly statesmanship that preserved Spain's neutrality during the Second World War; and his responsibility for initiating the economic and social modernization of the country in the 1960s. Similarly, many of the ideas entertained by the anti-Franco opposition, which portrayed him as an unintelligent, cruel tyrant in the service of Spanish capitalism, who rose to power only with the help of Hitler and Mussolini and survived 40 years through a combination of savage domestic repression and good luck abroad, have been abandoned.

The Forging of an *Africanista*

Francisco Paulino Hermenegildo Teódulo Franco Bahamonde was born in the Galician town of El Ferrol on 4 December 1892, to a lower middle-class family with a long naval tradition. The shy Francisco, nicknamed '*Cerillita*' ('Little Matchstick') by his classmates because of his height and scrawniness, grew up in this small provincial town under the influence of a conservative and pious mother and detached from his freethinking, philandering father. After failing in his attempt to become a naval officer due to the shortage of cadet places after the Disaster of 1898, and his father's final abandonment of the family, Franco managed to enter the Infantry Academy in Toledo in August 1907. It was in this old Castillian capital that much of his character and basic political philosophy was formed: 'That's where I became a man.'[8]

The Spanish army, with its rigid hierarchical command structure and closed ranks, obedience and discipline, completely fulfilled the emotional needs of this shy boy and gave him a new identity. Thereafter, Franco never wavered in his vocation and profession: 'I am a soldier.' This was confirmed in later years by both friends and enemies. Pedro Sainz Rodríguez, a conservative intellectual whom Franco met in Oviedo and who would end his days in the monarchist opposition, recalled in his memoirs: 'Franco was a man obsessed with his career and was above all a soldier.' Tomás Garicano Goñi, a comrade in arms, although slightly younger, and one of his last ministers of the Interior, agreed: 'Raised in a military environment, from a naval family, and naturally destined for the army, there's a feeling (and I think it is the reality) that Military Orders are his standard of living.'[9]

Indeed, with the trauma of the colonial Disaster of 1898, the growth of socio-political unrest in the country and the heat of a new and bloody war fought in northern Morocco, Franco, as a cadet, adopted to a large extent the political and ideological baggage of the soldiers of the Restoration. Above all he endorsed a fiery unitarian Spanish nationalism, a nostalgia for past imperial glories, a suspicion of the outside world which had remained impassive to Spain's unequal confrontation with the American colossus in 1898, and was extremely hostile to the emerging peripheral regionalist and nationalist movements that dared to question the unity of the fatherland. The prolific historical work of Marcelino Menéndez y Pelayo was the intellectual foundation for this hyper-nationalistic retrospection and identification of the country with Catholic orthodoxy:

> The Church nurtured us, with its martyrs and confessors, with its saints, with its admirable system of synods. Through it we were a nation and a great nation, instead of a multitude of nations, born to be the target for any greedy neighbour ... Spain, the evangelist for half of the world, Spain, the hammer of the heretics, the light of Trent, the sword of Rome, the cradle of St. Ignatius ... that is our greatness and our unity, we have no other. The day when that is lost, Spain will return to the fiefdoms of the *Arévacos* and the *Vectones*, or of the kings of the Taifas.[10]

Complementing his hard-line fundamentalism and nationalism was a milita-ristic view of political life and public order that saw the army as a praetorian institution virtually autonomous of civil power and in times of internal or external emergency, superior to it through its status as 'the spine' and 'backbone of Spain'. This was proclaimed by Alfonso XIII in 1902 when he ascended the throne at just 16 years of age: 'Blessed is the king who sees in you the firmest support of the social order, the surest foundation of public peace, the resolute defender of state institutions, the strongest basis for the welfare and happiness of the country.'[11]

As a direct result of this national militarism as well as the brutal experiences undergone in Morocco, a great number of the Spanish military (so-called '*Africanistas*' for having served in the Army of Africa) began to develop a strong authoritarian and anti-liberal mindset. They blamed liberalism, parliament and the party system for Spain's long decline, from the War of Independence of 1808–14 and throughout the nineteenth century, to the disaster of 1898. Over time, and especially after the watershed which was the Civil War, Franco would become the most genuine representative of this hard-line fundamentalist ideology prevalent among a large section of the Spanish military. In fact, at various times in his life, and throughout the early 1950s, he reiterated publically his furious criticism of liberalism as 'alien' and 'anti-Spanish' and his contempt for a 'decadent' and 'catastrophic' century.

> The nineteenth century, which we would have liked to erase from our history, is the negation of everything Spanish, the inconsistency for our faith, the denial of our unity, the demise of our empire, all the generations of our being, something foreign that divided us and turned brother against brother, destroying the harmonious unity that God had put on our land ... The consequence of liberalism was the degeneration of Spain. The neglect of the needs of the Spanish soul, kept undermining us throughout the nineteenth century and a large part of the 20th century, and cost us the loss of our empire and a disastrous decline.[12]

After finishing his studies in Toledo with a mediocre result (he only managed to be ranked 251 in an intake of 312 cadets), Franco sought and obtained in 1912 his transfer to the Spanish Protectorate in Morocco. The difficult conquest of this elongated, narrow territory lasted from 1904 (with the signing of the Franco-Spanish treaty) to 1926, owing to the fierce resistance offered by the native population. During his stay there, where he remained for over ten years of his life (only interrupted by short periods of leave in Oviedo in 1917 and 1920), he proved to be a serious officer, meticulous, courageous and effective, obsessed with discipline and the performance of duty: the archetypal *Africanista*, so different from the sedentary military bureaucracy who thrived in the quiet mainland barracks and opposed all forms of promotion that were not awarded for length of service (the so-called *junteros* named for their support of the embryonic military trade unions known as *Juntas Militares de Defensa*). Franco's qualities and courage (he survived a serious injury in June 1916) led to quick promotions 'for bravery in combat'. In 1926 he became the youngest brigadier general in Europe, at 33 years old.[13] By then, his name had acquired a certain notoriety in the peninsula with the publication in late 1922 of a small book (*Marruecos. Diario de una bandera*) in which he recounted simply and directly his war experiences as second in command of the Legion (or *Tercio de Extranjeros*), a unit of shock troops newly created for that conflict.[14]

His extensive service in Morocco, in the midst of a vicious colonial war and as commander of a crack task force like the Legion, reinforced Franco's political beliefs and contributed to a great extent to the hardening of his character. Not surprisingly, by fighting or negotiating with the rebel leaders of the Moroccan tribes, the young officer learned well the political tactics of 'divide and conquer' and the effectiveness of terror (imposed by the Legion) as the perfect military weapon to achieve the paralysis and submission of the enemy. In addition, his long experience in colonial Africa, where a de facto state of war prevailed and the military performed a wide range of administrative functions, confirmed in practice the supposed right of the army to exercise command without restrictions and above the distant and weak civil authorities on the mainland.[15] In fact, since then, Franco always understood political authority in terms of military hierarchy, obedience and discipline, calling it 'command' and considering dissenters and adversaries as little less than 'seditious'. In late 1938, and virtually victorious in the Civil War, he recalled the influence of his time in Morocco on the formation of his personality and that of his comrades in arms:

> My years in Africa live in me with an incredible force. There was born the possibility of rescuing a great Spain. There was formed the ideal that redeems us today. Without Africa, I can scarcely explain myself, nor can I explain myself fully to my fellow comrades.[16]

His promotion to general and his subsequent appointment (in January 1928) as the new Director General of the Military Academy of Zaragoza marked a notable shift in the trajectory of Franco's career path. Thereafter, the daring and brave officer of Morocco would become an increasingly cautious and calculating military leader, very conscious of his public standing and very jealous of his professional interests. Undoubtedly, his marriage in Oviedo in October 1923 to Carmen Polo Martínez-Valdés (1902–88), a pious and proud young woman from a rich, local family, accentuated this change and his previous conservative and religious inclinations. Franco had met his wife in the summer of 1917, during his brief leave on the mainland. He would have with her, in September 1926, his beloved only daughter *Nenuca* (Carmen Franco Polo), who grew to be 'the only person who can understand his personality'.[17] This marked change of character had its expression in his external physical appearance: the officer with teenage looks, short (1.64 metres), painfully thin with a high-pitched voice, would become a military leader with a tendency to obesity, markedly overweight at the waist. Moreover, his daily life remained relatively austere and humdrum: he didn't smoke, hardly drank and despite his notable appetite was not known for his culinary refinement. He had also cultivated an atypical habit during his years in Africa: he never took a siesta after lunch and instead spent that time sitting chatting with his few military friends.[18]

At this stage of his life Franco remained on the margins of the politics developed within the liberal parliamentary system of the Bourbon Restoration (1874–1923), the pseudo-democratic formal wrapping for 'oligarchy and *caciquismo* as the real form of government', as was angrily denounced by the author Joaquín Costa and the fin-de-siècle Spanish regenerationist writers. From the crisis in the summer of 1917, this system faced growing internal tensions: urban and rural labour conflicts, increasing pressure from Catalan and Basque nationalism, demands for democratization from the middle classes and petty bourgeoisie, and popular resistance to the bloody and endless war in Morocco. With the paralysis of the liberal oligarchic order and frightened by the revolutionary spectre of Bolshevism that emanated from Russia, in September 1923 King Alfonso XIII bet on a new solution to the protracted crisis through the establishment of a military dictatorship headed by General Miguel Primo de Rivera and supported with virtual unanimity across the army. During the entire dictatorship (1923–30), Franco was an enthusiastic supporter of the military regime which was comparable to those created in many other European countries where liberalism was in retreat from the two-pronged attack of revolutionary threat and reactionary appeal. Both the king and the dictator rewarded him with the appointment of Director of the Military Academy of Zaragoza.[19] Franco also continued to benefit from the king's public favour, appointing him gentleman of the bedchamber and acting as best man at his wedding.

It was in those years of the dictatorship when Franco began to receive and devour the anti-communist and authoritarian literature sent by the *Entente Internationale contre la Troisième Internationale*, an organization formed in Geneva by local radical right-wing forces and anti-Bolshevik Russians, dedicated to warning leaders across Europe of the danger of a universal communist conspiracy. This reactionary and Manichaean literature would be key to the formation of Franco's obsessive ideas about the hidden and divisive power of Masonry (synonymous with liberalism) and the existence of a universal Jewish–Bolshevik–Masonic conspiracy against Spain and the Catholic faith.[20] This firm anti-Masonic conviction would soon become 'second nature' to Franco, who would eventually turn his life into an 'anti-Masonic crusade' on which he accepted 'no discussion'.[21] In all likelihood, this same literature encouraged his instinctive distrust of intellectuals and the subtleties of contemporary socio-political thought for which he had always showed a blatant disregard and contempt. As recognized subsequently by one of his favourite ministers, the economist and military jurist, Mariano Navarro Rubio: 'Franco was not exactly an intellectual. He never presumed to be or boasted of being one. His political doctrine consisted of a few ideas, basic, clear and rich.'[22]

Prudence and Patience during the Second Republic

Given this context, Franco felt deep concern at the removal of Primo de Rivera in January 1930 and the subsequent and sudden fall of the monarchy after the municipal elections of April 1931. The arrival of democracy following the peaceful proclamation of the Republic on 14 April produced a notable setback to the hitherto brilliant career of the favourite general of Alfonso XIII. During the Republican–Socialist government of 1931–3, with Manuel Azaña at the head of the Cabinet and the War Office, the cautious and sly Galician general avoided open conflict with the new authorities yet still marked his distance from the established regime. 'I never cheered for the Republic,' he recalled proudly in 1964 to his cousin and military aide since 1927, 'Pacón' Franco Salgado-Araujo.[23] The closing of the Academy of Zaragoza, the review of his promotions during the Dictatorship and the progressive and anticlerical leanings of the government reinforced Franco's alienation. But it did not lead him to conspire recklessly against it, as did his superior in the Protectorate, General José Sanjurjo, head of an ill-fated reactionary military coup in August 1932. In fact, requested by Sanjurjo to act as his advocate in the subsequent court martial, Franco would refuse the request with a resounding argument: 'I shall not defend you. You deserve death; not for rebelling but for failing.'[24] That cold prudence and caution that was beginning to be proverbial (his own sister acknowledged, 'Cunning and caution define his character') motivated Sanjurjo's caustic comment on his former subordinate: 'Little Franco is a crafty so-and-so who only looks after himself' ('*Franquito es un cuquito que va a lo suyito*'). However, this did not prevent Sanjurjo from considering Franco to be the best Spanish military leader of the time: 'He's not Napoleon, but given what there is ...' Perhaps that is why Azaña believed 'Franco is the only one to be feared' of the potential military conspirators which the Republic might have to face.[25]

In any case, Franco's fears of the socio-political drift during the Republican–Socialist biennium would only last a short time. In November 1933, the breakdown and weariness of the coalition, due to the strong impact of the international economic crisis and its own divisions, brought about its electoral defeat by the conservative Radical party of Alejandro Lerroux and the powerful and authoritarian Spanish Confederation of Autonomous Right-wing Parties (CEDA), the new Catholic mass party led by José María Gil Robles.

Franco had voted for the CEDA in the general election as he identified with its Catholic and conservative ideology and with its pragmatic political strategy of transforming the regime from within so as to make it compatible with his principles. Therefore, he welcomed with great pleasure the political changes that would further his career prospects and reduce his instinctive repugnance to the Republican regime. In fact, under both Radical and Radical–CEDA governments of the biennium of 1934 and 1935, Franco became the most distinguished officer of the Spanish army and the favourite general of the authorities: he was promoted to major general in March 1934. As a result of his professional standing, when the socialists launched a general strike to prevent the entry of the CEDA into the Cabinet and revolution broke out in October 1934 (used by the Catalan autonomous administration for its own purposes), the government under Lerroux entrusted him with the task of crushing the insurrection with all military forces under his command, including the transfer to and the use of his beloved Legion in Asturias. This critical juncture provided Franco, already clearly ambitious, with his first taste of quasi-omnipotent state power. Following the declaration of a state of war and the handing over of governmental functions, the general was temporarily, for just over a fortnight, a real emergency dictator, controlling all military and police forces in what he perceived as a struggle against the revolution planned by Moscow and executed by its undercover agents and Spanish traitors. As he declared to the press in Oviedo after successfully quelling the last pockets of resistance, 'This war is a war fought on many fronts and the fronts are socialism, communism and all the forces that attack civilization in order to replace it with barbarism.'[26]

The overwhelming victory that he achieved in Asturias made him not only the hero of conservative public opinion but also reinforced his moral leadership within the officer corps, far above his recognized rank and seniority. His appointment as Chief of General Staff in May 1935 by Gil Robles, the new Minister of War, cemented that leadership in an almost unassailable way. As a result of this renewed public and professional prestige, Franco was courted by almost all parties of the political right. Besides his good connections with the conservative republicanism of Lerroux, his contacts with the CEDA were excellent given the friendship shown by Gil Robles and the presence of his brother-in-law, Ramon Serrano Suñer (married to his wife's younger sister), as a prominent CEDA deputy for Zaragoza.[27] In the case of Alfonsine monarchism, relations remained fluid through Pedro Sainz Rodríguez, one of the ideologues of the *Acción Española* journal, who Franco had met in Asturias when Sainz was a professor of literature at the University of Oviedo.[28] With regard to the Spanish Falange, the new small fascist party founded in 1933 by the son of former dictator, José Antonio Primo de Rivera, contact was spare but revealing. The Falange leader had sent a personal letter to Franco (through Serrano Suñer, a friend of both) on the eve of October 1934 to alert him to the danger of revolution. Franco replied by asking him to 'keep faith with the military and give them support if the crisis erupted'.[29]

In this context, Franco's concern at the lengthy crisis that forced the government to call new general elections for 16 February 1936 is not surprising. In fact, against a backdrop of severe economic depression, strong political bipolarization and acute social antagonism, the elections were won with a slim majority by the leftist coalition of the Popular Front over the right-wing parties. A left-wing republican government presided over again by Azaña, supported in parliament by the Socialist and Communist parties, was returned to power.

The narrow victory of the Popular Front tempted Franco to take part, for the first time, in a coup. He sought to obtain during the next two days the authorization of the government and that of the President of the Republic (the conservative and Catholic Niceto Alcalá Zamora) to declare a state of war and avoid the transfer of power. This initiative was thwarted by the resistance of the civil authorities to take that crucial step, the lack of material resources to execute the plan and the decision of the ever-cautious Chief of Staff not to act until almost completely certain of success. When the Prime Minister suggested to him on the 18th that the military should act on their own initiative, Franco replied with complete sincerity: 'The Army does not have the moral unity necessary to undertake this task.'[30]

Consequently, Franco had to resign himself to the return to power of *azañista* reformism, which as a precautionary measure, on 21 February, ordered his transfer from Madrid to the distant but important military command of the Canary Islands. It was a considerable professional and political setback which affected Franco deeply. He was also concerned about the continuing political crisis experienced during the first half of 1936, and the actions of a decidedly reformist Popular Front government, which faced a double-pincer attack. This came, on one side, from the revolutionary stance of the anarchist unions, supported by the radical faction of the socialist movement, which undermined the crucial collaboration between bourgeois republicanism and reformist socialism, pillars of the ruling coalition and its interclass nature; on the other side, from the convergence of the right-wing parties around a reactionary strategy which put all its hopes on military intervention to stem the crisis and overthrow a reformist democracy that was seen as merely a front for revolution.

By virtue of his rank and influence, Franco was, from the outset, although with his usual caution, in touch with the broad anti-republican conspiracy brewing within the army under the technical direction of General Mola (the last Chief of Security for Alfonso XIII) from Pamplona. Finalized throughout the months of April and May, Mola's plan was to orchestrate a simultaneous uprising of all military garrisons to seize power within a few days, after crushing any possible resistance in the large cities and manufacturing centres. Franco's hesitation to commit himself definitively to the plot (which exasperated the rest of the conspirators) stemmed mainly from his fear of the consequences of failure ('We do not have the whole army'). Many years later he confessed to his cousin and aide the sincere reasons for his caution:

> I was always a supporter of the military movement, since I realized that the time had come to save Spain from the chaos that was the Socialists and all the forces of left, who united marched resolutely to proclaim a dictatorship of the proletariat ... What I always feared was that the lack of concerted action by the majority of the Army would bring a repeat of 10 August [1932].[31]

Despite his initial scepticism, Franco persuaded his co-conspirators to accept that the hypothetical rising would have no defined political profile (monarchist or otherwise) and was 'only for God and for Spain'. He also repeatedly insisted that the operation was purely military and without reliance on any right-wing party: 'No consideration was given by the Movement to political forces.'[32] He met with no opposition as all the conspirators agreed with both these judgements. As General Mola, 'technical director' of the conspiracy, swiftly proclaimed, '[The reconstruction of Spain] must be initiated exclusively by the military: it is our right, because that is the nation's wish, because we have a clear idea of our power.'[33]

Finally, already deeply concerned by the strike wave of May and June 1936, Franco's vacillations that unnerved the other conspirators were swept away by the murder, on 13 July 1936, of the monarchist leader José Calvo Sotelo, committed by a group of Assault Guards who wanted to avenge the death of one of their commanders, a socialist sympathizer, in a Falange attack in Madrid the previous day. Concluding that the assassination showed that the Republican government lacked authority and that real power lay in the street, Franco prepared himself to fulfil his role in the planned coup: to conquer the Canary Islands and to proceed immediately to Morocco to take charge of the best and most seasoned Spanish troops, the Army of Africa.

Divine Providence and Civil War

On 18 July 1936, as the military uprising began in Morocco, Franco fulfilled his expected role. He assumed command of the insurgents in the Canary Islands and the Protectorate with the same mixture of caution and determination that he had shown during his years as an officer. In case things went wrong, having previously shipped his wife and daughter to France, he procured a diplomatic passport and shaved off his moustache to go unnoticed on the trip from the Canaries to Tetuán. To the dismay of the military rebels, the insurrection succeeded initially in only half the country (the most agrarian and rural), but was crushed in the other half (the most developed and urbanized) by a combination of troops loyal to the government and quickly-armed syndicalist militias. Consequently, the military coup in a few days became a long and bloody Civil War that pitted a military reaction, on one side of the trenches, against an unstable forced alliance of reformists and revolutionaries on the other. In any case, the outbreak of hostilities marked the beginning of the meteoric rise of Franco to Generalissimo of the rebel army and the Leader of a so-called 'New State' where Falangism would serve as the modernizing garb for a socio-political regime that was reactionary and ultra-conservative.

The Civil War fought between 18 July 1936 and 1 April 1939 set, therefore, the foundations of what would be the Francoist state while also providing an excellent political and diplomatic learning ground for Franco. To his amazing good fortune, which he took as a sign of Divine Providence, most of the politicians and generals who might have challenged his prominence in the insurgent camp were removed from the scene: the charismatic Calvo Sotelo had been murdered previously; Sanjurjo was killed in plane crash shortly after; generals Fanjul and Goded failed in their revolt in Madrid and Barcelona respectively and would be shot by the Republicans, as would the Falange leader José Antonio, who had been in a Republican jail since March.

Furthermore, it was Franco who promptly obtained the vital Italian and German military and diplomatic aid, who was recognized as the rebel leader by Hitler and Mussolini, who attracted the largest personal support of the Church hierarchy and the Vatican, and who led the march of the victorious rebel troops, advancing unchecked from Sevilla to Madrid (the official capital whose occupation would lead to international legal recognition). In late September 1936, during a crucial meeting of leading rebel generals, Franco's military and diplomatic successes and the expectation of a final assault on Madrid raised the need to concentrate strategic and political direction in a single command to increase the effectiveness of the war effort. The show of strength represented by the military junta could not be sustained without internal and diplomatic difficulties. In two subsequent meetings held at an airfield near Salamanca, on 21 and 28 September, the generals decided to choose Franco as 'Generalissimo of the Army, Navy and Air Force' and 'Head of Government of the Spanish State', giving him specifically 'all powers of the New State'.[34']

The political elevation of Franco meant the conversion of the collegiate military junta into a personal dictatorship, with a single individual invested by his comrades as the absolute representative of the only dominant power within insurgent Spain: the military. Significantly, Franco said after his election, 'This is the most important moment of my life.'[35] On 1 October 1936, in Burgos, in his first public statement after accepting the office, he announced emphatically both his style and his basic political intentions: 'You place Spain in my hands. My hand will be firm, it will not tremble and I will try to raise Spain to its rightful place according to its history and its past.'[36]

The failure of successive offensives against Madrid (November 1936– March 1937) forced Franco to focus his attention on the political problems presented by the consolidation of his own absolute personal dictatorship. He was fortunate to have for this task the legal and political support of Serrano Suñer, who had escaped from Madrid and arrived in Salamanca (the Generalissimo's headquarters) in early 1937. With the so-called *Cuñadísimo* (supreme brother-in-law) as his political and ideological mentor, Franco

Figure 5.1 Franco and his wife, Carmen Polo, in 1938.

proceeded to take a crucial step in the institutionalization of his 'New State'. On 19 April 1937, without prior consultation with those concerned, Franco decreed the forced unification of all right-wing parties 'under my leadership, in a single national political entity, which will be named "*Falange Española Tradicionalista y de las JONS*"' (*FET y de las JONS*). The purpose of this 'Great Party of the State' was, 'as in other totalitarian regimes', to serve as a link 'between Society and the State' and promote the 'political and moral virtues of service, hierarchy and brotherhood'. The measure was accepted with alacrity by monarchists, Catholics and Carlists and was only subject to reservations, soon silenced, from a reduced sector within the Falange, itself weakened by the disappearance of José Antonio and the failure to appoint a successor acceptable to all.[37]

From then on, the new single party, tightly controlled by the central headquarters, became the second institutional pillar (after the army) of a personal dictatorship that can already be described as *Franquismo*. Serrano Suñer was the architect of this transformation of 'a battlefield state' into a 'regime of single command and single party that took some of the universal external features of other modern regimes'. Inspired by him and the wave of political fascistization of the times, FET was closer to the old Falange than to Carlism, the CEDA or monarchism: 'in the choice of symbols, terminology and doctrine, preference was given to the Falange'.[38] However, despite these trappings, the emerging Francoist regime always reflected the simple political philosophy of its *Caudillo*: anti-communism, anti-liberalism, anti-Masonry and a determination to safeguard national unity and the existing social order through a military dictatorship. On this point, in 1933 Manuel Azaña had already noted the lack of modernizing whims entertained by the Spanish right:

> There are or might be as many fascists as you want. But there will not be a fascist regime. If force triumphs against the Republic, we would fall back under the power of a traditional military and ecclesiastical dictatorship. No matter how many slogans are translated and how many mottos are used. This country offers nothing but swords, cassocks, military parades and homages to the Virgin of Pilar.[39]

This traditional and reactionary orientation of the regime was firmly underpinned by its third institutional pillar: the Catholic Church. Indeed, the military uprising had been able to count very soon upon the crucial assistance of the Spanish episcopal hierarchy and the masses of faithful Catholics. In line with its previous hostility to the secular programme of the Republic and terrified by the anticlerical fury unleashed in government areas (with 6,832 victims), the Spanish Church resolutely sided with the military. Catholicism rose to become one of the major national and international supporters of the rebel war effort, exalted to the rank of crusade for Christ's faith and the salvation of the fatherland from atheist communism and anti-Spain[40].

Its resolute support transformed the Church into a social and institutional force of great influence, second only to the army and ahead of the Falange, in shaping the political structures that sprouted in insurgent Spain under Franco. The compensation for this vital support could not be more enthusiastic or generous. A flood of legislation was passed revoking the Republican reforms (secular education, elimination of state funding, etc.) and giving back to the clergy control of civil society and the intellectual and cultural life of the country. On their part, given Franco's fervent Catholicism, the Spanish episcopal hierarchy did not take long to bless him as *homo missus a Deo cui nomen erat Franciscus* and 'Caudillo of Spain by the Grace of God'. This would be no mere formality for public consumption used by Franco (despite the benefits it brought internally and diplomatically), but a deeply-rooted conviction that led him to consider himself a new 'hammer of the heretics' in the style of Philip II (he would later try to replicate *El Escorial* with his own pharaonic temple, the Valley of the Fallen). It is somewhat revealing of his Tridentine Catholic devotion that, in his bedroom, Franco had with him, from February 1937 and throughout the war until his death, the relic of the incorruptible hand of St Teresa of Jesús (the 'saint of the Race').[41]

The strategic and tactical skills of Franco during almost three years of Civil War caused great concern among his Italian and German backers. In December 1936, General Wilhelm Faupel, German Ambassador in Salamanca, reported confidentially to the authorities in Berlin:

> Personally, General Franco is a ruthlessly brave soldier, with a strong feeling of responsibility; a man who is likeable from the very first because of his open and decent character, but whose military training and experience do not fit him for the direction of operations on their present scale.[42]

In Rome there were also serious doubts about the military capability of the Generalissimo to conduct the nationalist war effort effectively and according to modern military strategies. Count Ciano, Mussolini's son-in-law and Foreign Minister, noted in his diary on 20 December 1937, 'Our generals [in Spain] are restless and quite rightly. Franco has no idea of synthesis in war. His operations are those of a magnificent battalion commander. His objective is always ground, never the enemy.'[43]

However, the exultant *Caudillo* did not act from mere military considerations nor did he seek a quick victory in the style of *blitzkrieg* (lightning war) or *guerra celere* (fast war), as intended by the German and Italian strategists. His aim was wider and more profound: to exploit military operations to achieve the total physical removal of an enemy considered the anti-Spain and

Figure 5.2 General Varela decorates Franco with the Great Laureate Cross of Saint Ferdinand, at the 'Victory Parade' in Madrid, 19 May 1939.

as racially despicable as the rebel tribesmen in Morocco. In the telling words of Franco to Lieutenant Colonel Emilio Faldella, deputy head of the Italian military contingent serving under his command, 'In a civil war, the systematic occupation of territory, accompanied by any necessary purging, is preferable to the quick defeat of adversaries which may still leave the country infested with enemies.'[44]

For that reason he insisted on waging, with tenacity and perseverance, a slow war of attrition that literally decimated the ranks of a more poorly equipped enemy and approved a ruthless crackdown on the disaffected rearguard which stifled resistance and paralyzed all opposition among the vanquished for many years to come. At the beginning of the insurrection, the intention of the repressive violence had been the physical elimination of the most important enemies and the creation of an atmosphere of paralyzing terror that prevented active resistance among the potential disaffected. Franco later confessed an unusual personal distance from the phenomenon: 'the authorities had to anticipate any backlash against the Movement by leftist elements. That's why they shot the most prominent among them.'[45] However, with the extension of the war and the rise of Franco, this initial repression became a persistent policy of purging, 'redemption' and 'cleansing' so that the so-called *paseos* and less organized murders, more or less irregular in the first few months, were replaced by summary trials in brutal military courts. The political aim and social 'redemption' of that repression was respon- sible for a high number of fatalities that probably reached a figure close to 100,000 during the war (with another 40,000 after the victory and in the immediate post-war period, compared to 55,000 victims of the repression in the Republican zone).[46] With his full consent and legitimization of that harsh, ruthless repression, Franco reaped a huge political benefit: a 'pact of blood' that would guarantee forever the blind allegiance of his supporters to the 'Leader of the Victory' for fear of the possible vengeful return of the bereaved and vanquished. That same bloodletting also represented a useful 'insurance' against the defeated Republicans themselves: for a long time those who had not died in the process were silenced and paralyzed out of sheer terror.

With the army as an instrument for victory, with 'National Catholicism' as the supreme ideology and the Falange as a means to organize his supporters and discipline civil society, Franco built his own dictatorship between 1936 and 1939 and victoriously waged a war against liberal-democratic reformism and subversive social revolution. In April 1939, the unconditional victory achieved over an isolated, internationally abandoned Republic opened the way for the consolidation of what was already Franco's personal rule. As a result of a systemic policy of flattery, the *Caudillo*'s character had become markedly more cold, imperturbable, calculating, and guarded, surprising even his closest friends. The end of the war intensified his tendency to succumb to this folie de grandeur and to surround himself with a sycophantic court. Consequently, even though he decided not to occupy the Royal Palace in Madrid, thus avoiding the open alienation of his monarchist supporters, Franco installed himself in the nearby Palace of El Pardo with all the pomp and ceremony worthy of royalty (including the exotic Moorish Guard, a faithful reminder of his *Africanista* past). The signs of his willingness to stay in power for life were unambiguous, as was his determination not to proceed with the restoration of the monarchy in the person of Alfonso XIII or his rightful heir and pretender to the throne, Don Juan de Borbón.

Temptation and Opportunism in the Second World War

Despite the profound process of fascistization that the Francoist dictatorship had experimented with during the Civil War and the regime's political and diplomatic proclivity toward the German–Italian Axis, Franco was forced to remain on the margins of the European war which began in September 1939 following the German invasion of Poland. Exhaustion and destruction caused by the Civil War, along with a state of deep economic depression and growing starvation, left the Spanish regime at the mercy of an Anglo-French fleet which controlled Spain's maritime access to food and oil supplies, vital to its post-war recovery. Under these conditions, neutrality was followed out of necessity rather than from choice. For this very reason, it was accompanied by an official public identification with Germany's cause and limited covert military and economic support to her war effort.[47]

The striking German victories in the summer of 1940, with the defeat of France and the imminent attack on Britain, as well as Italy's entry into the war, allowed for a significant change in the Spanish position. Franco was seriously tempted to enter the war on the side of the Axis in order to achieve the irredentist and imperial dreams for his regime: the recovery of Gibraltar from British hands and the creation of a great North African empire at the expense of France. The problem remained the same: Spain could not sustain a prolonged war effort, given its enormous economic and military weakness and the British naval control of its deliveries of oil supplies and foodstuffs. Therefore, the cautious *Caudillo* tried to reconcile his expansionist goals with Spain's plight by means of a last-minute military intervention on the side of the Axis, at the hour of a German–Italian victory, and so participate as a belligerent in the subsequent division of imperial spoils.

Fortunately for Franco, Hitler scorned as unnecessary the costly and dubious offer of belligerency made secretly in mid-June 1940, at the time of

Germany's apparent triumph over France and Britain's imminent defeat. In August, Admiral Wilhelm Canaris, head of the German secret service, aptly summarized the nature and dangers of Franco's offer to the German high command:

Franco's policy from the start was not to come in until Britain was defeated, for he is afraid of her might (ports, food situation, etc.) … Spain has a very bad internal situation. They are short of food and have no coal … The consequences of having this unpredictable nation as a partner cannot be calculated. We shall get an ally who will cost us dearly.[48]

A few weeks later, when Britain's stubborn aerial resistance in the Battle of Britain showed that the end of the war was not imminent, the Hispano-German disagreement deepened. According to Francoist propagandists, at the crucial meeting at Hendaye on 23 October 1940, the *Caudillo* had firmly and astutely resisted threatening pressure from Hitler to enter the war with Germany. Through the writings of Sánchez Silva and Saenz de Heredia this central myth was magnified even further: 'The ability of a man to contain what all the armies of Europe could not, including the French'.[49] In fact, as made clear by the German and Italian documents from the aforementioned summit, captured by the Allies at the end of the conflict, Franco merely refused to enter the war if Hitler did not accept his demands for military aid and food and the future delivery of a large part of the French empire. However, the Führer neither wanted nor could accept this. He concluded that the priority was to keep collaborationist France under Marshal Pétain on his side, which guaranteed the benevolent neutrality of the French colonial empire in the struggle against Britain. Therefore, he refused to promise a dismemberment of that empire that would have pushed France's colonial authorities into the enemy arms of De Gaulle and Churchill. Quite simply, he could not risk the advantages brought by French collaboration for the sake of a costly and uncertain belligerence from Franco's hungry, defenceless and half-devastated Spain. The Italians also believed that Spanish belligerence 'would cost more than it is worth'.[50]

Thereafter, the Franco regime maintained its strong alignment with the Axis powers without overstepping, by virtue of its material incapacity, the threshold of official non-belligerence. The beginning of the Nazi offensive against the Soviet Union (June 1941) would offer a practical way to identify with the Axis cause: 47,000 volunteers and officers of the Blue Division would fight with the Wehrmacht on the Russian front until late 1944. It was the contribution of Spanish blood to the Axis war effort that, in Franco's mind, would substantiate any territorial claims in the future.[51]

However, with the entry of the United States into the war (December 1941) and the military situation turning in favour of the Allies, Franco's foreign

Figure 5.3 Official portrait of Franco after the Civil War. He appears as a victorious *Caudillo*, wearing on his chest the Great Laureate Cross of Saint Ferdinand.

policy was gradually returning to its usual mixture of pragmatic caution and sense of opportunism. Since November 1942, with the Anglo-American Allied landings in North Africa destroying his imperial dreams, Franco retreated to a neutrality increasingly acceptable to the Allies, determined to survive at any cost the collapse of the Axis in Europe. In April 1943, shortly before the Allied invasion of Sicily provoked the fall of Mussolini, the Caudillo reiterated to the Italian ambassador the cause of his inactivity: 'My heart is with you and

I wish the Axis victory. It is something that is in my own interest and that of my country, but you cannot forget the difficulties I face both internationally and domestically.'[52]

A year later, faced with a short and excruciating oil embargo by the British and Americans, Franco yielded fully to Allied demands to adopt a more neutral policy and end his remaining surreptitious help to the Germans: wolfram exports, complicity with the Nazi spy network, maintenance of the Blue Division on the Eastern Front, and so on. In fact, Western diplomatic analysts had by then realized his desire for political survival at any cost. As was noted confidentially by a senior official at the British Foreign Office in March 1944, 'Under Franco's canny Gallegan control, I do not think that the Spanish Government will remain either too blind or too proud to reach a settlement. Franco is the Sancho Panza rather than the Don Quixote type of Spaniard!'[53]

With chameleon-like cunning and without the slightest embarrassment, Franco began to rewrite history and, thanks to the cooperation of a controlled press much given to flattery, he was portrayed as an honest and impartial neutral who had saved Spain from the horrors of war. The now demonized Serrano Suñer was conveniently loaded with all the blame for past fascist proclivities. In mid-December 1944, after meeting with Franco in the Palace of El Pardo to relay Allied protests at his past conduct, the British ambassador in Madrid informed his government of the degree of confidence and self-assurance that still oozed from the Caudillo:

He showed no signs of being worried about the future of Spain and had evidently convinced himself that the present regime is in the forefront of human progress and the best that Spain has ever possessed. Whether this appearance of complete complacency is a pose or not, it is impossible to say. My own view is that he is genuinely convinced that he is the chosen instrument of Heaven to save Spain, and any suggestions to the contrary he regards as either ignorant or blasphemous ... It was only when I was leaving that I noticed a sign that the wind had begun to blow in this unventilated shrine of self-complacency. Photographs of the Pope and President Carmona (of Portugal) had taken the place of honour previously held on his writing table by Hitler and Mussolini.[54]

Resistance and Survival in the Post-War World

The end of the Second World War and the beginning of the ostracism of the Franco regime allowed the *Caudillo* again to demonstrate his political skills in a difficult situation. On 19 March 1945, Don Juan de Borbón published his *Manifiesto de Lausana* requesting Franco's withdrawal in favour of a monarchy open to national reconciliation and democratic transition. Shortly thereafter, on 2 August, the conference of the victorious Allies in Potsdam (Germany) issued a statement vetoing the entry of Franco's Spain into the UN 'in view of its origins, its nature, its record and its close association with the aggressor States'.[55] Beset by both international condemnation and internal pressure in favour of monarchical restoration, Franco fought his last great battle for survival, reviving the hatreds of the Civil War and the spectre of a Masonic–Bolshevik conspiracy against Catholic Spain. He was convinced that very soon there would be unleashed upon Europe a fierce clash between the Soviet Union and the United States and that the latter would turn to Spain for its invaluable strategic importance and strongly anti-communist policy. Until this break came, there was no other choice but to follow the private recommendation given him by his political alter ego since the ousting of the *Cuñadísimo*, Admiral Luis Carrero Blanco:

> The only formula for us can be no other than order, unity and endurance ... Because the Anglo-Saxons will accept anything from Spain if we do not let ourselves be pushed around, because in no way do they want disorder that may lead to a pro-Communist regime in the Iberian Peninsula.[56]

Before the generals and monarchist politicians, Franco made clear his determination to remain in power without surrendering the state headship to the pretender. He could not be more explicit: 'As long as I live, I shall never be a Queen Mother'; 'I will not make the same mistake as Primo de Rivera. I do not resign, from here to the cemetery.'[57] In late 1945, he coldly warned the most prominent and dangerous of the monarchist officers, General Varela, High Commissioner in Morocco, about the risks of breaking the unity of the victors in the Civil War: 'If they succeed in overcoming the goalkeeper, we would all fall one by one; if we are united they will not dare to attack with the utmost ferocity.'[58] Faced with the dilemma of enduring him sine die or removing him by force at the risk of war and the hypothetical return of the Republic, the majority of monarchists resigned themselves to Franco's pompous uncrowned reign.

He achieved another similar success with the victorious democratic powers: faced with the alternative of supporting a harmless Franco or provoking political destabilization in Spain with an uncertain outcome, both the new British Labour government and the US Democratic administration bore his presence as a lesser evil and preferable to a new civil war or a communist regime in the Iberian Peninsula. This was despite the profound personal and political displeasure this caused in official circles. In June 1946 a senior British Foreign Office official confided the reasons that precluded any effective allied pressure, economic or military, to topple Franco: 'The fact remains that Franco is not a threat to anybody outside Spain, odious though his regime is. But a civil war in Spain would bring trouble to all the Western democracies, which is what the Soviet Government and their satellites want.'[59]

The success of the strategy of stubborn resistance displayed by the *Caudillo* was evident in 1948 when the French government ordered (on 10 February) the reopening of its Spanish border which had closed two years earlier, and when Don Juan met with Franco (28 August) and yielded to his demand that Prince Juan Carlos be educated in Spain under Franco's tutelage. The victory was formalized conclusively in 1953 with the signing of the Concordat with the Vatican (28 August) and the Spanish–US agreements for the installation of American military bases in Spain (26 September). The Cold War between the former allies against the Nazis, formalized in 1947, had arrived in time to save him from his 'original sin', as it emphasized in Washington and London the political and strategic value of an anti-communist Spain in case of conflict in Europe with the Soviet Union.[60]

From that point, no real danger threatened either Franco's all-embracing 'command' in Spain or his diplomatic recognition in the West, albeit as a junior partner and despised for his political structure and recent past. In this sense, the regime's survival was achieved at a high political and economic price for Spain: the exclusion in 1947 from the benefits of the US Marshall Plan for aid to help European reconstruction and the veto of the continental democracies on admission to the Council of Europe, NATO and the emerging Common Market.

A Long Reign without a Crown

From the late 1940s, secure in his position and recognized as supreme and final arbiter for all the Francoist political 'families' (Falange, Carlist, Catholics, monarchists and military), the *Caudillo* could spend more time on his favourite hobbies and leisure activities. Only during the crucial year of 1957 was he forced to make a decisive political intervention when faced with a double crisis: that of the autarkic economic model adopted since the victory and the provocative policy of the Falange in attempting to expand its sphere of influence within the regime. The outcome was the reduction of the presence of the Falange in the new government and the promotion of the so-called technocrats, Catholics linked to *Opus Dei* and supporters of an economic and institutional modernization that would enable the survival of the regime. After approving the implementation of the Stabilization Plan of 1959, Franco

virtually retired from active daily politics. The deep social and economic transformations that occurred during this decade of technocratic development
emphasized this withdrawal because, quite simply, Franco did not understand
the complexity of the new situation. In addition, Carrero Blanco began to
occupy himself with the work of the presidency of the government in a way
as faceless and loyal as it was effective and satisfactory.

The technocrats' liberalizing policies allowed the Spanish economy to
benefit from the general expansion experienced by Western economies during
the 1960s. Under these conditions of intense economic modernization and
sociological changes, the ideological discourse within the dictatorship tended
to replace the 'legitimacy of the victory' with the 'legitimacy of success' in the
hope that material prosperity would cement the social peace and conformist
political apathy desired by the regime's hierarchy. However, Franco remained
immersed in the doctrinal legacy of the Civil War and immune to the calls for
tolerance and political openness that began to emerge in Spain. Indeed, the
only limitation imposed on the technocratic governments lay in the political
arena: nothing should diminish his supreme decision-making power because
'it is unthinkable that the victors of a war cede power to the losers, as if
nothing had happened here and we could go back to the starting point'.[61]

From the late 1960s, the noticeable physical decline of Franco turned the
fearsome dictator of previous eras into a weak and trembling old man who
ruled, as a stern father figure, a Spain unrecognizable to his generation and
increasingly more unstable. His last major political act, in July 1969, was the
appointment of Prince Juan Carlos de Borbón as his successor with the title
of king, in the belief that his regime could outlast him. However, the murder
of Carrero Blanco by the Basque terrorist organization ETA in December 1973
disrupted much of the succession plans because it eliminated the intended
guardian of the orthodoxy. Around the same time, the fall of the Portuguese
dictatorship, changing global economic conditions and growing social and
political questioning of the regime, triggered in Franco a surge of repressive
reaction to his significant cost: his approval of five executions in September
1975 caused the largest wave of international protests against the regime
since the time of ostracism. No other event of late Francoism revealed more
clearly the gap between a dramatically modernized society and an anachro-
nistic political system lacking in civil legitimacy.

That is why the last two years of Franco's life were a time of anxiety and
frequent depressions that were worsened by his problems with phlebitis,
gastric ulcers and Parkinson's disease. While his supporters were dividing
between reformists and *continuistas* and preparing to face an uncertain
future, the *Caudillo* finally died on 20 November 1975 after a long and painful
illness. With his demise, the dilemma was whether the regime could initiate
internal reform of a democratic nature or whether a forced break with the

past favoured by opposition forces was necessary. In the end and largely because of the ubiquitous memory of the Civil War and the general desire not to repeat it, the political transition was a result of both.

In short, the most recent historiography on the figure of Francisco Franco clearly shows that he was neither an intelligent statesman, as promoted by his hagiographers, nor an incompetent man blessed by good fortune, as claimed by his opponents. He was much more complex and, at the same time, more commonplace, as highlighted by the evident contrast between the skills that allowed him to achieve great triumphs and the intellectual mediocrity that led him to believe the most banal ideas. Perhaps here lies the impenetrability of the imperturbable General Franco. Beyond this, probably the only constant that guided his conduct was that which Salvador de Madariaga detected and described long ago:

> Franco's political strategy is straightforward. There is not an act of his that proposes anything other than his survival. Beneath the appearance of ever varied and even contradictory tactics (peace, neutrality, bellicosity; amnesty, prosecution; monarchy, regency), the only thing that Franco thinks about is Franco.[62]

Endnotes

1 These were not extemporaneous invocations but titles used in official publications. See, as an example, the decree of *Junta de Defensa Nacional* printed in the *Boletín Oficial del Estado* (30 September 1936); the article 'Caudillo de España' in *Extremadura. Diario católico* (1 April 1944); and the book of Luis de Galinsoga and Francisco Franco Salgado-Araujo, *Centinela de Occidente. Semblanza biográfica de Francisco Franco* (Barcelona: AHR, 1956).

2 José María Pemán, *La historia de España contada con sencillez para los niños ... y para muchos que no lo son* (Cádiz: Cerón y Librería Cervantes, 1939), Vol. 2, p. 213.

3 Antonio Muñoz Molina, 'La cara que veía en todas partes', *El País*, 19 November 2000.

4 Joaquín Arrarás Iribarren, *Franco* (Valladolid: Santarén, 1939); Galinsoga and Franco Salgado-Araujo, *Centinela de Occidente*; José María Sánchez Silva and José Luis Sáenz de Heredia, *Franco, ese hombre* (Madrid: Lidisa, 1964); Ricardo de la Cierva, *Francisco Franco: un siglo de España* (Madrid: Editora Nacional, 1973), 2 vols; and Luis Suárez Fernández, *Francisco Franco y su tiempo* (Madrid: Fundación F. Franco, 1984), 8 vols.

5 Luis Ramírez, *Francisco Franco. Historia de un mesianismo* (París: Ruedo Ibérico, 1964) (in later editions the subtitle was changed: *La obsesión de ser, la obsesión de poder*). Salvador de Madariaga, *Sanco Panco* (Mexico, Latino Americana, 1964). Amando de Miguel, *Franco, Franco, Franco* (Madrid:

Ediciones 99, 1976). Francisco Umbral, *La leyenda del César visionario* (Barcelona: Seix Barral, 1991). Manuel Vázquez Montalbán, *Autobiografía del general Franco* (Barcelona: Círculo de Lectores, 1992).

6   Juan Pablo Fusi Aizpurúa, *Franco: autoritarismo y poder personal* (Madrid: El País, 1985). Javier Tusell, *Franco en la guerra civil. Una biografía política* (Barcelona: Tusquets, 1992). Paul Preston, *Franco. A Biography* (London: Harper Collins, 1993). Spanish translation published in Barcelona by Ediciones Grijalbo in 1994 under the title *Franco. Caudillo de España*.

7   Alberto Reig Tapia, *Franco, 'caudillo'. Mito y realidad* (Madrid: Tecnos, 1995). Bartolomé Bennassar, *Franco* (Madrid: Edaf, 1996). Andrée Bachoud, *Franco* (Barcelona: Crítica, 2000). Fernando García de Cortázar, *Fotobiografía de Franco* (Barcelona: Planeta, 2000). José Luis Rodríguez, *Franco. Historia de un conspirador* (Madrid: Oberón, 2005). We cannot fail to mention our own contribution: *Francisco Franco. Crónica de un caudillo casi olvidado* (Madrid: Biblioteca Nueva, 2002).

8   Confession of Franco in October 1973. Reproduced in the major hagiographic work of the journalist Rogelio Baón, *La cara humana de un Caudillo. 400 anécdotas* (Madrid: San Martín, 1975), p. 49.

9   Opinion recorded in the book *Franco visto por sus ministros* (Barcelona: Planeta, 1981), 195. The previous quote in Pedro Sainz Rodríguez, *Testimonio y recuerdo* (Barcelona: Planeta, 1978), p. 324.

10 Reproduced in Marcelino Menéndez y Pelayo, *Historia de España (seleccionada en la obra del maestro)* (Madrid: Gráfica Universal, 1934), pp. 352, 354. The book, published at the height of the Republic by General Jorge Vigón, is a compilation of writings *menendez-pelayistas* that had an undoubted widespread influence among military and right-wing circles. For the impact of Menéndez y Pelayo on this national conservative concept, see Juan Pablo Fusi, *España. La evolución de la identidad nacional* (Madrid: Temas de Hoy, 2000), pp. 188, 241–2.

11 Cited by Stanley G. Payne, *Los militares y la política en la España contemporánea* (París: Ruedo Ibérico, 1968), p. 80. Cf. Carolyn P. Boyd, *La política pretoriana en el reinado de Alfonso XIII* (Madrid: Alianza, 1990); and Manuel Ballbé, *Orden público y militarismo en la España constitucional, 1812–1983* (Madrid: Alianza, 1983).

12 The first fragment was from his speech in the town hall of Baracaldo (21 June 1950). The second was in a statement to the Parisian daily newspaper *Le Figaro* (13 June 1958). Both are included in the anthology, *Pensamiento político de Franco* (Madrid: Servicio Informativo Español, 1964), pp. 54, 57.

13 Esteban Carvallo de Cora, *Hoja de servicios del Caudillo de España* (Madrid: Biosca, 1967). Understandably, the author omits the low ranking achieved by Franco in his first promotion.

14 Francisco Franco, *Papeles de la guerra de Marruecos* (Madrid: Fundación Nacional F. Franco, 1986).

15 Sebastian Balfour, *Abrazo mortal. De la guerra colonial a la guerra civil en España y Marruecos (1909–1939)* (Barcelona: Península, 2002). Gustau Nerín, *La guerra que vino de África* (Barcelona: Crítica, 2005).

16 Declarations of Franco to the journalist Manuel Aznar, 31 December 1939. Taken from the anthology *Palabras del Caudillo (19 Abril 1937–31 Diciembre 1938)* (Barcelona: Ediciones Fe, 1939), p. 314.

17 Opinion expressed by the Catalan Falangist and later union official, José María Fontana, *Franco. Radiografía del personaje para sus contemporáneos* (Barcelona: Acervo, 1979), p. 28.

18 Notes on his private life in Baón, *La cara humana de un Caudillo*, pp. 30, 37, 52, 126.

19 Carlos Blanco Escolá, *La Academia General Militar de Zaragoza, 1928–1931* (Barcelona: Labor, 1989).

20 José Antonio Ferrer Benimeli, 'Franco y la masonería', in Josep Fontana, ed., *España bajo el franquismo* (Barcelona: Crítica, 1986), pp. 246–68. On the origin of this conspiracy theory, see Norman Cohn, *El mito de la conspiración judía mundial* (Madrid: Alianza, 1983); and Herbert R. Southworth, *El lavado de cerebro de Francisco Franco. Conspiración y guerra civil* (Barcelona: Crítica, 2000).

21 According to Ricardo de la Cierva, *Historia del Franquismo* (Barcelona: Planeta, 1975), Vol. 1, p. 102.

22 Confession of a decorated ex-serviceman and Minister of Finance between 1957 and 1965. Found in *Franco visto por sus ministros*, p. 88.

23 Francisco Franco Salgado-Araujo, *Mis conversaciones privadas con Franco* (Barcelona: Planeta, 1976), p. 425.

24 Testimony recorded in Cierva, *Franco*, p. 121. This is a revised and expanded version of the two-volume biography published in 1973.

25 Manuel Azaña, *Memorias políticas y de guerra (1931–1939)* (Barcelona: Grijalbo-Mondadori, 1978), Vol. 1, pp. 47, 100. The first quotation by Sanjurjo is in Preston, *Franco*, p. 119. The opinion of his sister is in Pilar Franco, *Nosotros, los Franco* (Barcelona: Planeta, 1980), p. 73.

26 Cited in Claude Martin, *Franco, soldado y estadista* (Madrid: Fermín Uriarte, 1965), pp. 129–30.

27 Ramón Serrano Suñer, *Entre el silencio y la propaganda, la Historia como fue. Memorias* (Barcelona: Planeta, 1977).

28 Pedro Sainz Rodríguez, *Testimonio y recuerdos* (Barcelona: Planeta, 1978). On the influence of *Acción Española* on Franco and his regime, see Raúl Morodo, *Los orígenes ideológicos del franquismo: Acción Española* (Madrid: Alianza, 1985).

29 The relations between them are analysed in Stanley G. Payne in *Franco y José Antonio. El extraño caso del fascismo español* (Barcelona: Planeta, 1997).

30 Arrarás, *Franco*, p. 226. A more detailed version of Franco's actions in February 1936 is in Joaquín Arrarás, *Historia de la Segunda República Española* (Madrid: Editora Nacional, 1968), Vol. 4, pp. 56–9.

31 Annotation of 27 April 1968. Franco Salgado-Araujo, *Mis conversaciones privadas*, p. 526. This opinion on the lack of military unity was delivered by Franco to Orgaz during his visit to the Canary Islands at the beginning of the spring of 1968. Preston, *Franco*, p. 168.

32 Annotation of 27 April 1968. Franco Salgado-Araujo, *Mis conversaciones privadas*, p. 527. Arrarás, *Historia de la Segunda República*, Vol. 4, p. 304. Suárez Fernández, *Francisco Franco*, Vol. 2, pp. 24–5.

33 Claim made at the very beginning of the insurrection in Pamplona, 18 July 1936. Reproduced in Fontana, ed., *España bajo el franquismo*, p. 13.

34 *Boletín Oficial del Estado*, 30 September 1936.

35 Preston, *Franco. Caudillo de España*, p. 234.

36 Francisco Franco, *Discursos y escritos del Caudillo* (Madrid: no publisher, 1939), p. 12.

37 On the role of the new party, see Ricardo Chueca, *El fascismo en los comienzos del régimen de Franco. Un estudio sobre FET-JONS* (Madrid: Centro de Investigaciones Sociológicas, 1983). Sheelagh Ellwood, *Prietas las filas. Historia de Falange Española* (Barcelona: Crítica, 1984). Joan Maria Thomàs, *La Falange de Franco. El proyecto fascista del régimen* (Barcelona: Plaza y Janés, 2001). Ismael Saz, 'Salamanca, 1937: los fundamentos de un régimen', in *Fascismo y franquismo* (Valencia: Universidad de Valencia, 2004), pp. 125–50.

38 In his own words, Ramón Serrano Suñer, *Entre Hendaya y Gibraltar* (Madrid: Nauta, 1973), pp. 57, 59, 117.

39 Azaña, *Memorias políticas y de guerra*, Vol. 2, p. 313.

40 María Luisa Rodríguez Aisa, *El cardenal Gomá y la guerra de España* (Madrid: CSIC, 1981). Alfonso Álvarez Bolado, *Para ganar la guerra, para ganar la paz. Iglesia y guerra civil* (Madrid: Universidad Pontificia de Comillas, 1995). Hilari Raguer, *La pólvora y el incienso. La Iglesia y la Guerra Civil española* (Barcelona: Península, 2001).

41 Giuliana di Febo, *La santa de la raza. Un culto barroco en la España de Franco* (Barcelona: Icaria, 1988). Annotation of 8 March 1958 in Franco Salgado-Araujo, *Mis conversaciones privadas*, p. 90.

42 Despatch of 10 December 1936. Found in the collection of documents from the German archives captured by the Allies in 1945 and published as *Documents on German Foreign Policy, 1918–1945*, Series D, Vol. III, *Germany and the Spanish Civil War* (London: His Majesty's Stationery Office, 1951), p. 159.

43 Galeazzo Ciano, *Ciano's Hidden Diary, 1937–1938* (New York: E. P. Dutton, 1953), p. 46.

44 Reproduced in Preston, *Franco*, p. 278.

45 Franco Salgado-Araujo, *Mis conversaciones privadas*, p. 78. Annotation of 5 February 1955.

46 Santos, Juliá, coord., *Víctimas de la guerra civil* (Madrid: Taurus, 1999), pp. 407–12. Julián Casanova, et al., *Morir, matar, sobrevivir. La violencia en la dictadura de Franco* (Barcelona: Crítica, 2002). On the debate about 'extermination' as the basic purpose of Francoist repression, see the thoughtful reflections of Javier Rodrigo, '1936: guerra de exterminio, genocidio, exclusión', *Historia y Política*, 10 (2003): 249–58; and Julius Ruiz, 'A Spanish Genocide? Reflections on the Francoist Repression after the

Spanish Civil War', *Contemporary European History*, Vol. 14, No. 2 (2005): 171–91.

47 Javier Tusell, *Franco, España y la Segunda Guerra Mundial* (Madrid: Temas de Hoy, 1995). Luis Suárez Fernández, *España, Franco y la Segunda Guerra Mundial* (Madrid: Actas, 1997). Enrique Moradiellos, 'El régimen franquista y la Segunda Guerra Mundial', in *La España de Franco. Política y sociedad (1939–1975)* (Madrid: Síntesis, 2000), pp. 237–61. Manuel Ros Agudo, *La guerra secreta de Franco, 1939–1945* (Barcelona: Crítica, 2002).

48 Minute from the diary of General Franz Halder (Chief of Staff of the Army) on Canaris's report, 27 August 1940. Charles Burdick and Hans-Adolf Jacobsen, eds, *The Halder War Diary, 1939–1942* (London: Greenhil Books, 1988), p. 252. Cf. Stanley G. Payne, *Franco y Hitler. España, Alemania, la Segunda Guera mundial y el Holocausto* (Barcelona: Planeta, 2008).

49 Sánchez Silva and Sáenz de Heredia, *Franco … ese hombre*, p. 139.

50 A note by Count Ciano, 28 September 1940, *Diarios*, p. 480. Cf. Javier Tusell and Genoveva García Queipo de Llano, *Franco y Mussolini. La política española durante la II Guerra Mundial* (Barcelona: Planeta, 1985).

51 Xavier Moreno Juliá, *La División Azul. Sangre española en Rusia, 1941–1945* (Barcelona: Crítica, 2005).

52 Tusell and García Queipo de Llano, *Franco y Mussolini*, p. 193.

53 Minute of Mr Roberts, 3 March 1944. Reproduced in Enrique Moradiellos, *Franco frente a Churchill. España y Gran Bretaña en la Segunda Guerra Mundial* (Barcelona: Península, 2005).

54 The report of Hoare on his meeting with Franco, 12 December 1944, in Moradiellos, *Franco frente a Churchill*, p. 399.

55 Enrique Moradiellos, *La Conferencia de Potsdam de 1945 y el problema español* (Madrid: Instituto Universitario Ortega y Gasset, 1998).

56 Fragments of a report of late August 1945 sent by Carrero to Franco. Reproduced in Florentino Portero, *Franco aislado. La cuestión española (1945–1950)* (Madrid: Aguilar, 1989), pp. 105–6; and Javier Tusell, *Carrero. La eminencia gris del régimen de Franco* (Madrid: Temas de Hoy, 1993), pp. 128–30.

57 Alfredo Kindelán, *La verdad de mis relaciones con Franco* (Barcelona: Planeta, 1981), 287. Baón, *La cara humana de un Caudillo*, p. 171.

58 Tusell and García Queipo de Llano, *Franco y Mussolini*, p. 290.

59 Minute of Oliver Harvey, 7 June 1946. Moradiellos, *Franco frente a Churchill*, pp. 440, 443.

60 Viñas, Ángel, *Los pactos secretos de Franco con Estados Unidos* (Barcelona: Grijalbo, 1981). Javier Tusell, *Franco y los católicos. La política interior española entre 1945 y 1957* (Madrid: Alianza, 1984).

61 Comment by Franco to his cousin and secretary, Francisco Franco Salgado-Araujo, 4 February 1963, *Mis conversaciones privadas con Franco*, p. 369.

62 Salvador de Madariaga, *España. Ensayo de historia contemporánea* (Madrid: Espasa-Calpe, 1979), p. 511.

6

Juan Antonio Suanzes: Industry, Fascism and Catholicism

MIGUEL ÁNGEL DEL ARCO BLANCO

It is probable that Juan Antonio Suanzes saw the arrival at port of the reduced Spanish fleet following its defeat in the Spanish-American War of 1898. The ruination of an old and decrepit Spain, which had lost everything, had left behind what it once was, 'abandoning the way of tradition', would remain with him forever.

Juan Antonio Suanzes Fernández was born in Ferrol, Galicia, at one o'clock in the afternoon of 20 May 1891.[1] His father, Saturnino Suanzes Carpegna, belonged to the General Corps of the navy and had served for three years during the Spanish-American War: the loss of the colonies and the consequent notion of Spanish decadence would pervade the atmosphere in which Juan Antonio Suanzes grew up.[2]

Traditional and numerous, his family was deeply marked by a military and Catholic spirit. He attended a religious school with his brothers and, along with some of them, embarked upon a military career. This in a Spain that, at the beginning of the century, was tired, with the shadow of 'the Disaster' more present than ever, in a city where the navy was everything and a country where it was hardly anything. The same city where another personality central to the Spanish twentieth century would grow up, with whom our subject would share a childhood, friendship and future battles: Francisco Franco.

Suanzes began his military career in 1903 as a naval cadet, when he was only 12 years old.[3] He studied in the Naval School of his city and was promoted to midshipman (1906), frigate ensign (1908) and navy Ensign (1909), sporadically stationed on evocatively named vessels: *Numancia, Pelayo, Carlos V, Reina Regente* and *España*.

In 1915 his life took an unexpected turn. Without abandoning his military aspirations, these took on a technical hue as he began to study naval engineering in Ferrol. By 1917 he was already captain of Naval Engineers and taught in the Naval Military School of San Fernando (Cadiz). By 1919 he was commander of Engineers and continued his technical specialization with a course on submarines in the School of Cartagena (Murcia). There his professional future was reoriented: in 1920 he was named head of the shipyard of the Spanish Society of Naval Construction. For some time he worked simultaneously in the navy and the company and, in 1921, at only 30 years of age, he was promoted to the rank of commander of Engineers. In 1922 he became a supernumerary of the navy, in this way obtaining a licence to move away from military life to work for the private company.

The military spirit accompanied Suanzes throughout his life. He belonged to a generation of military men, that of 1915, which would be marked by a short education and a long African war; a generation that shared a military ideology, in which loyalty and order were axiomatic. Nevertheless, his status as an engineer led him to consider himself a distinct element, better trained than his colleagues of the '*armas generales*' (the rank and file of the military, as distinct from the '*cuerpos facultativos*', the recipients of technical training).[4]

Suanzes would never conceive of his technical work as something removed from his service to the fatherland. Through his management of the shipyards he attempted to endow Spain with a fleet appropriate to the times. His experience as a marine in a limited and antiquated navy would be the spur: doubtless he never forgot the unfortunate incident of 1912 when, on board the *Reina Regente* in the course of an important mission on the coast of Morocco, the cruiser suffered a breakdown that forced it to be towed back to Cartagena.

In January 1908 the 'Ferrándiz Law' had entrusted the construction of a new fleet to the Spanish Society of Naval Construction, the company for which Suanzes was to begin working. But in this vocational struggle to provide Spain with a powerful navy he would come across an unforeseen obstacle: half of the society was constituted by English capital, belonging to the hugely powerful naval company Vickers.[5]

Suanzes's experiences in the world of naval military construction were to become the genesis of his political choices and of his visions for the future. He learned that under no circumstances could the interference of private capital in the affairs of the 'fatherland' be tolerated, still less if it was foreign capital; in this case, British. Sovereignty, exaltation of the nation and progress were to be inseparable.

Suanzes viewed the arrival of the Primo de Rivera Dictatorship with sympathy. As a supernumerary of the navy he saw from a distance the military reforms undertaken by General Miguel Primo de Rivera, as well as the conflicts produced by the policy on promotions, particularly in the shipyard corps (and to a lesser extent that of Engineers).[6] By contrast, the military successes (the liquidation of the Moroccan problem through the Spanish victory at Alhucemas), the re-evaluation of the army, the project of warship construction in 1926, the work of the 'commissions of industrial mobilization' that were to be so decisive in their later evolution, or the attempt to nationalize Spanish society in those years, would be key in the communion of his ideology and interests with those of the new regime. So much so that the words that General Mola would go on to write some years later could have been his own: 'Never, since the times of O'Donnell and Prim, has our army achieved as much prestige abroad as under the command of General Primo de Rivera.'[7]

On the professional terrain his first years in the Spanish Society of Naval Construction (*La Naval*) were positive in terms of his aspirations. He ran the shipyards at Cartagena until 1926, when he was assigned to that of Ferrol. He learned then to combine his work with his political thought: the construction plan of the Dictatorship provided a boost to the programme of naval construction, which Suanzes would link to the progress and strengthening of the nation.[8] The Spain of General Primo de Rivera and the shipyard directed by Suanzes walked hand in hand, securing the greater glory of the nation – that is, until republican democracy crossed their path.

The Time of Radicalization: The Second Republic

The beginning of the Republic coincided with Suanzes moving to Madrid in January of 1932, where he settled with his family. Attentive to preserving traditional morality, he enrolled his sons and daughters in the conservative religious colleges *El Pilar* and *Nuestra Señora de Loreto*, both in the Barrio de Salamanca district. He entered into relations with some conservative circles of Madrid society, while bearing witness to the progressive measures taken by the first Republican government. The arrival of democratic liberties, the military reform of Azaña, the secularizing measures, the law of religious congregations, the projected agrarian reform and the increase in power of the unions and parties went against the mentality and beliefs of the old naval officer who, now in the capital, continued to see in the nation, order and Catholicism the core of his life. There he took the position of Inspector General of Construction in *La Naval*, which would confer maximum responsibility on him for all the projects developed in the shipyards of the company. At the same time, however, he would enter into relations – and conflict – with its highest representatives.[9]

At the beginning of the 1930s the situation of *La Naval* was complicated. Over 25 million pesetas in debt to the British company Vickers, the latter organization made an inspection trip to its Spanish affiliate with the intention of reducing production costs. For Suanzes this was an authentic attack on the interests and independence of the company and of Spain: he did not consider his job to be a private activity but 'the work of building warships for my country'.[10] To his mind, the English wanted to prevent *La Naval* from becoming progressively more independent and autonomous. Since his arrival at the company he had attempted to 'nationalize' it, encouraging technological independence and designating to Spaniards the posts of greater responsibility. In this way, 'an enthusiastic and patriotic spirit substituted the previous English one, which was cold, uninterested, and tinged with perfectly explicable colonial aspects.'[11]

The conflict around *La Naval* reveals some of the convictions and the strong character of Suanzes. His behaviour and the events which took place would make him believe, in the first place, that the development of national industry was closely linked to the progress and independence of the nation and, secondly, that this was to be necessarily propelled by state intervention and the work of men of faith, will and enthusiasm.

Suanzes considered *La Naval* to be helpless before the jaws of British capitalism. Even at this early stage he opted for the solution that he would adopt so many times in the future: direct state intervention. The problem of *La Naval* 'had to be put in its totality and with total clarity into the hands of the state; in collaboration with it, it had to move towards a rationalization of society, disregarding the necessary sacrifices, it had to ensure, paying the English debt at any cost, that foreign influence ... did not cross certain limits'.[12] The state did not come to his aid, however, and Suanzes would look on astonished at the unfolding of events.

The acid test was to be a competition for the building of ships for Brazil. *La Naval* participated with a concrete proposal. Before it could be sent, however, the British obliged the sales price to be raised so that Vickers, also participating, would be assured of the concession. Suanzes' ire was provoked, and he resigned from the company at the beginning of 1934: 'Is it admissible that .... the competition fixes our price? Is national work to be thus played with?'[13]

The importance of the affair brought Suanzes into the political arena. He met with José María Gil Robles, leader of the CEDA. The esteem in which Suanzes held this politician is demonstrated not only by the fact that he turned to him but also by his own words: he 'received him amiably', was completely informed of everything; the 'national interest' was 'the only thing which seemed to concern him'.[14]

The subject was broached by parliament in March of 1934, in the government presided over by the Radical Alejandro Lerroux, which as yet had no CEDA ministers. The naval minister, the lawyer Juan José Rocha García, proposed a naval construction plan for the fleet, approved by the right. The Socialist party opposed it.[15] For Suanzes the postures of the left were intolerable: as a naval officer, it was inconceivable that Spain should renounce having a strong war fleet at her disposal.

The conflict around *La Naval* was also brought up in those sessions. Gil Robles warned of the danger of entrusting construction to 'societies that, with a Spanish denomination, operate with the intervention, perhaps decisive, of foreign capital, that could at some time cause problems for the defence of our Fatherland'. The politician from Salamanca made the ideas of Suanzes his own, but also denounced 'the elimination of Spanish technicians' from the leadership of the business, 'under pressure from foreign houses'. For Gil Robles this 'denationalisation' was intolerable, and he demanded 'an energetic and decisive intervention on the part of the Spanish state, so that something as serious as national defence did not rest in foreign hands'.[16]

Nevertheless, the Radical Party supported continued collaboration with English capital. The deputy Pérez Madrigal recognized Spain's technical limitations ('Do we have patents, inventors, workshops?') and even affirmed that the exit of Suanzes and other engineers from the company was due to discontent caused by the 'reduction of their salaries' brought about by cuts to production costs.[17] We learn from Suanzes' own pen his opinion on this matter: Pérez Madrigal was nothing more than a 'distinguished defender' of British interests.[18] In his eyes, he was but one further example of the corrupt and disastrous political class that served not Spain but their own selfish interests and those of international capital.

In 1934, after some time without employment, Suanzes was named director general of the company *Boettichery Navarro*, a manufacturer of lifts based in Madrid. Once again he would encounter foreign 'interference', as the business relied on Austrian participation. Suanzes did not hesitate in showing his 'serious reserves about the foreign personnel'.[19] His ideas remained intact and were even radicalized. The Asturian insurrection fanned the flames: like the rest of the employer class, Suanzes considered these events to be an authentic 'revolution', coldly planned by the leaders of the left.[20]

In February 1936 the Popular Front won the general election. Conservatives received the result with real dread, and the Catholics of *Acción Española* openly called for armed rebellion. In March the first conspiratorial movements began within the army.[21].

Social unrest was again on the rise and Suanzes, as director of Boetticher, was a witness to it. The amnesty and social reforms undertaken by the Popular Front were not at all to the liking of the employers. Between February and July there were frequent violent demonstrations and armed clashes. Businesses obstructed the readmission of fired workers, and businessmen called for a 'Policy of order' that would put an end to the 'disruptive and revolutionary' movement that was endangering the nation. In June and July, Boetticher was affected by an important construction strike and another, of lifts, called by the UGT and CNT.[22] In the climate of tension and polarization of those days, and in view of his temperament and political credo, Suanzes took an active and inflexible position. It was then that he was imprisoned.

Here we come to an obscure point in the life of Suanzes. Did he belong to a right-wing party or union? We have not found a trace of political affiliation prior to July 1936. He does not seem to have been affiliated to the Falange. Historians of diverse tendencies have described him as a 'technician' and have concentrated on his economic programme for the future of Spain.[23] Some time ago, without referring to a concrete source, some linked him to 'corporatism' and the Catholicism of *Acción Popular*: he belonged to the board of *Editorial Católica*, publisher of the newspaper *El Debate*, bulwark of corporatist Catholic ideology.[24] As we have shown, Suanzes' ideology before the coup d'état, if it did not coincide exactly, was very close to that of the increasingly radicalized Catholic right represented, for example, by the CEDA. If he did not participate actively, he was very close to their opinions, ideology and also to their most notable personalities. Proof of this can be found in his close relationship with Ángel Herrera Oria, promoter of social Catholicism in Spain.[25]

Suanzes was jailed a short time before the outbreak of the Civil War. By then his opposition to the Republic was evident, seeing in it from his ultranationalist Catholic perspective a pit of intolerable anarchy, atheism, anti-Spanish sentiment and separatism. He regained his freedom eight days before the coup d'état, on 12 July 1936. On the following day, José Calvo Sotelo was assassinated.

On 18 July 1936, the military coup did not succeed in the capital: General Fanjul rebelled in the Montaña barracks but was crushed. The Republican state was overwhelmed and, in spite of the efforts of some leaders to stop them, *paseos* (the practice of searching out political enemies for summary execution) and executions were widespread.[26]

Frightened by the events, the Suanzes family abandoned their home in *El Viso*, later expropriated by the CNT. Several militiamen took Suanzes prisoner along with his brother Luis and Francisco Dopico, another military man from Ferrol. They were released thanks to the intervention of General Masquelet, chief of the military HQ of the President of the Republic and former Minister of War, from Ferrol and loyal to the Republic. Suanzes then found refuge in the Polish embassy. On 23 March 1937 he left for Valencia, from where he set sail for Marseilles. Eight days later he entered the 'national zone' by Fuenterrabía, ready to offer his services to Franco as one who had been persecuted and imprisoned by 'the red horde'. For Suanzes, the 'Crusade' had begun: the march had begun for the regeneration and exaltation of the fatherland.[27]

At Spain's Service: in the 'National Zone'

'By the hand of Providence', Suanzes found that his friend Francisco Franco was the *Caudillo* who would guide the destiny of the 'New Spain'. At his side was his brother, Nicolás Franco, with whom his friendship was even closer. These relationships would result in his carrying out, within a short time, activities of ever growing responsibility.

Suanzes the military man was ready for the struggle. With his lack of political antecedents confirmed, he began to lend his services to the High Command of the navy. On 10 April 1937 he was sent to San Fernando at the service of the Commander General of the Maritime Department of Cadiz, Juan Cervera Valderrama. There he managed to recover the *Republic*, an out of service cruiser in the shipyard that would now be launched, armed and made ready for combat under the name *Navarra*.[28]

After winning the confidence of Cervera, he became his consultant in the acquisition of ships for the 'Crusade'. He was commissioned on several occasions to travel to Italy. His execution of this important task was due to his naval and technical knowledge, and also to his friendship with Francisco Franco and, still more, with Nicolás Franco, a key operator in the management of German and Italian aid during the Civil War.[29]

In fascist Italy he came into contact with ideas essential for the confirmation of his ideology: the managed economy, corporatism and, of course, state intervention in the organization of industry through the *Istituto per la Riconstruzione Industriale*, the inspiration for the future National Institute of Industry (INI). On 26 June 1937 he explained in Rome the perilous situation of the Spanish fleet to Admiral Somigli, department head of the Royal Italian Navy. In spite of their initial refusal, thanks to the direct intervention of Mussolini, Suanzes was able to send in a series of ships that Italy would renovate and arm. His management enabled the 'national' navy to count on

Figure 6.1 Suanzes dressed in a navy uniform during the Civil War.

five warships that would become known as the 'fleet of death'.[30] This success earned Suanzes the appreciation and trust of the Generalísimo.

Suanzes received an education from such trips and negotiations. As he told Cervera, the Italian ships were 'very old' and expensive to maintain.[31] His attempts to make them battle ready in Ferrol were fruitless. Had it not been for the decision of 'Il Duce', Suanzes would not have been able to obtain them. For him, this was another example of dependence on abroad, of Spain's defencelessness and sorry state.

During the years of conflict, Suanzes attempted to encourage the construction of warships in Spain. It proved impossible, however, again due to the hated Vickers, who refused to provide the construction plans, alleging that the only copies were in the headquarters of *La Naval* in Cartagena and

Madrid.[32] Now, in days crucial for the 'salvation of the fatherland', obscure foreign interests had re-emerged. Private initiative had again hindered Spain's supreme destiny.

In the rebel rearguard the Civil War was conceived of as a mythical and crucial moment that would decide the salvation of the country. In it 'the sons of the true Spain' duelled with foreign, anti-Spanish, atheist and harmful forces.[33] Suanzes would share this vision due, not only to his personal experience – for example, his brush with death in the days immediately following the coup – but also to that of his family. His wife and children remained in Republican Madrid after his exit, escaping the 'red terror' and arriving in 'national Spain' in August 1937.[34] His brother José died in December 1936 on the northern front, in Villareal de Álava: for Suanzes, he was one of the 'martyrs' of the 'Holy Crusade' who, with their blood, fertilized the ground and future of the fatherland, contributing to its salvation.[35] The engineer from Ferrol would guard his memory throughout his life, as shown in numerous speeches in which he called for the remembrance of the fallen and of the Civil War.

On 30 October 1937 Franco sent Suanzes to Gijón, where he would direct the salvage operations undertaken on boats sunk in the port of Musel.[36] He managed to refloat the Republican destroyer *Císcar*, sunk in an aerial attack days before the fall of Asturias. The rebels, who, until then, had relied on the single, antiquated destroyer in their fleet (the *Velasco*), thus added a modern ship to their forces that would prove decisive in the outcome of the war.[37]

His efficacy in the positions entrusted him after his arrival in rebel Spain, combined with his friendship with the Franco brothers, would contribute decisively to his being named Minister of Industry and Commerce. Nevertheless, Suanzes was not Franco's first choice. A confidential British diplomatic report does not include his name among the candidates for the government of Burgos.[38] According to Serrano Súñer, the Generalísimo wanted to nominate his brother Nicolás. If we give credit to Serrano's memoirs – on occasion somewhat difficult to do –Serrano suggested to his brother-in-law that 'there was too much family in the government', and offered to leave his own department so that Nicolás might be nominated. Then it would be the same Serrano who suggested the name of Suanzes to Franco, hoping to distance the *Caudillo* from a character such as Nicolás, who could vie with him for his influence. Serrano knew the engineer from Ferrol vaguely from the years of the Congress, when he had revealed to the deputies of the CEDA his problem in *La Naval*. According to him, he proposed Suanzes because he had heard Franco praise him, something 'he did very rarely'. Franco accepted his advice.[39]

From the summer of 1937 Suanzes formed part of the Generalísimo's circle of advisors and collaborators. This would be proven by the 'guidelines' he drew up and which, after a time, would be taken up by Franco himself to form the spine of his 'economic programme'.[40] This is the first document that provides evidence of his political ideas and the Civil War's great influence upon them. We find an amalgam typical of the times and of early Francoism: elements of the Spanish Catholic right and of Falangism. He considered Catholicism vital for the future 'New State': a 'pure and clean religion', 'externalised' and present in 'all aspects of social and political life'. He repeats the old idea of a 'Judeo-Masonic conspiracy' against Spain, linking it to democracy, calling for a 'constant war on masonry, on politics', on 'Judaism and Marxist International organisations', on 'regionalism' and on 'anti-national spirit'. Spain had to be regenerated: the 'moral reconstruction' of the country was necessary. He therefore called for an 'initial and permanent administrative purification' of public positions and the implantation of 'religious, patriotic and social education'. The end was in sight for the politicians and vices of the liberal state: he declared war on 'pessimism', on 'recommendation', on lack of faith, incompetence and indiscipline. It was time for the fulfilment of duty to the fatherland 'with firmness, purity, discipline, urbanity and happiness'. Family and home were to be the 'bases of the new state' that had to be protected to stimulate the birth rate. Fascist influence on his thinking is revealed in his plans for the organization of free time: the promotion 'of games and sports', the implantation of an organization 'similar to the [Italian] Dopolavoro' or the Nazi 'Strength Through Joy' (Kraft durch Freude), control of the means of communication and the importance of propaganda, and so on.

The concept of 'autarky' was already present in his thought. Once again corporatist and fascist elements were emphasized in Suanzes' ideology. He criticized the pernicious effects of 'capital', the 'noxious and excessive concentration of wealth' and of 'luxury'. He therefore declared 'war on speculation and on the middle man' and decreed the 'abolition of usury'. He conceived of work as a 'duty' and an 'authentic social obligation' that the state would protect. There would be no place for individual interests, only those of the fatherland. Economically he defended the 'total nationalisation of consumption (autarky)', and therefore imports had to be restricted and the export of national products ('typical products, of Spanish brand') promoted. Resources could be found within the country that had until then been bought abroad. State intervention in the economy had to be total: he even assumed the radical Falangist postulate of the 'nationalisation of the banking system', which he would later abandon. Private initiative could not be trusted: the state, through 'Unions', 'Corporations' and its institutions would take the initiative in economic policy. To ensure the greater glory of Spain, the 'nation-alisation' of companies would be undertaken where necessary, particularly in the 'War Industries'. The economy would be a key element in the expansion and development of the country that would proceed hand in hand with virile military power to safeguard the 'Empire' to which Spain, resuscitated by arms, was now marching.[41]

Thus when Franco recruited Suanzes to continue the struggle from the Ministry of Trade and Industry, he was already clearly identified with and committed to the 'National Cause'. More than friendship, it would be their ideas and experiences that bound them together over the years; the same as those shared by many who, proceeding from the diverse tendencies of the Spanish right, would find in the Civil War the decisive event and ideological linkage that would unite them forever.

The 'Crusade' from the Offices: Minister of Trade and Industry

The ministerial Department of Trade and Industry was essential to the development of the war. From its offices, Suanzes organized the supply of the rebel army and of the rearguard, contributing to the consolidation of the 'New State'. In addition, he had to mobilize Biscayan industry, in the hands of the insurgents from June of 1937. Independent of the results of the policy of autarky developed later in the 1940s, it is certain that the management of Suanzes during the Civil War was beneficial to the rebels, and contributed to the victory of 1939 and the consolidation of Francoism. This strengthened the esteem in which Suanzes held himself and his ideas, and the faith and confidence that Franco would have in him for the future.

The Ministry of Trade and Industry was situated in Bilbao. Suanzes assigned the post of Chief of the National Service of Industry to José María de Areilza. Areilza represented the model politician that Suanzes wanted to have at his side: young (only 29 years of age), religious, committed to the Crusade, a man of will and organizational gifts.[42] During his career, the engineer from Ferrol would surround himself with men who were committed and loyal to the uprising and its principles, who had demonstrated their fidelity, their spirit of sacrifice and their religiosity; men, as Franco himself would say, 'with brains, not stuffing, in their heads; men of substance, with hearts not dripping in ink for their dossiers but red blood for the people'.[43]

Suanzes would conceive of his task as a 'service to Spain'. His work desk was a 'trench' from which to continue the struggle and ensure the 'salvation of Spain'. For him, motivation, morality and beliefs were essential. Discipline, sacrifice and faith were key. He always arrived early to work, dressed in the uniform of colonel of Engineers.[44] Camaraderie and union among the administrative staff were considered vital and to promote them he had a canteen set up in the ministry.[45] He was also mindful of the spiritual welfare of his subordinates, punctuating ministerial work with Mass, religious acts and even spiritual retreats.

In 1938, a Portuguese journalist from the daily *O Seculo* described the ministry as the 'engine room' of 'the immense ship' that was the 'New Spain'. When Suanzes granted him an interview, he appeared in it as the 'Chief Engineer of the ship', arriving 'sweating and panting from the machine room' with 'his military jacket unbuttoned'. Overlooking his office was a portrait of the *Caudillo*, hung beneath 'an admirable Calvary scene'.[46]

The situation of the ministry and its early days are also worth recounting. It was located in the heart of Bilbao, in the sumptuous Palace of the Provincial Deputation, an 'old fortress of separatist misunderstandings'.[47] The space had been purified: the meeting room was now presided over by a 'great cross with a yellow centre and red borders' and by 'the highly Spanish del Pilar Virgin'. After Suanzes took possession of it, mass was celebrated daily, attended by all employees: minister, chiefs of service, typists, and so on. On the first Friday of every month communion was received together, symbolizing the spiritual unity of the redeemed fatherland.[48]

His activity during the Civil War demonstrates that Suanzes was far from being a mere technician within Francoism; we now see a man politicized and imbued with all the ideals of the Crusade. According to him, the Civil War was a providential event. During a radio talk of July 1938, commemorating the passage of Franco's troops over the Straits of Gibraltar, he even alluded to the Virgin del Carmen 'who was necessarily present at that initial miracle of the Crusade'. The war was a mythic moment when the destinies of Spain and Western civilization would be redeemed ('Spain in a unique opportunity in her history, Spain, bulwark of civilisation'). The blood of true Spaniards, fallen on the soil of the fatherland, was the way of redemption for past sins, but also the seed of an immediate future ('Spain, purified by the blood of its best, is going to enter immediately on the way to Greatness'). Violence, as in the rest of Europe, was a creative and necessary force[49].

In the opinion of Suanzes, until 18 July 1936 Spain had been submerged in absolute decadence: it had fallen into foreign hands and its political, economic and spiritual degradation had reached their culmination in the Second Republic. The country had to close ranks on itself around a strong state that would put an end to the secular economic backwardness that weighed down its destiny. As his life had taught him, private initiative was antinational and harboured secret interests. It had to be the state that resolved the problems of the country, taking the reins of the economy, strengthening industrialization and development. Also necessary to resolve the problems of the country was a 'spirit', a 'mood'. Impregnated with clearly fascistic elements, Suanzes joined those men who recognized that the crisis of modernity could only be resolved by uniting the material and the spiritual, will and faith.[50]

The new Spaniards had to be possessed of a 'furious patriotism, in living flesh' that would make the greater glory of Spain possible. It had to manifest itself in work, which he equated to the struggle in the trenches, given that if it was not carried out in a satisfactory manner it would endanger 'the life of the Fatherland'. Spain had to be worked for until exhaustion: 'It is necessary that the tool should shake in the hands and the pen [be] dropped through fatigue.' As in other nationalist speeches of interwar Europe, the nation was placed above individual interests, and daily life seen as one further war against reality, against the obstacles that impede the destiny and exaltation of the fatherland. Sacrifice, abnegation and belief in abstract and eternal values identified with Spain were necessary.

His nationalism led him to speak, explicitly, of a 'Spanish race': 'an intelligent, sober, and heroic race, creator of twenty flourishing nations'. The race that, with the cross in its hand and 'a profound spirituality based on a religious sense of life', had discovered America and civilized half of the world, but which had been contaminated by foreign and anti-Spanish influences.[51]

Suanzes repudiated democracy. Like Franco, he thought it bad for economic growth and order in the countr[52] He conceived of parliamentary politics and of the Second Republic as something pernicious for Spain. Politicians were nothing more than 'groups of layabouts, imbeciles and cretins', gurus of the country's 'moral degradation'. Republican politicians were 'a bunch of bandits, the dregs of society', who had 'poisoned the masses'. 'We have let them rob us of spiritualism, we have allowed the disappearance of religion and the higher feelings.' Some Spaniards were 'capable of becoming wild beasts'.

The moment to act had now arrived. The sick body of the nation had to be purged: 'sacrifice' and 'Catholicism' would be the keys to redemption. The Catholic religion was, together with nationalism, the other pillar of Suanzes's ideology. He linked it to that traditionalist conception of Spain that, at least since the War of Independence, associated the nation with Catholicism and that, in the Crusade, had reached its extreme: 'To love God above all things' was to 'love Spain, our mother, because she has formed us and given us our character'. Outside of God, outside of Spain, lay atheism, wickedness and anti-Spanish sentiment. With God and with a united and healthy nation, 'The Spain, One, Great and Free that the crucified Fatherland, our mothers in tears, our yearning children, our dead and our History demands' would finally rise.[53]

No sooner had he had taken possession of the ministerial department, with a military and determined air, than Suanzes began to put into practice his economic programme which, had it not been for the cessation of his ministerial role amidst the Falangist ascent of 1939, would have given rise to the creation of the INI before 1941. In his 'notes for the cultural attachés', we find evidence of his intentions, clearly influenced by the experiences of the totalitarian and corporatist 'industrial mobilisation' of other European regimes in the interwar period.[54] A 'unitary and totalitarian state' was necessary that, with 'confirmed faith', would 'take sides before the problems of the times' – in contrast to that 'sceptical, indifferent' liberal state, that allowed itself to be dragged to and fro by the class struggle or a 'materialist' conception of history. The new 'totalitarian state' would, therefore, have to submit the material, the economy, to politics; that is, to the 'spiritual, historical and political ends of the state'.[55]

Figure 6.2 Suanzes heading towards the Francoist Ministry of Trade and Industry in Bilbao in January 1939.

Two complementary objectives were proposed: 'To affirm the Spanish character in the European concert' abroad; and, domestically, to secure 'the wellbeing of the Spanish social community'. Industry would be essential to this process. It would not be, as in the liberal state, a 'modern money-making process' to satisfy suspicious private interests. Rather, it would be an essential instrument for 'national independence and the ends of war and of peace'. Therefore, the 'New State' could not neglect it or leave it in foreign hands. It would have to intervene in its orientation, development and functioning. It would have to be tenaciously protected, not only through indirect measures (trade barriers, customs laws, various exemptions or fiscal policies), but also through the state taking charge of 'the prosperous life of a strong and robust industry' and determining 'its orientation towards the sectors held to be most useful to the national economy'. It would be 'total, absolute' protection.[56]

His work as a minister was decisive. He traced the guidelines of what would be the autarkic economy of the 1940s, becoming one of its supreme ideologues. Until recently it was upheld that autarky was an economic system, the primary goal of which was to achieve the economic independence of Spain, substituting its imports for products that from then on would be produced inside the country, obtaining a favourable balance of payments.[57] But it was much more than this. As the ideas of Suanzes show, for such men the economy was closely linked to their politics. Autarky was, therefore, also a cultural and political programme that, isolating Spain from abroad and closing it in on itself, hoped to purify and regenerate it.[58]

Autarky was a policy adopted intentionally and was not the product of circumstances, as some authors have attempted to argue.[59] Suanzes himself affirmed explicitly that Spain had to aspire to a 'partial autarky' that would allow it to be self-sufficient 'regardless of circumstance'.[60] He did not pursue absolute autarky, far from any contact with the exterior, but wanted to drive through rapid industrialization in deficient sectors of the country, in this way strengthening its independence. In practice, however, this implied an autarky that was far from 'partial'. As he himself would describe, this forced indus-trialization would have to stretch to a highly varied range of products and industries.[61] In this way, renouncing the importation of those same products from abroad, Spain would achieve a favourable balance of payments that would launch her towards her dreamed of 'imperial destiny'. Factors such as production costs, opportunity costs and the reality of the country's resources were ignored. Optimism and faith in Spain and her destiny meant that politics and the economy would go hand in hand in search of a dream that would never be realized.

The work of Suanzes as a minister was frenetic. He developed projects and proposed laws and decrees to domesticate Spain's economic destiny.

By the end of the war, he had planned the industrial policy of the New State: nationalization of industries in case of industrial mobilization with military ends and equilibrium in the balance of payments, which would from then on be 'a recurring refrain that would last until his disappearance from public life'.[62] Rejecting private initiative, he was already thinking of creating an organism that would strengthen the industrialization of the country. In his last months as minister, Suanzes asked for the statutes and balance sheets of the *Istituto per la Reconstruzione Italiana* (IRI) to be sent to his office.[63] What is more, Suanzes elaborated fundamental regulations that would herald the industrial policy of the post-war period, and which consecrated the state as the supreme manager of the economy.[64].

The weight of Suanzes in the first government was notable. His ideology was felt not only in the guidelines of economic policy, but in the construction of the Francoist state. He took an active part in the elaboration of the '*Fuero del Trabajo*' (Charter of Labour), in which the New State defined its nature, ideology and aspirations.[65] As the engineer would remember later, he had the 'honour of forming a part' of the committee that would elaborate the draft which would later be 'clarified and improved by the First National Council' of the FET and the JONS.[66] The committee was made up of Suanzes; Raimundo Fernández Cuesta of the old guard, Minister of Agriculture, Secretary General of the Movement and moderate Falangist; and Pedro González Bueno, Minister of Union Action and Organization and more radical Falangist. Two drafts emerged from these sessions: one, more radical and revolutionary, backed by González Bueno; and the other more socializing and moderate, proposed by Fernández Cuesta.[67] The latter was imposed with the support of Suanzes: its content is notable for markedly Catholic elements, the conception of the economy as something 'subordinate to politics', and the determined intervention of the state in the economy. Suanzes' ideas contributed to the fact that the *Fuero*, in spite of its fascistic character, would contain important elements of social Catholicism.

Suanzes never felt closely connected to Falangist thought. Like many others, his adoption of elements of fascism was determined, not so much by his proximity to or complete acceptance of the postulates of the Falange, but by the experience of the Civil War and the conformation of discourse, symbols and myths born at that time. His distance from Falangism can be observed in his alignment during the internal struggles of Franco's first government.

The Council of Ministers of Burgos was far from being a peaceful entity. Initially, in the midst of a victorious Civil War, the ministers maintained good relations. Progressively, however, conflicts emerged. The role of Serrano Súñer, in propaganda and in his attitude to government, invading ministerial territories that had nothing to do with his own, the Ministry of Governance, marred relations. By the summer of 1939 the situation was unsustainable.

As the Count of Rodezno wrote in his personal notes, the 'breakdown was absolute'; hardly any minister would exchange greetings with Serrano, 'either at the entrance or the exit of the Council of Ministers'.[68] Martínez Anido demonstrated his repulsion at the young and impetuous Falangists; the Treasury Minister, Amado, confessed to being 'unable to live under the same roof' as Franco's brother-in-law; Rodezno, of Justice, ridiculed anything related to Serrano; and Jordana, who had initially enjoyed cordial relations with him, complained insistently to Franco about the attitude of the Minister of Governance and 'his extreme eagerness to encroach on everything'.[69]

Suanzes, too, lined up against Serrano. His distrust of Franco's brother-in-law had begun early; in October 1938 he was absent from a Council of Ministers, pretending to be 'sick from discomfort caused by Serrano'.[70] By that time, when the defeat of the Republic seemed imminent, some international powers attempted to put some form of mediation into place between the rebels and the Republicans; Serrano, opposed to this, made a personal decision to carry out a survey among the military and notable figures of the regime that could have had the opposite effect to that intended; Suanzes, bothered by the decision and a firm supporter of total victory, refused to respond to the survey, defying the powerful minister.[71] The relationship became ever more embittered, and in March 1939, Suanzes declined the decoration awarded him by the Italian government because it was of a lower rank than that awarded his Falangist rival.[72]

By the summer of 1939 the situation was unsustainable. Vice-President Jordana had spent six months asking Franco to restructure the government. The decision of the *Caudillo* came in August: the majority of the ministers accepted their removal as a relief. In the formation of the new Cabinet the orientation and influence of Serrano took precedence. 'Those who were not among his favourites' left government. Juan Antonio Suanzes was among them.[73]

Interlude: The General Management of Naval Constructions

The zenith of the Falangist period personified by Serrano Súñer put the breaks on Suanzes's meteoric career for a time. It would not be until the fall of the Generalísimo's brother-in-law in 1941 that he would return to hold a position of high responsibility. Nevertheless, he would not remain away from political life; according to Franco's personal wishes, on 23 September 1939 he accepted his nomination as Director General of Naval Constructions.[74]

His appointment is explained by the prestige he acquired during the war years, as well as his, until that time, good relationship with the naval minister, his cousin Salvador Moreno. He would develop, in this small sphere of activity, a similar programme to that later propounded in the INI: the nationalization of the sector, stimulating production and attempting to create a state institution that would promote naval construction.

For Suanzes, a war fleet was crucial to the destiny of a country: 'without a navy there can be no Spain. Or, at least, no dignified and free Spain.'[75] Now he would be the man responsible for ensuring its existence. In the midst of the dramatic socio-economic situation of the post-war period, he began to enact his programme. He reorganized the construction of warships in Spain, suspended concessions to *La Naval*, nationalized the centres of production and created new institutions to develop them.[76] He also put forward an ambitious construction plan so that, finally, Spain would have an armada worthy of the great destiny that awaited it.[77] He also proposed the creation of an entirely state body to direct naval construction in Spain. The old naval officer from Ferrol did not achieve his proposals, however. Once again, *La Naval* blocked his path; technical difficulties, in spite of his trips to and negotiations in Italy, impeded the development of the ambitious construction plan; and Minister Moreno did not accept his proposal to create a public body.[78]

Suanzes presented his resignation to the minister, who left it to gather dust on his desk. His resignation only took effect in July 1941, after he had directed it personally to Francisco Franco.[79] In this letter he affirmed that he had run into 'the traditional obstacles, those that have always blocked the path of our businesses: private interests without control or breaks'. He had 'lacked authority'. Suanzes had lost another battle with private capital, and condensed into a single sentence his attitude and the solution for victory: 'little can be expected of state action which has neither faith nor energy'.[80] He abandoned his charge and retired to Puentedeume, in Galicia, to await the call to launch the definitive battle from the INI. In the meantime, the dreams of the old naval officer from Ferrol were shipwrecked on a Spain besieged by hunger and ration cards.

The (Long) Final Battle: The National Institute of Industry

On 25 September 1941 the National Institute of Industry (*Instituto Nacional de Industria* (INI)) was created; a body that would intervene decisively in the economy and in the industrialization of Spain, with varying results. It would appear doubtful that Suanzes was its creator. Some historians hold that the idea came from Franco himself; arguing that the IRI 'had done a lot of good in Italy', he requested a similar project from Demetrio Canceller, Minister of

Industry, in 1941.[81] Nevertheless, Suanzes was the chief inspiration: already as a minister in Bilbao he had in mind the formation of a state institution that would direct the industrialization of Spain. In fact, before the law for the creation of the INI was made public, an old collaborator congratulated him on the body's imminent creation ('Like El Cid you win battles after officially dying').[82] It is probable that it was Suanzes who commented to Franco on the need to create an institution that would force industrialization. Some time later, a key man in the Francoist regime who was surely aware of his plans, Luis Carrero Blanco, rescued the project. In only a few months the loyal sub-secretary, like Suanzes, a naval man, produced a draft law for the creation of the INI[83].

The INI was not an original institution. The Italian IRI has traditionally been recognized as its closest precursor, although the practices of 'industrial mobilisation' developed during the Great War and in the interwar years in various European countries and in Spain should also be taken into account. Suanzes wanted an industry that could, at any moment, be redirected according to the necessities of war; for this reason it was necessary to limit the free market and involve the state and army in the economy.[84]

Juan Antonio Suanzes was named President of the INI on 17 October 1941. It would appear that Franco had previously offered the presidency to José Larraz, until May of that year Minister of the Treasury, who had resigned due to his unease at the direction the dictatorship was taking economically.[85] Franco then remembered his old friend, comrade of the Crusade, loyal, hard working, with a will to sacrifice and faith in Spain.

Now the struggle continued on the front of the INI, and the lieutenant needed brave warriors. During his long presidency of the Institute (1941–63), Suanzes would demonstrate a clear predilection for motivated personnel, combining the warlike with the monastic, with faith, bravery and a spirit of sacrifice. He showed an especial predilection for military men. Perhaps influenced by Costa's regenerationist theories, he also believed in the necessity of 'iron surgeons' beyond individual interests who, with authority and faith, would direct the industrialization of the country. Suanzes looked after the 'spiritual health' of the Institute staff; there were frequent spiritual exercises and religious tutelage to lead their work in the right direction. His faith in these practices was such that, he confessed, 'If, by some divine miracle, it were possible that all Spaniards took part in them, I firmly believe that the exaltation and ... the salvation of our dear country would be guaranteed.'[86]

Suanzes attempted to recruit so many military men that the ministers of the three armies opposed him. He then resorted to higher authorities to attain his objective: in a letter to Carrero Blanco he justified his attitude by asserting the necessity of 'infusing the organisation with spirit, leadership qualities and all that is proper to the military elements'. This was vital because '*without men* I cannot adequately carry out my work, and without an indus-trial rearguard there can be no military force'.[87] The industrialization of Spain was a further stage in her rebirth, the first episode of which was the Civil War.

Here we see the high opinion in which Suanzes held the labour he had been entrusted with, and the instrument with which it was to be brought about, the INI. The Institute was the key to the future of Spain – so much so that he would protest energetically, on many occasions directly to Franco, when his authority was not respected or when the Institute received treatment that, in his opinion, undermined it. And so, in July of 1942, he directed himself to the *Caudillo*, demonstrating his unease at not having been invited to the commemorative acts of 18 July, which damaged the 'indispensable prestige of the Institute'.[88]

There were frequent rivalries and conflicts with other ministries: with Trade and Industry, over the control of fossil fuels and of *Telefónica* or the creation of an automobile industry; with the Treasury, over funding for the Institute or the intervention and control of its accounts; with the navy, over naval construction; even with Public Works. For Suanzes, the Institute had been called to a supreme labour, providential, in which nothing and nobody could interfere. The supporters of greater economic rationality or less intervention were, in his eyes, representatives of dubious individual interests that had held back the greater glory of the country.

To impose his opinion, Suanzes always resorted to his privileged relationship with Franco. Proof of this can be found in the ministerial tensions alluded to around the year 1943. His unease with other ministers had him request of the *Caudillo* the relief of his charge for reasons of health in a concise and cold letter of July 1943. Franco, as was his custom, let time pass and met his request with silence. On 25 November the president of the INI again presented his resignation in the same terms. Before the continued silence of the Generalísimo, he repeated the action on 20 December, ceding his functions to the Vice-President of the Institute. He also resigned as Attorney to the Cortes, as National Minister, and requested his separation from the service of the naval ministry. It was a high-risk strategy.[89] That same 20 December he explained to Carrero Blanco the reasons for his resignation, alleging that the work of the Institute was being boycotted by members of the government ('The Institute is being taken apart from the Government').[90] In an extensive memorandum of January 1944 that he would later send to Franco, he set out the divergences and clashes to which we have referred. He said that he had had to confront elements of the 'old politics', the interests of a few, in order to defend the supreme interest of Spain. For having battled for the well-being of his fatherland he counted, in his words, on the enmity 'of a number of ministers, of the bankers, of big industrialists, of the Pretender to the Crown, and of a series of foreign representatives'.[91]

Franco finally reacted and received him at the Palace of Pardo on 1 February 1944. He convinced Suanzes to continue at his post; Suanzes confessed to returning to his position 'lacking faith in the attempt' due to the absence of 'the support indispensable to carrying out the difficult labour with which I have been entrusted'. He declared that he would continue through loyalty and fidelity to the *Generalísimo*: 'Now and forever, and until death, you will have at your will unconditionally those well born Spaniards, such as myself, as well as their absolute loyalty.'[92] The old combatants continued in the struggle.

Francoism Enclosed: Suanzes at the Apex of Power

From 1943, the unanticipated evolution of the Second World War and the increasingly likely Allied victory worried the regime. Francoism's turn to neutrality were viewed with suspicion by more conservative elements. This could have been the case of some Carlists, such as the one who, in January 1944, wrote to Suanzes alerting him as to how the spirit of 'our Crusade' was being distorted. This was due to many 'reds' having put on 'a blue shirt' in order to approach 'the reins of power' and of, course, because 'the red-separatists return to Spain in their hundreds, as do the Masons, through the imposition of England'. Suanzes shared these ideas and fears: 'There is no other way or salvation save that of practising, entrenching and fermenting

Figure 6.3 Franco and Suanzes at a National Institute of Industry event in the 1950s.

a strictly Christian spirit ... defending it against everything and everyone, without the slightest concern for one's own life, which in such conditions is not lost, but gained'.[93] Catholicism and the nation remained one: the spirit of the Civil War, of the martyrs, of the heroes and of the labour that remained to be done was unscathed in Suanzes's mind.

Their worst fears were confirmed. In May 1945 Soviet troops entered Berlin. The defeat of the Axis had been accomplished and the future of Franco's regime was less than certain. In March of that year Don Juan de Borbón disseminated the 'Lausanne Manifesto' in which he rejected Franco's dictatorship and proposed the restoration of a constitutional monarchy in his name. On 19 June, the Conference of the United Nations meeting in San Francisco excluded Spain due to its close relationship with the defeated fascist powers. On 2 August 1945 the principal Allied powers, meeting at Potsdam, reaffirmed the decision of the United Nations, confining Spain to theoretical isolation. Franco then put his balancing acts and propaganda into play so as to not lose power. On 17 July the '*Fuero de los Españoles*' ('The Charter of the Spanish') had been enacted, which theoretically guaranteed rights and duties, now far from fascistic rhetoric. On 18 July the government had been reorganized: those ministers closest to the Third Reich were deposed, he left a limited Falangist presence and surrounded himself with Catholics of unswerving loyalty. Juan Antonio Suanzes, then named Minister of Trade and Industry, was one of these. Franco had formed a 'cabinet of ferociously loyal Francoists, a crew that could leave to one side party loyalties in the common interest of keeping the ship afloat'.[94] Finally, in October, the *Caudillo* met with his government for over a week. They then decided upon the cosmetic measures to be taken to ensure the survival of the regime: relaunching the application of the *Fuero de los Españoles*, and announcing a future law of succession, a referendum and municipal elections that would not take place until 1948.[95] On 12 October 1945 the agreements adopted appeared in the press, preceded by a note drawn up by Suanzes, giving evidence of his weight and that of his position within the regime[96].

In those deliberations Suanzes had aligned himself with the most reactionary ministers and identified himself with the well-known invariant positions of Carrero ('order, unity and endurance').[97] Suanzes perfectly embodied the archetypal Francoist profile: the experience of the Civil War had infused and augmented the amalgam of Catholicism, militarism and authoritarianism of many pre-war rightists. In a report put forward in the Council of Ministers we find evidence of his vigorous defence of the Manichean ideas so typical of Francoism that were to bring him so close to the dictator. For him, the siege of Spain was one facet of 'a great process of moral and material decomposition to which the world is being subjected'. The 'real enemy' was 'Russian communism which, as always, uses at its direct service all the forces of wickedness and treachery that have infiltrated every country'. He saw in everything an international conspiracy that hoped to trick a society 'put to sleep by the opium of democracy', attacking Spain and Franco in order to drive them 'towards a communist system and government'. He also sustained that providential and mystical conception of the Francoist regime, ' 'the only regime' that could 'point a viable way to others', 'the firmest base of militant Catholicism and of a system of life that opposed Christian spirituality to prevailing materialism'. If Franco were to disappear, in a question of 'months, perhaps weeks, the horde would have the run of Spain, and life, honour, the family and the Christian spirit would be myths dragged across the floor'. He conceived of the world in a dichotomous form: 'either Franco or chaos'; there were no 'viable and stable intermediate solutions'. There was only one path, fidelity to 'Franco and to what he represents': the key was 'total, absolute resistance, until death, with all the material and spiritual characteristics of the Crusade'. Abroad, Spain had to close in on itself, to save itself from external dangers. In the interior, as always: 'to keep morale alert and upright and maintain the spirit of service and of sacrifice'. In that Council of Ministers, Suanzes advised the displacement of the monarchists less faithful to Franco from positions of responsibility, identifying them with obscure private interests. Regarding the cosmetic reforms of the regime, he supported all save that of greater liberty for the press, as well as advising caution with regard to the calling of a referendum. It was necessary to close ranks; he even proposed a return to organizing armed militias. As the culmination of all these measures of resistance there was something no less important: to obtain a 'plan of industrialisation' that would develop the economy of the country in order to guarantee 'measures of a social character' for Spaniards.[98] His autarkic proposals, of closure to the exterior, resistance and self-sufficiency, took on greater topicality and vigour in those moments so crucial for the future of Francoism.

His appointment as minister in July of 1945 is explicable through this prism. Franco gravitated towards his loyal collaborator at one of his most critical moments, days during which the autarkic proposals of Suanzes seemed to be the best shield with which to face pronounced international isolation. This in spite of the terrible socio-economic consequences they were having.

The year 1945 saw the peak of Suanzes's power. He simultaneously occupied the presidency of the INI and the department of Trade and Industry. Finally he could carry out his work without being bothered by external interference. He had previously sent a report to Carrero in which he had maintained the necessity of 'identifying' both positions as those disposing of sufficient 'authority' to bring about his planned objectives, even suggesting some trusted names for the post of minister. Franco shared Suanzes's vision: so much so that it was him he named.[99].

In his inauguration speech, Suanzes showed himself to be the same as always. 'Enthusiastic and completely satisfied', he crowned his words with three affirmations that characterized his work: the 'spirit of justice' towards 'private interests', attempting to allay the fears of those who – with reason – identified him as a fierce partisan of state interest; 'faith', as it was necessary 'to believe' in a Spain that 'must be great'; and, of course, the eternal fidelity of that effective and industrious collaborator of Franco ('Absolute loyalty to ourselves and supreme loyalty to the Head of State, and loyalty to the country, to our Spain').[100]

The problems of the regime did not cease, however. The cause of monarchic restoration in the figure of Don Juan put the regime in one of the most complicated positions in its history. Consequent upon the action taken by the monarchist and Catholic Martín Artajo, Foreign Minister, there was to be an interview between Franco and the heir to the throne in Portugal at the beginning of 1946. In those days some monarchists had already begun to abandon the regime and explicitly advocated restoration in the figure of the Borbón heir. The best example of this was the 'Saluda' ('Note') that, on 13 February, was signed by high-ranking personalities of the regime, demonstrating their support for Don Juan and advocating a restoration in his name. Franco reacted violently and, in a heated Council of Ministers two days later, at which Suanzes was present, he brandished all the ideas related to the communist and Masonic conspiracy against the regime. 'The regime has to defend itself and sink its teeth even into the soul,' affirmed the *Caudillo*. This was to be demonstrated: the withdrawal of passports and suspension of the signatories was agreed upon.[101] Suanzes, loyal as ever, then sent a cascade of letters to those high-ranking collaborators who, in the INI or the ministry, had signed the document. To the explanations presented by these individuals following their suspension he responded with cold and identical letters, in which he regretted that 'differences in interpretation of matters deemed fundamental' prevented him from being able to continue counting on 'their valuable advice'. Loyalty to Francoism and, in short, to politics, remained above all else[102].

Epilogue: The Dejection of the Greatest Servant

The labour of Juan Antonio Suanzes rested for a long time on the myth that Francoism concerned itself with constructing. Franco and consequently Suanzes had been the artisans of Spanish industrialization. Various historians have, however, stripped the legend of its legitimacy and have demonstrated that the work of the Institute and its creator was not so beneficial for Spain.

Practically all economists coincide in affirming the limited results, above all in the 1940s, of Francoist industrial policy; some of them have even termed the period 'the night of Spanish industrialisation'.[103] Even when there were advances, various works question the opportunity costs of Spanish modernization, as well as its structural consequences.[104] In addition, some historians have highlighted the harmful consequences the work of the INI had for private initiative.[105] In complete coherence with the thought of Suanzes, the Institute not only failed to encourage private investment in the sector but hindered and impeded it.

By the 1950s the situation was unsustainable. American aid, the consequence of the agreements of 1953, gave a break to a regime that had no option but economic liberalization. This came at the end of the decade, accompanied by the technocratic ministers of *Opus Dei*, like Suanzes, Catholics and loyal to Franco, but against interventionism and economic nationalism. In those years of stabilization and economic liberalism, Suanzes and his INI became ever more of a nuisance to the system. It saw its powers progressively cut back; it lost the freedom of action and strength it had enjoyed in previous years and became dependent on the decisions of the government. The old naval officer continued to use the privilege of his closeness to Franco to recover the authority of the INI: he sent innumerable letters of resignation to the *Caudillo* in those days. All were rejected by the dictator, save for one of 1963.[106] On that occasion, Franco accepted the resignation of his old collaborator: 'I would have liked for us to have fallen together of old age in this transcendent collaboration of so many years; but it will not surprise you that I will not now fight to retain you. Your state of mind suggests that the post is now considerably affecting your resistance and your health, which you should now place at the forefront of your concerns.'[107] And there it all ended. Juan Antonio Suanzes retired from public life until his death in 1977. He made no declarations. He accepted no further positions. He refused to normalize relations with Franco. Nor did he attend the burial of his old comrade-in-arms. Certainly the engineer of Ferrol would have considered that the *Caudillo* had betrayed the ideas that had united them and for which they had struggled together in the Civil War. Ultimately, in the life of Suanzes, everything had been subordinate to politics. Even his relationship with Francisco Franco.

Endnotes

1   Real Academia de la Historia (RAH), Juan Antonio Suanzes archive (AJAS), box 1, register 2, birth certificate of Juan Antonio Suanzes, issued 17 November 1942.

2   General Archive of the Navy (AGM). Services page of Saturnino Suanzes Carpegna.

3   AGM, service record of Juan Antonio Suanzes Fernández.

4   Julio Busquets, *El militar de carrera en España* (Barcelona: Ariel, 1984), pp. 97–8. Gabriel Cardona, *El gigante descalzo. El ejército de Franco* (Madrid: Aguilar, 2008), p. 55. On this attitude among the 'cuerpos facultativos', see Antonio Cordón, *Trayectoria: memorias de un militar republicano* (Barcelona: Crítica, 1977), p. 49.

5   Stefan Houpt and José M. Ortiz-Villajos, eds, *Astilleros Españoles, 1872–1998* (Madrid: LID, 1998), pp. 95–8.

6   Carlos Navajas Zubeldia, *Estado y Sociedad en España (1923–1930)* (Logroño: Instituto de Estudios Riojanos, 1991), pp. 277–85.

7   Emilio Mola Vidal, *Obras Completas* (Vallodolid: Santarén, 1940), p. 1030.

8   Houpt and Ortiz-Villajos, *Astilleros*, p. 100.

9   Alfonso Ballestero, *Juan Antonio Suanzes, 1891–1977. La politica industrial de la postguerra* (León: LID, 1993), p. 47ff.

10 RAH, AJAS, box 36, register 2672. Letter to Francisco Cervera, 31 March 1934.

11 Ibid.

12 Ibid.

13 Ibid.

14 Ibid.

15 See the positions adopted by Indalecio Prieto and Julián Besteiro: *Diario de Sesiones de Cortes* (DSC), numbers 50 and 51, sessions 14 March 1934 and 15 March 1934 respectively.

16 DSC, No. 49, Session 13 March 1934.

17 DSC, No. 50, Session 14 March 1934.

18 RAH, AJAS, box 36, register 2672. Letter to Francisco Cervera, 31 March 1934.

19 Ballestero, *Juan Antonio Suanzes*, pp. 59–60.

20 Mercedes Cabrera, *La patronal ante la II República. Organizaciones y estrategia (1931–1936)* (Madrid: Siglo XXI, 1983), pp. 240–2.

21 Pedro Carlos González Cuevas, *Historia de las derechas españolas. De la Ilustración a nuestros días* (Madrid: Biblioteca Nueva, 2000), p. 354.

22 Sandra Souto Kustrín, *Y ¿Madrid? ¿Qué hace Madrid? Movimiento revolucionario y acción colectiva (1933–1936)* (Madrid: Siglo XXI, 2004), pp. 392–3, 400; Cabrera, *La patronal*, pp. 298–303. Quotation in pp. 302–3.

23 Ricardo de la Cierva would say of him that he belonged to a 'technocratic sector highly pleasing to Franco'. See *Historia de la guerra civil española* (Madrid: Fénix, 2006), p. 705.

24 Pedro Schwartz and Manuel Jesús González, *Una historia del Instituo Nacional de Industria (1941–1976)* (Madrid: Tecnos, 1978), pp. 25–6.

25 Years later they would maintain regular correspondence. For example, RAH, AJAS, box 102, registers 7052, 7053, 7050, year 1944.

26 Helen Graham, *The Spanish Republic at War* (Cambridge: Cambridge University Press, 2002), p. 90.

27 Ballestero, *Juan Antonio Suanzes*, pp. 66–8.

28 Juan Cervera, *Memorias de Guerra: mi labor en el Estado Mayor de la Armada afecto al Cuartel General del Generalísmo durante la Guerra de Liberación Nacional, 1936–1939* (Madrid: Editora Nacional, 1968), pp. 159–60.

29 Ángel Viñas, *Guerra, dinero, dictadura. Ayuda fascista y autarquía en la España de Franco* (Barcelona: Crítica, 1984), pp. 179–80.

30 Cervera, *Memorias*, pp. 185–9.

31 Ibid., pp. 185, 201.

32 Ibid., p. 216.

33 Francisco Cobo Romero and Teresa Ortega López, 'Pensamiento mítico y energías movilizadoras: la vivencia alegórica y ritualizada de la guerra civil en la retaguardia rebelde andaluza, 1936–1939', *Historia y Política* 16 (2006): 131–58

34 Ballestero, *Juan Antonio Suanzes*, pp. 70–1.

35 Fundación Nacional Francisco Franco (FNFF), Documento 10870, 'Carta de Camilo Alonso Vega a la viuda de José Suanzes Fernández', 27 December 1936.

36 'Oficio de Juan Cervera', 30 October 1937, in Ballastero, *Juan Antonio Suanzes*, pp. 395–6.

37 Michael Alpert, *La Guerra civil española en el mar* (Barcelona: Crítica, 2007), pp. 51, 64, 256.

38 The National Archives, Foreign Office, 371/21298. Report from the British embassy in Hendaye, 2 August 1937.

39 Ramón Serrano Súñer, *Memorias* (Barcelona: Planeta, 1977), pp. 257–8.

40 Included without reference in Ballestero, *Juan Antonio Suanzes*, pp. 391–5. Elena San Román, *Ejército e industria: el nacimiento del INI* (Barcelona: Crítica, 1999), p. 148, n. 20.

41 Ibid.

42 José María Areilza, *A lo largo del siglo* (Barcelona: Planeta, 1983), pp. 81–2.

43 José García Mercadal, *Ideario del Generalísimo* (Zaragoza: La Académica, 1937), p. 58.

44 Prior to this he had dressed in the uniform of ensign colonel. He was promoted to colonel on 19 October 1938. AGM, Service record of Juan Antonio Suanzes Fernández.

45 Areilza, *A lo largo*, p. 82.

46 RAH, AJAS, box 37, register 2719, 1938.

47 RAH, AJAS, box 37, register 2723. 'Acta de entrega del Palacio Provincial', 30 March 1938.

48 RAH, AJAS, box 36, register 2670. 'Un mes en un ministerio nuevo. Hábil designio del Caudillo', 1938.

49 RAH, AJAS, box 37, register 2717. 'Texto taquigráfico de la conferencia pronunciada por radio por el Excmo. Ministro de Industria y Comercio el día 16 de Julio de 1938'.

50   RAH, AJAS, box 37, register 2674. 'Conferencia pronunciada por S.E. el Señor Ministro de Industria y Comercio con motivo del Primer Consejo Técnico de FET y de las JONS', 29 April 1938.

51   RAH, AJAS, box 37, register 2717. 'Texto taquigráfico . . .'.

52   Josep Fontana, 'La utopía franquista: la economía de Robinson Crusoe', *Cuadernos de Historia del Derecho*, Extra (2004): 99.

53   RAH, AJAS, box 37, register 2674. 'Conferencia pronunciada . . .'.

54   San Román, *Ejército*, pp. 68–9.

55   RAH, AJAS, box 37, register 2676. 'Nota sobre política industrial del Estado para los nuevos agregados comerciales', December 1938.

56   Ibid.

57   For example, Carlos Barciela et al., *La España de Franco (1939–1975). Economía* (Madrid: Síntesis, 2001), pp. 28–30.

58   Michael Richards, *A Time of Silence, Civil War and the Culture of Repression in Franco's Spain, 1936–1945* (Cambridge University Press, 1998), pp. 2–23.

59   Ricardo De la Cierva, *Historia del franquismo. Orígenes y configuración (1939–1945)* (Barcelona: Planeta, 1975), p. 133.

60   RAH, AJAS, box 37, register 2676. 'Nota sobre política industrial . . .', pp. 6–7.

61   Such as motor and automobile, nitrogen, rubber manufacture, machinery, electrical material, cellulose, artificial silk, pharmaceutical products, film and photographic material, aniline and all types of paper, and many more. RAH, AJAS, box 37, register 2676. 'Nota sobre sobre política industrial . . .', p. 10.

62   San Román, *Ejército*, p. 76.

63   RAH, AJAS, box 37, register 2677.

64   Perhaps the most notable law was that of the Bases of Industry, 11 November 1939 (BOE, 15 December 1939). The other great regulation of that time, the Law of New Industries, 24 October 1939 (BOE, 25 October 1939) was not the work of Suanzes, following a less interventionist tendency. See San Román, *Ejército*, pp. 79–84.

65   Decree, 9 March 1938 (BOE, 10 March 1938).

66   Juan Antonio Suanzes, 'Franco and the economy'. Lecture in Burgos, 28 November 1961, in *8 discursos de Suanzes* (Madrid: INI, 1963), pp. 136–7.

67   Javier Tusell, *Franco en la Guerra Civil. Una biografía política* (Barcelona: Tusquets, 1992), pp. 257–8.

68   Cited in ibid., p. 367.

69   Francisco Gómez-Jordana Souza, *Milicia y diplomacia. Diarios del Conde de Jordana* (Burgos: Dossoles, 2002), p. 116.

70   Ibid., p. 98.

71   Tusell, *Franco en la Guerra*, pp. 215–16.

72   Gómez-Jordana Souza, Francisco, *Milicia*, p. 118.

73   Ibid., p. 129.

74 Decree, 23 September 1939 (BOE, 25 September 1939).

75 *Gaceta del Norte*, 'La entrega de premios a los marinos', 21 June 1939.

76 Law, 2 September 1939 (BOE, 30 September 1939).

77 Law, 8 September 1939 (reserved law).

78 Ballestero, *Juan Antonio Suanzes*, pp. 127–8

79 Decree, 1 July 1941 (BOE, 2 July 1941).

80 FNFF, Document 1498, 17 June 1941.

81 Law, 25 September 1941 (BOE, 30 September 1941). Schwartz and González, *Una historia*, p. 15.

82 RAH, AJAS, box 38, register 2786. Letter from J. de Zamayo, 7 September 1939.

83 San Román, *Ejército*, 158.

84 Ibid., pp. 89–92.

85 Decree, 17 October 1941 (BOE, 18 October 1941). Schwartz and González, *Una historia*, 16.

86 RAH, AJAS, box 106, register 7369, 24 November 1943.

87 The italics are underlined in the original. RAH, AJAS, box 38, register 2737, 23 July 1942.

88 RAH, AJAS, box 38, register 2736. Letter to Franco, 22 July 1942.

89 Respectively: RAH, AJAS, box 39 (registers 2788, 2789, 2790, 2791, 2792, 2793, 2803).

90 Two of his closest collaborators also resigned: Joaquín Planell, President of ENCASO, and General Dávila, advisor to the INI. RAH, AJAS, box 39 (registers 2799, 2800). Written document to Carrero: box 39, register 2807.

91 RAH, AJAS, box 39, register 2796, 10 January 1944.

92 RAH, AJAS, box 39, register 2794.

93 RAH, AJAS, box 106, register 7367. Letter from Luis Llaguno and the reply of Suanzes, 31 January 1944.

94 Paul Preston, *Caudillo de España* (Barcelona: Grijalbo, 1994), p. 671.

95 Ibid., p. 679.

96 In the Suanzes Archive there are two notes, one written by his hand, more rhetorically aggressive (box 20, register 2130, October 1945) and another typed that is much more moderate (box 20, register 2131, 9 October 1945).

97 Javier Tusell, *Franco y los católicos. La política interior y exterior española entre 1945 y 1957* (Madrid: Alianza, 1984), pp. 101–10.

98 RAH, AJAS, box 39, register 2830. 'Note about domestic and foreign policy in the present moment', 3 October 1945.

99 RAH, AJAS, box 26, register 2368, 13 July 1945.

100 RAH, AJAS, box 26, register 2367, 13 July 1945.

101 Tusell, *Franco*, p. 151.

102 Four advisors were removed from the INI: state attorney Manuel López Calderón, Mariano Traver, Antonio Melchor de la Heras and Tomás Trenor. RAH, AJAS, box 20, registers 2133, 2134, 2135, 2136, all from February 1946.

103 Albert Carreras, 'La producción industrial española, 1842–1981: construcción de un índice annual', *Revista de Historia Económica* II, 1 (1984): 144–7.

104 For example, Manuel Jesús González, 'La economía española desde el final de la Guerra civil hasta el Plan de Estabilización de 1959', in *Historia económica de España. Siglos XIX y XX*, ed. Gonzalo Anes (Barcelona: Galaxia Gutemberg-Círculo de Lectores, 1999), pp. 625–65.

105 Antonio Gómez Mendoza and Elena San Román, 'Competition between Private and Public Enterprise in Spain, 1939–1959: An Alternative View', *Business and Economic History* 26, 2 (1997): 696–707. Antonio Gómez Mendoza, ed., *De mitos y milagros. El Instituto Nacional de Autarquía (1941–1963)* (Barcelona: Duques de Soria-Universitat de Barcelona, 2000). Others believe that the actions of the INI did not influence the creation of new private enterprises: Pablo Martín Aceña and Francisco Comín, *INI, 50 años de insustrialización en España* (Madrid: Espasa-Calpe, 1991).

106 FNFF, Document 4575, 'Carta de Suanzes a Franco', 9 October 1963.

107 FNFF, Documento 4575, 'Carta de Franco a Suanzes', 11 October 1963.

7

Juan Tusquets:
A Catalan Contribution
to the Myth of the
Jewish-Bolshevik-
Masonic Conspiracy

PAUL PRESTON

One of the principal contributions to right-wing violence in the Civil War was the accusation that the Second Republic was the anti-Spanish instrument of the "Jewish-Bolshevik-Masonic Conspiracy". The idea of an evil Jewish conspiracy to destroy the Christian world went back to the middle ages but it was given a modern spin in Spain by the dissemination from 1932 onwards of *The Protocols of the Elders of Zion*. Drawing on French, German and Russian myths, this fantastical concoction purveyed the idea that a secret Jewish government, the Elders of Zion, was plotting the destruction of Christianity and Jewish world domination.[1] The first Spanish translation of *The Protocols* had been published in Leipzig in 1930. Another translation was made available in Barcelona in 1932 by a Jesuit publishing house which then serialized it in one of its magazines. Awareness and approval of *The Protocols* was helped greatly by the enormous popularity of the work of the Catalan priest, Juan Tusquets Terrats (1901–98), author of the best seller *Orígenes de la revolución española*. Tusquets was born into a wealthy banking family in Barcelona on 31 March 1901. His father was a descendant of Jewish bankers, a committed Catalanist and a friend of Francesc Cambó. His mother was a member of the fabulously wealthy Milà family, the patrons of Antoni Gaudí. As a teenager, Tusquets was also a militant Catalan nationalist. During the revolutionary disturbances of 1917, he had taken to the streets with his schoolfriends and chanted Catalanist slogans. His secondary education took place in a Jesuit school and then he studied at the University of Louvain and the Pontifical University in Tarragona, where he wrote his doctorate. He was ordained in 1926. Described by one of his ecclesiastical patrons as 'slim, supple and hyperactive', the young scholar was regarded as one of the brightest hopes of Catalan philosophy. Renowned for his piety and his enormous culture, he became a teacher in the seminary of the Catalan capital, where he was commissioned to write a book on Madame Blavatsky's theosophism. In the course of his research and in the wake of its success, he developed an obsessive interest in secret societies.[2]

Despite, or perhaps because of, his own remote Jewish origins, by the time that the Second Republic was established, his investigations into secret societies had developed into a fierce anti-Semitism and an even fiercer hatred of Freemasonry. In a further rejection of his family background, he turned violently against Catalanism and gained great notoriety by falsely accusing the Catalan leader Francesc Macià of being a Freemason.[3] Working with another priest, Joaquim Guiu Bonastre, he built up a network of what he regarded as his 'informants', that is to say, Freemasons who told him about lodge meetings. His ostentatious piety notwithstanding, Tusquets was not above spying or even burglary. One of the principal lodges in Barcelona was in the *Carrer d'Avinyó*, next to a pharmacy. Since Tusquets' aunt lived behind the pharmacy, he and Father Guiu were able to spy on the Freemasons from her flat. On one occasion, they broke into another lodge and set a fire, in order, in the ensuing confusion, to steal a series of documents. These 'researches' were the basis for the regular, and vehemently anti-Masonic, articles that he contributed to the Carlist newspaper *El Correo Catalán* and for his book *Orígenes de la revolución española*. This immensely successful book was notable both for popularizing the notion that the Second Republic was the fruit of a Jewish–Masonic conspiracy and also for publishing the names of those he considered its most sinister artificers. He later alleged that, in retaliation for his writings, the Freemasons twice tried to assassinate him. From his account, it seems that they did not try very hard. On the first occasion, he cheated death simply by getting into a taxi. On the second, he claimed, curiously, that he was saved by an escort provided by the anarcho-syndicalist newspaper *Solidaridad Obrera*. This benevolence on the part of the anarchists was all the more curious given their passionate anticlericalism.[4]

Tusquets used *The Protocols* as 'documentary' evidence of his essential thesis that the Jews were bent on the destruction of Christian civilization. Their instruments would be Freemasons and socialists who do their dirty work by means of revolution, economic catastrophes, unholy and porno-graphic propaganda and unlimited liberalism. In Spain, he denounced the Second Republic as the child of Freemasonry and accused the President, the piously Catholic Niceto Alcalá Zamora, of being both a Jew and a Freemason.[5] The message was clear – Spain and the Catholic Church could be saved only by the destruction of Jews, Freemasons and socialists, in other words, of the entire left of the political spectrum. Tusquets' book *Orígenes de la revolución española* not only sold massively but also provoked a noisy national polemic which served to give even greater currency to his ideas. His central notion that the Republic was a dictatorship in the hands of 'Judaic freemasonry' was further disseminated through his many articles in *El Correo Catalán* and a highly successful series of fifteen books (*Las Sectas*) attacking Freemasonry, communism and Judaism. The second volume of *Las Sectas* included a complete translation of *The Protocols* and also repeated his slurs on Macià.[6] Among those influenced by the publication of *The Protocols* was his brother-in-law Víctor Guillén who would give copies of it to his family and friends. After the Second World War, he would deny the existence of the Holocaust and kept a substantial museum in his house full of photographs of Hitler and Eva Braun and of Nazi flags and artefacts.[7]

So great was the wider impact of his writings that in late 1933 Tusquets was invited by the International Anti-Masonic Association to visit the recently established concentration camp at Dachau. He commented that 'they did it to show what we had to do in Spain'. Dachau was established as a camp for various groups that the Nazis wished to quarantine: political prisoners (Communist, Socialist, liberal, Catholic and monarchist opponents of the regime) and those that they defined as asocials or deviants (homosexuals, gypsies, vagrants). More than fifty years later, he would claim to have been shocked by what he saw. Nevertheless, at the time, the flow and the intensity of his anti-Semitic and anti-Masonic publications did not abate.[8]

Tusquets would come to have enormous influence within the Spanish right in general and specifically over General Franco who enthusiastically devoured his anti-Masonic and anti-Semitic diatribes.[9] However, Tusquets did more than just develop the ideas that justified violence. He was on the periphery of the military plot against the Republic through his links with Catalan Carlists. In late May 1936, he approached Joaquim Maria de Nadal, private secretary to the Catalan plutocrat, Francesc Cambó, and requested financial assistance for the forthcoming coup d'état. He was emboldened to do so because Cambó, as a friend of Tusquets' father, had written and congratulated him on the success of *Orígenes de la revolución española*. It appears that the financial help did not materialize.[10] Nevertheless, he was able to make an important contribution to the rebel cause. From the early 1930s, with the help of Joaquim Guiu, Tusquets had assiduously compiled lists of Jews and Freemasons in part on the basis of information provided by a network of what he called 'mis fieles y audaces informadores'. Their search for the enemy extended to societies of nudists, vegetarians, spiritualists and enthusiasts of Esperanto. When Tusquets finally became a collaborator of Franco in Burgos during the Civil War, his files on alleged Freemasons would provide an important part of the organizational infrastructure of the repression.[11]

With the collapse of the structures of law and order in the immediate aftermath of the military uprising, right-wingers of all kinds, industrialists, landowners and clerics, were often in danger in Republican Spain. This was especially true for Father Juan Tusquets who, given the immense notoriety achieved by his books and the polemic occasioned by his attacks on Macià, had managed to make enemies of the entire spectrum of the left. His faithful collaborator, Joaquim Guiu, would be murdered on 30 January 1939 in Collell (Gerona).[12] Tusquets' two brothers, Jaime, a lawyer, and Manuel, a pharmacy student, were civilian volunteers who supported the rebellion having been assured by Juan that 'religion was in danger from atheistic Communism'. They both died in the fighting in Barcelona in the early hours of 19 July 1936. Accordingly, Father Tusquets went into hiding, moving first to the house of Gertrudis Milà, a relative of his mother's, and then to the apartment of his brother, Magí.

The scale of the danger facing Tusquets was further underlined when Emili Blay, the husband of his sister María Teresa, was murdered in Vilafranca del Penedés on 26 July 1936. Three days later, a patrol of the anarchist FAI was about to search the building containing Magí's flat. Despite claiming to have been saved from the murderous intentions of Freemasons by anarchists, there was every reason to believe that, if the patrol caught him, they would kill him. Magí went out and found a detachment of the middle-class nationalist organization, Estat Català, which obliged the anarchists to move on without searching the building. Finally, Emili Blay's brother Andreu, who was acting Consul of Paraguay, managed to get hold of a Portuguese passport for Tusquets. On 31 July, with that document, Tusquets managed to get aboard a German ship bound for Genoa. From there he went to Rome where he stayed until the end of August. Finally, with permission from the Vatican, he made his way through France and finally reached Pamplona.[13] There, he made contact with Father Luis de Despujol Ricart, the intimate friend and collaborator of Cardinal Isidro Gomá, Archbishop of Toledo and Primate of all Spain, who had taken up residence in the Navarrese capital. Tusquets soon moved to Burgos where he looked after his bereaved sister and her two children. Amongst his numerous activities there, he assiduously maintained close relations with Gomá.[14]

Highly popular in military circles as the leading Spanish opponent of Freemasonry, Tusquets was assured of a warm reception.[15] The fact that both Mola and Franco, who were paranoid in their hatred of Freemasonry, were known to be enthusiastic readers of Tusquets ensured that he would find preferment within the Nationalist establishment. He worked for a time in Burgos with Mola, alongside one of the most sinister figures to be found on the Nationalist side, the general's friend and one-time subordinate, the policeman Julián Mauricio Carlavilla del Barrio. Carlavilla, specialized in undercover work, infiltrating left-wing groups where he would then act as an agent provocateur.[16] When General Mola became Director General of Security in early 1930, Carlavilla informed him of his clandestine activities, which he described as 'my role as catalyst within the highest circle of the revolutionaries'.[17] Between 1932 and 1936, Carlavilla had written a series of best-sellers, using the pseudonym Mauricio Karl.[18] The first, *El comunismo en España*, described the various socialist, anarchist and communist elements of the working-class movement as the enemy of Spain that would have to be defeated. The second and third, *El enemigo* and *Asesinos de España*, argued that the enemies masterminding the left-wing assassins of Spain were the Jews who controlled Freemasonry, 'their first army', the Socialist and Communist Internationals and world capitalism. The only hope of stopping the destruction of Christian civilization and the establishment of the empire of Israel lay in joining German Nazism and Italian fascism in defeating the 'sectarians of world Jewry'. He asserted that General Primo de Rivera, who died of natural causes, had been poisoned by a Jewish Freemason and that the Catalan financier, Francesc Cambó, was both Jewish and a Freemason.

One hundred thousand copies of the third of Carlavilla's books, *Asesinos de España*, were distributed free to army officers. It ended with a provocative challenge to them: describing Jews, left-wingers and Freemasons as vultures hovering over the corpse of Spain, he wrote, 'The Enemy howls with laughter while the nations that serve Zion play diplomatic dice for the cadaver's land. Thus might be the real end of Spain who was once feared by a hundred nations. And so it will be because her sons no longer know how to die. Nor how to kill.'[19]

Carlavilla was expelled from the police in 1935 as a result of what he would later describe as persecution for his anti-Masonic revelations. In May 1936, after being involved in an attempt to assassinate Manuel Azaña, he fled to Portugal. Carlavilla had lived and worked in Lisbon on the fringes of the group gathered around General Sanjurjo. Shortly after the outbreak of war, he went to Burgos where he was welcomed onto the staff of General Mola. At some point while Tusquets worked in Mola's headquarters, Carlavilla helped him scour the press for evidence of Masonic or Jewish influences.[20] Carlavilla joined the column of exiled rightists organized by Comandante Lisardo Doval.

In Salamanca, Carlavilla helped Doval organize and recruit for his column as well as briefly participating in it as a rank-and-file soldier. Doval sent him back to Portugal to buy arms and supplies for the column. There he began to work as an agent for Nicolás Franco in the Nationalist embassy, seeking out dissident Falangists. As a result of his investigations of the followers of Manuel Hedilla, in May 1937, he was the victim of an attempt on his life in Valladolid, as a result of which he returned to Portugal. He was arrested by the Portuguese police on suspicion of involvement in black market currency dealings and was expelled from Portugal. Despite his personal corruption, he was regarded as an efficient agent on behalf of Nicolás Franco.[21]

After Franco was installed in Salamanca as Head of the Nationalist State on 1 October 1936, Tusquets' stock rose rapidly. He was helped immensely by the fact that a friend and one-time fellow student from Barcelona, Father José María Bulart, at the time secretary to the Bishop of Salamanca, Enrique Plá i Deniel, was appointed chaplain to the Franco family on 4 October. Whenever Father Bulart was not available, Tusquets would go to the Episcopal Palace to say Mass for the General's family. He was also appointed tutor ('preceptor') to the dictator's daughter, Carmen. He became a frequent visitor to the *Palacio Episcopal* where the Franco family had taken up residence at the gracious insistence of Bishop Plá i Deniel. Moving frequently between Salamanca and Burgos, by November, Tusquets was also tutor to the two daughters of General Fidel Dávila, the President of the rebel 'government', *la Junta Técnica*. Luis de Despujol reported to Cardinal Gomá from Salamanca that 'Tusquets is well placed and highly thought of. His principal activity is the search for Masonic documents and everything related to that subject. The Government has set up an office with this purpose and Tusquets is employed there and indeed is the very soul of the enterprise.' Tusquets was also appointed *consejero de la Comisión de Cultura y Enseñanza de la Junta Técnica del Estado*, advising on matters relating to religious education. While Tusquets continued his anti-Masonic investigations, Carlavilla moved to Salamanca where he began to work for Nicolás Franco as a spy within the Falange.[22]

Like others who had suffered bereavement at the hands of the other side, Tusquets seems to have felt a mixture of vengefulness and suicidal thoughts. Perhaps that is why this pale and elegant priest established such a close friendship with the similarly traumatized Ramón Serrano Suñer after the *Caudillo*'s brother-in-law arrived in Salamanca on 20 February 1937. Echoing the deranged General José Millán Astray, Tusquets told a Carlist friend in Burgos 'I am in love with death. And death is the most disdainful and ungrateful lover. When she realizes that she is desired, that she is idolised, that she is truly loved, she flees, she escapes, she deserts'.[23]

Not long after Franco established his headquarters in Salamanca, Tusquet's desire for vengeance found an outlet in the office to which

Figure 7.1 Enrique Pla y Deniel, Bishop of Salamanca, giving the fascist salute. Following the military uprising, the Spanish Church supported the Francoists in a war that it labelled as a 'crusade'.

Father de Despujol had referred in his report to Cardinal Gomá. Together with Comandante Antonio Palau, he was placed in charge of the *Sección Judeo-Masónica*, the anti-Jewish and anti-Masonic section of the rebel intelligence services, the *Servicio de Información Militar*. His job was to collect and systematize all information on Freemasons, both gathered by the intelligence services and published in the Republican and international daily press. From this material, he inflated his existing lists, dossiers and files on Freemasons who were assumed to be enemies of the rebel cause. This often inaccurate information would play a crucial role in the repression. However, Tusquets was equally assiduous in exposing possible Freemasons among those who had supported the military uprising.[24] In the words of the Falangist Maximiano García Venero, 'he would seek out traces of Freemasonry in the writings, words and private conduct of supporters of the National Movement. Tusquets saw Freemasons everywhere.' He once told Ramón Garriga, a close collaborator of Serrano Suñer in the press service, that he could spot a Freemason by the way in which his handkerchief was placed in his top pocket. From this material, he wrote reports about *'nuestros adversarios'* that were sent both to the army high command and to the ecclesiastical hierarchy.[25] Cardinal Gomá was delighted and informed Cardinal Pacelli, the Vatican Secretary of State, that the military authorities were now stepping up 'the elimination of freemasonry'. He explained that 'to this end an investigative office has been set up along the lines of the French Deuxième Bureau, directed by specialists and installed within the headquarters of the President of the Government in Burgos'.[26] Tusquets himself described the scrutiny of the Republican press and of captured documentation, and the building up of his files on suspected Freemasons, as the work of the '*policía intelectual*' of the new regime.[27]

Father Tusquets complained constantly that his salary from his work was exiguous ('*petit, molt petit*'). In February 1937, he wrote to Cardinal Gomá lamenting that, from what he earned, he had to maintain his sister 'whose husband was barbarously murdered' and her two children. To increase his income, he was keen to accept an invitation from General Fidel Dávila, *Presidente de la Junta Técnica*, to join the Nationalist army's corps of chaplains. It was necessary to seek Gomá's leave to join because large numbers of Navarrese priests had simply gone to war abandoning their parishes without permission. After Gomá granted permission, Tusquets was given the rank of lieutenant ('*alférez-sacerdote*') in the army and worked briefly as a chaplain to units of the Falangist militia. He joined the Falange, figuring in the lists of the party's Catalan members.[28] Despite his new post and success as a writer and lecturer, Tusquets was still short of money and he complained to the colonel in charge of pay who came up with the solution of giving him a horse. Thereafter, whenever Tusquets needed money for his sister, he simply requested that amount to have the horse shoed.[29]

In late 1936, Franco's *Cuartel-General* had helped Tusquets set up a publishing house, *Ediciones Antisectarias*. Over the next two years, he would publish 20 volumes denouncing the sinister machinations of Spain's Jewish and Masonic enemies. Apart from four titles attributed to Tusquets, another, the rabidly anti-Semitic *El Judaísmo*, signed by the non-existent 'Barón de Santa Clara', may well have been by him. At least three of his authors also worked in the *Sección Judeo-Masónica* of the SIM and based their books on its documentation. This suggests that *Ediciones Antisectarias* functioned as the propaganda arm of the anti-Masonic section of the secret services. However, the publishing house was run as a family business owned jointly by Father Tusquets and his brother Carlos. Despite Tusquets' claims of penury, the books he published were massive best-sellers with sales in the tens of thousands. Serrano Suñer collaborated with him and wrote the prologue to his virulently anti-Semitic tract, *Masones y pacifistas*. He particularly praised Tusquets' earlier publication of the *Cuadernos de Información* which had been widely circulated amongst the retired army officers who took part in the military conspiracy and was thus a significant contribution to 'the creation of the atmosphere which led to the National uprising'.[30]

The tall, blonde-haired Tusquets was an inspiring public performer and he made lecture tours propagating his conspiratorial theories to huge and

Figure 7.2 *Masones y pacifistas* was one of the best-sellers written by Juan Tusquets during the Civil War.

appreciative audiences. In November 1936, he gave the lecture subsequently published as *La Francmasonería, crimen de lesa patria*, which went into several editions and sold massively. In it, he accused Freemasonry of being a Jewish creation, a weapon of English imperialism and responsible for the bloodshed in the Mexican and Russian revolutions. Freemasonry had, Tusquets absurdly alleged, directly organized the murder of José Calvo

Sotelo. He also described it as a cancer in the body and a poison in the veins of the nation. He claimed that among the instruments of Freemasonry were nudism, esperantism and vegetarianism – accusations that would lead to police persecution for the practitioners of such innocuous activities.[31] In the equally best-selling *Masonería y separatismo*, he blamed Freemasonry for the loss of Spain's empire and for the birth of Catalan and Basque nationalisms.[32] In a lecture given in Zaragoza on 21 March 1937, with the title '*La Masonería y el obrero*', he took his anti-Semitism to new heights, arguing that the workers' movement was the puppet of Jewish revolutionaries.[33] A regular feature of his lectures was a spine-chilling recitation of the crimes which he attributed to the Freemasons. His normally quiet delivery would turn into a howl of rage as he called for the extermination of all Freemasons in Spain.[34]

Masones y pacifistas was Tusquets' most virulently anti-Semitic tract. He blamed the Civil War on Jewish machinations:

> The determination to multiply the number of Masonic temples in Spain and turn Spain into the slave of Judaism has led to the burning of the most beautiful altars and has destroyed thousand year-old churches ... The Devil and freemasonry are motivated by the same purpose: to destroy Christian civilization, to build on its ruins the materialistic and despotic temple of Judaism.[35]

His efforts in the SIM would eventually be eclipsed by the creation and growth of the *Delegación del Estado para la Recuperación de Documentos* (DERD). Under the dynamic direction of Marcelino Ulibarri, all efforts to gather material on Freemasons and other enemies of the rebel cause were centralized. This was not entirely to the liking of Father Tusquets, who resisted efforts to make him hand over his personal archive to Ulibarri, although he did eventually collaborate with the DERD. Until the occupation of Catalonia in January 1939, he continued to work in a much reduced *Sección Judeo-Masónica* within the SIM. In 1941, a proposal was made that he be rewarded for his services by the granting of two medals, the *Medalla de campaña con distintivo de campaña* and the *Cruz roja de mérito militar*.[36]

Despite the disappointment of the clash with Ulibarri, Tusquets had become an immensely influential figure within the Nationalist zone. He had always put immense effort into creating links with those in power. His assiduous links with Cardinal Gomá and generals Franco and Dávila demonstrated his readiness to take full advantage in terms of jobs and preferment. In July 1937, for instance, he wrote a sycophantic letter congratulating Pedro Sainz Rodríguez on his recent appointment as *Jefe Nacional de Educación* within the *Junta Técnica* and offering his services.[37] He had also made successful efforts to establish a relationship with Ramón Serrano Suñer. The opportunity arose in March 1938 when the distinguished French Catholic philosopher Jacques Maritain criticized the Nationalist bombing raids on Barcelona, which he described as 'the most violent bombing carried out since air forces came into being'. He wrote that 'if humanitarian reasons alone are enough to condemn such a massacre of non-combatants, this massacre is all the more repugnant if such a thing is possible given that those responsible for the operations claim to be defending Christian civilisation'. Maritain, who was a convert to Catholicism married to a Jewish woman, was denounced as 'this converted Jew', by Ramón Serrano Suñer on 12 May and again in a speech on 19 June 1938 commemorating the fall of Bilbao. Claiming that the words of Maritain echoed *The Protocols of the Elders of Zion*, he described him as the darling of Masonic lodges and synagogues. A week after Serrano Suñer's first declaration, Joan Tusquets came out in support of the minister, publishing an article attacking Maritain for his links with Jews, Freemasons and Catalan nationalists.[38]

This paid off in early 1938, when Serrano Suñer created the *Servicio Nacional de Propaganda*, and gave Tusquets the job of selecting material which the Catholic Church would wish to see published.[39] He wrote proudly of his connections: 'I write at the orders of the ecclesiastical hierarchy. The Generalísimo approves of my campaigns. They have been supported by the Minister of the Interior Serrano Suñer.' In the autumn of 1938, on the eve of the great Nationalist offensive against Catalonia, Franco and Serrano Suñer asked him to suggest names to head the institutions to be set up by the occupying forces. On the basis of his advice, Franco selected the future Mayor of Barcelona, Miquel Mateu, and other important appointees.[40]

After the Civil War, Father Tusquets returned to Barcelona where, with Freemasonry eliminated from Spanish life, and perhaps traumatized by the activities of the occupying forces in Catalonia, he turned his back on the possibility of preferment. At the end of the war, Serrano Suñer offered him the post of *Director General de Prensa y Propaganda*. He refused on the grounds that he wished to return to his ecclesiastical duties.[41] Similarly, when Franco later offered him the position of religious adviser to the *Consejo Superior de Investigaciones Científicas*, he declined, alleging that he did not want to live in Madrid and be separated from his widowed sister and his niece and nephew. Given that in previous years, Tusquets had revelled in his closeness to the epicentres of power and had, on the grounds of penury, shamelessly sought to accumulate salaries, the refusal of two such important and well-paid posts is noteworthy. There are reasons for suspecting that he was shocked by the brutality of the occupying Francoist forces in Catalonia and perhaps felt some guilt for his part in fomenting the hatreds that drove it. Certainly, he claimed later that he had made a special effort to get people of his acquaintance out of concentration camps. This may be true but no evidence has come to light.

Figure 7.3 Priests collaborated with the rebels and carried out decisive propaganda campaigns in the Civil War. Above, Fermín Yzurdiaga, *Jefe Nacional de Propaganda* of Falange, in conversation with the Falangist leader Raimundo Fernández Cuesta.

Moreover, in several interviews, he asserted that he prevented major Catalan treasures such as the Archive of the Crown of Aragón and the *Biblioteca de Catalunya* from suffering the fate of so many other Catalan institutions whose books, documents and papers were seized and sent to Salamanca, a process which he had encouraged.[42] Having contributed so substantially to the mentality of hatred that lay behind the repression of Catalonia, it is not unreasonable to speculate that he was horrified by the practical consequences of his anti-Masonic and anti-Jewish campaigns.

Instead of accepting official preferment, he returned to religious education. He founded the journals *Formación Catequista* and *Perpectivas Pedagógicas*. *Ediciones Antisectarias* was converted into the publishing house Editorial Lumen. Under the direction of his brother Carlos, Lumen specialized in religious texts. Juan Tusquets was given a chair of Pedagogy in the University of Barcelona and wrote several books on the subject as well as on Ramón Llull, the thirteenth-century Mallorquín philosopher. Nevertheless, he remained proud of his work and of his connection with Franco, delighted to be asked occasionally for advice on issues such as student unrest. He also maintained his friendship with Franco's chaplain, José María Bulart. Throughout these years, he lived quietly in Barcelona with his widowed mother, his sister María

Teresa and her two children. The family's banking wealth had long since been dissipated.

In interviews given in old age, Juan Tusquets tried in various ways to dissociate himself from his past. He alleged that, in the early 1930s, it was his sidekick, Joaquim Guiu, and not himself, who had been obsessive about Freemasonry.[43] He denied any participation in the repression, even claiming mendaciously that he had categorically refused to let his lists of names be used by the Francoist authorities. In a tone of disgust, he distanced himself from his wartime collaborator in the compilation of lists, Mauricio Carlavilla, telling the historian Jordi Canal that Carlavilla was a 'a passionate Nazi who made up more even than Comín Colomer' – a reference to another policeman who wrote polemical books attacking the left. Tusquets tried to give his own anti-Masonic work a retrospective respectability by insinuating that it had been commissioned by the much revered liberal Cardinal Francesc Vidal i Barraquer. In fact, the only commission every given him by Vidal i Barraquer was for his book on theosophism. Vidal i Barraquer also wrote a prologue for his *Manual de catecisme*. However, he was hardly responsible for Tusquets' subsequent anti-Masonic and anti-Semitic campaigns. Indeed, Tusquets' attacks on both Francesc Macià and Niceto Alcalá Zamora had caused the Cardinal considerable embarrassment.[44]

Despite his attacks on Francesc Macià, Tusquets even claimed, somewhat incredibly, 'I always made an effort to do my work without ever renouncing my identity as a Catalan and a Catalanist, whether with Franco or with anyone else.' Even more implausibly, he claimed that, in his reports to Franco during the Civil War, he had denounced the Nazi persecution of the Jews as a result of being shocked by the visit that he made in 1934 to the concentration camp at Dachau on the invitation of the International Anti-Masonic Association. He said

... they were camps aimed at killing the Jews through exhaustion. I had gone to Germany with some hope of learning about Hitler and his promises. But I was disillusioned when I saw that it was all paganism and they were persecuting the Jews. When Franco commissioned me to do a daily resumé of the press, I did so stressing what the Nazis were doing and that the Falange with all its liturgy was just another sect, just like freemasonry.

His memory was surely faulty since, at the time of the visit, the mass detentions of Jews were still four years away. This later description is clearly coloured by what he came to know about Nazi death camps as they operated during the Second World War. When Tusquets visited Dachau in 1934, there is no way he could have known which of the prisoners happened to be Jewish since they were not yet classified as such. Moreover, his claim sits uneasily with his membership of the Falange and the fact that he continued to make anti-Semitic propaganda in his lectures and writings and did so with ever-greater vehemence as the Civil War progressed.[45]

Endnotes

1 On the genesis of the *Protocols*, see Norman Cohn, *Warrant for Genocide. The Myth of Jewish World Conspiracy and the Protocols of the Elders of Zion* (Harmonsworth: Pelican Books, 1970).

2 On Tusquets, see Antoni Mora, 'Joan Tusquets, en els 90 anys d'un home d'estudi i de combat', Institut d'Estudis Tarraconenses Ramón Berenguer IV, *Anuari 1990–1991 de la Societat d'Estudis d'Història Eclesiàstica Moderna i Contemporània de Catalunya* (Tarragona: Diputació de Tarragona, 1992), pp. 231–42; José Antonio Ferrer Benimelli, *El contubernio judeo-masónico-comunista. Del Satanismo al escándolo del P-2* (Madrid: Ediciones Istmo, 1982), pp. 191–7; Jordi Canal, 'Las campañas antisectarias de Juan Tusquets (1927–1939): Una aproximación a los orígenes del contuberio judeo-masónico-comunista en España', in José Antonio Ferrer Benimeli, ed., *La masonería en la España del siglo XX*, 2 vols (Toledo: Universidad de Castilla-La Mancha, 1996), pp. 1193–214; Javier Domínguez Arribas, 'Juan Tusquets y sus ediciones antisectarias (1936–1939)', in José Antonio Ferrer Benimeli, ed., *La masonería española en la época de Sagasta*, 2 vols (Zaragoza: Gobierno de Aragón, 2007), II, pp. 1157–96.

3 On Tusquets' accusations against Macià, see Tusquets, *Orígenes*, pp. 150–1; Juan Tusquets, *Masones y pacifistas* (Burgos: Ediciones Antisectarias, 1939), pp. 104–5; Hilari Raguer, *La Unió Democràtica de Catalunya i el seu temps (1931–1939)* (Barcelona: Publicaciones de l'Abadia de Montserrat, 1976), pp. 279–80; Arxiu Vidal i Barraquer, *Esglesia i Estat durant la Segona República espanyola 1931/1936*, 4 volumes in 8 parts (Monestir de Montserrat: Publicacions de l'Abadia de Montserrat, 1971–1990), II, pp. 386, 638, III, p. 935.

4 On the burglary and the alleged assassination attempts, see Mora, 'Joan Tusquets', pp. 234–5.

5 Tusquets, *Orígenes*, 101, 137. Alcalá Zamora wrote in protest to Archbishop Vidal i Barraquer, 26 March 1932, Arxiu Vidal i Barraquer, *Esglesia i Estat* II, pp. 644–6.

6 *Los poderes ocultos en España: Los Protocolos y su aplicación a España – Infiltraciones masónicas en el catalanismo – ¿El señor Macià es masón?* (Barcelona: Editorial Vilamala, Biblioteca Las Sectas, 1932); Tusquets, *Orígenes*, pp. 35–6, 41, 99, 126–7; Jordi Canal, 'Las campañas antisectarias', pp. 1201–7.

7 Esther Tusquets Guillén, *Habíamos ganado la guerra* (Barcelona: Editorial Bruguera, 2007), pp. 62–6.

8 Joan Subirà, *Capellans en temps de Franco* (Barcelona : Editorial Mediterrània, 1996), p. 25; interview with Lluís Bonada, *Avui*, 28 February 1990.

9 Ignasi Riera, *Los catalanes de Franco* (Barcelona: Plaza y Janés, 1998), pp. 126–7.

10 Hilari Raguer, *Salvador Rial, Vicari del Cardenal de la pau* (Barcelona: Publicacions de l'Abadia de Montserrat, 1993), p. 40; Joaquín María de Nadal, *Seis años con don Francisco Cambó (1930–1936). Memorias de un secretario político* (Barcelona: Editorial Alpha, 1957), p. 265.

11 Tusquets, *Orígenes*, pp. 51–7, 95–6, 122–6, 170, 177, 207–15. On the compilation of lists, see also the 'Declaración del testigo Francesc Casanova a la Causa General, Provincia de Barcelona, 8 June 1942', Archivo Histórico Nacional.

12 Josep M. Solé i Sabaté and Joan Villarroya i Font, *La repressió a la reraguardia de Catalunya (1936–1939)*, 2 vols (Barcelona: Publicacions de l'Abadia de Montserrat, 1989), II, p. 536.

13 Magí Tusquets was a doctor and a publisher. He was father of the architect Oscar and the publisher Esther. Antoni Mora, 'Joan Tusquets', p. 237; Ignasi Riera, *Los catalanes de Franco* (Barcelona: Plaza y Janés, 1998), pp. 126–7, 274; Jordi Canal, 'Las campañas antisectarias de Juan Tusquets (1927–1939): Una aproximación a los orígenes del contuberio judeo-masónico-comunista en España', in José Antonio Ferrer Benimeli, ed., *La masonería en la España del siglo XX*, 2 vols (Toledo: Universidad de Castilla-La Mancha, 1996), pp. 1207–8.

14 Archivo Gomá, *Documentos de la guerra civil. 1 Julio-diciembre 1936*, José Andrés-Gallego and Antón M. Pazos, eds (Madrid: Consejo Superior de Investigaciones Científicas, 2001), pp. 216–20, 488; *Documentos de la guerra civil. 3 Febrero de 1937* (Madrid: Consejo Superior de Investigaciones Científicas, 2002), pp. 55–6, 217–18; *Documentos de la guerra civil. 4 Marzo de 1937* (Madrid: Consejo Superior de Investigaciones Científicas, 2002), pp. 212–13.

15 As he put it himself, 'La meva popularitat va a repercutir entre el militars i la gent que preparava el cop d'Estat. De manera que quan aconsegueixo fugir a l'Espanya nacional, sóc rebut amb entusiasme.' Interview with Lluís Bonada, *Avui*, 28 February 1990.

16 He gave his own account of this in *Asesinos de España*, pp. 60–8, 76–81.

17 Mauricio Carlavilla, *Anti-España 1959. Autores, cómplices y encubridores del comunismo* (Madrid: Editorial NOS, 1959), pp. 18, 434–8. In his memoirs, *Obras*, p. 758, General Mola describes the work of an unnamed undercover policeman. Carlavilla, *Anti-España*, p. 436, claims that this was a reference to his activities.

18 Mauricio Karl, *Asesinos de España. Marxismo, Anarquismo, Masonería* (Madrid: Ediciones Bergua, 1935). On Carlavilla, see Southworth, *Conspiracy*, pp. 207, 212–13; Gonzalo Álvarez Chillida, *El antisemitismo en España. La imagen del judío (1812–2002)* (Madrid: Marcial Pons, 2002), pp. 320–1. According to Ricardo de la Cierva, *Bibliografía sobre la guerra de*

España (1936–1939) y sus antecedentes (Barcelona: Ariel, 1968), pp. 115, 140, 365, his name was Mauricio Carlavilla de la Vega. However, one of his later books, published when he no longer felt the need for a pseudonym, is signed 'Mauricio Carlavilla del Barrio "Mauricio Karl"', *Sodomitas* (Madrid: Editorial NOS, 1956). Mola acknowledged knowing Carlavilla well, Mola, *Obras*, 624.

19 Mauricio Karl, *Asesinos de España. Marxismo. Anarquismo. Masonería* (Madrid: Imprenta Saez Hermanos, 1936), pp. 21–4, 85–9, 196–207 (on Hitler and Mussolini), pp. 320–1 (army). On Cambó, pp. 74–5; Julio Rodríguez Puértolas, *Literatura fascista española*, 2 vols (Madrid: Ediciones Akal, 1986, 1987), I, 309; Maximiano García Venero, *Falange en la guerra civil de España: la unificación y Hedilla* (Paris, Ruedo Ibérico, 1967), 309.

20 Joaquín Arrarás, *Historia de la Cruzada española*, 8 vols, 36 books (Madrid: Ediciones Españolas, 1939–43), II, pp. 9, 503; Guillermo Cabanellas, *Los cuatro generales*, 2 vols (Barcelona: Planeta, 1977), I, p. 274.

21 Expediente 1736, Expediente personal de Julián Mauricio Carlavilla del Barrio, Archivo General del Ministerio de Interior, Doc 238, 4 March 1947, Doc 272; Maximiano García Venero, *Falange en la guerra de España: la Unificación y Hedilla* (Paris: Ruedo Ibérico, 1967), pp. 309, 343.

22 Interview with Lluís Bonada, *Avui*, 28 February 1990; interview in Joan Subirà, *Capellans en temps de Franco* (Barcelona: Editorial Mediterrania, 1996), pp. 5–16; Ramón Garriga, *La Señora de El Pardo* (Barcelona: Editorial Planeta, 1979), p. 182; Maximiano García Venero, *Falange en la guerra de España: la Unificación y Hedilla* (Paris: Ruedo Ibérico, 1967), pp. 309, 343; Interview with José María Bulart, María Mérida, *Testigos de Franco: retablo íntimo de una dictadura* (Barcelona: Plaza y Janés, 1977), p. 31; Archivo Gomá, *Documentos 1*, p. 336.

23 Antonio Pérez de Olaguer, *Lágrimas y sonrisas* (Burgos: Ediciones Antisectarias, 1938), pp. 67–8.

24 On Tusquets' role in the SIM, see Javier Domínguez Arribas, 'Juan Tusquets y sus ediciones antisectarias (1936–1939)', in José Antonio Ferrer Benimeli, ed., *La masonería española en la época de Sagasta*, 2 vols (Zaragoza: Gobierno de Aragón, 2007), II, pp. 1165–7. In the autumn of 1938, Tusquets referred to 'mi buen amigo el comandante Palau' in a letter to Gomá, José Andrés-Gallego, *¿Fascismo o Estado católico? Ideología, religión y censura en la España de Franco 1937–1941* (Madrid: Ediciones Encuentro, 1997), p. 176. He also admitted his familiarity with the material collected by the SIM, Tusquets, *Masones y pacifistas*, p. 218.

25 Testimony of Ramón Serrano Suñer to the author; García Venero, *Falange*, p. 343; Ramón Garriga, *El Cardenal Segura y el Nacional-Catolicismo* (Barcelona: Editorial Planeta, 1977), p. 200; Subirà, *Capellans*, p. 32; Ferrer Benimeli, *El contubernio judeo-masónico-comunista*, pp. 191–7; Jordi Canal, 'Las campañas antisectarias de Juan Tusquets (1927–1939): Una aproximación a los orígenes del contuberio judeo-masónico-comunista en España', in José Antonio Ferrer Benimeli, ed., *La masonería en la España del siglo XX*, 2 vols (Toledo: Universidad de Castilla-La Mancha, 1996), pp. 1207–8.

26 Gomá to Pacelli, 8 April 1937, Archivo Gomá, *Documentos de la guerra civil 5 Abril-Mayo de 1937*, José Andrés-Gallego and Antón M.Pazos (eds) (Madrid: Consejo Superior de Investigaciones Científicas, 2003), pp. 81–3.

27 Tusquets, *Masones y pacifistas*, p. 258.

28 Subirà, *Capellans*, p. 32; Tusquets to Gomá, 17 February 1937, Archivo Gomá, *Documentos de la guerra civil 3*, pp. 247–8; Hilari Raguer, *La pólvora y el incienso. La Iglesia católica y la guerra civil española (1936–1939)* (Barcelona: Ediciones Península, 2001), pp. 207–8; Joan Maria Thomàs, *Falange, guerra civil, franquisme. F.E.T. y de las J.O.N.S. de Barcelona en els primers anys de règim franquista* (Barcelona: Publicacions de L'Abadia de Montserrat, 1992), p. 465.

29 Subirà, *Capellans*, p. 32.

30 Domínguez Arribas, 'Juan Tusquets y sus ediciones antisectarias', pp. 1171–9, 1195–6; Ramón Serrano Suñer, 'Prólogo', in Juan Tusquets, *Masones y pacifistas*, p. 7.

31 Juan Tusquets, *La Francmasonería, crimen de lesa patria* (Burgos: Ediciones Antisectarias, 1936), pp. 3–4, 7–8, 13, 19, 24, 45. On his lecture style, see Pérez de Olaguer, *Lágrimas y sonrisas*, pp. 109–11.

32 Juan Tusquets, *Masonería y separatismo* (Burgos: Ediciones Antisectarias, 1937), pp. 28–34, 62–6.

33 Juan José Morales Ruiz, *El discurso antimasónico en la guerra civil española, 1936–1939* (Zaragoza: Diputación General de Aragón, 2001), pp. 335–7.

34 Antonio Ruiz Vilaplana, *Doy fe … un año de actuación en la España nacionalista* (Paris: Éditions Imprimerie Coopérative Étoile, n.d. (1938)), p. 193.

35 Tusquets, *Masones y pacifistas*, pp. 21–2, 92.

36 On Ulibarri's clash with Tusquets, see Javier Domínguez Arribas, 'Juan Tusquets y sus ediciones antisectarias (1936–1939)', in José Antonio Ferrer Benimeli, ed., *La masonería española en la época de Sagasta*, 2 vols (Zaragoza: Gobierno de Aragón, 2007), II, pp. 1167–9; Josep Cruanyes, *El papers de Salamanca. L'espoliació del patrimoni documental de Catalunya* (Barcelona: Edicions 62, 2003), pp. 234–5.

37 Pedro Sainz Rodríguez, *Testimonio y recuerdos* (Barcelona: Planeta, 1978), p. 387.

38 Herbert Rutledge Southworth, *El mito de la cruzada de Franco* (Paris: Ediciones Ruedo Ibérico, 1963), pp. 108–12; Ramón Serrano Suñer, *Siete discursos* (Bilbao: Ediciones Fe, 1938), pp. 54–7; Hilari Raguer, *La pólvora y el incienso. La Iglesia y la guerra civil española* (Barcelona: Ediciones Península, 2001), pp. 285–7. Tusquets, *Masones y pacifistas*, pp. 100–1.

39 José Andrés-Gallego, *¿Fascismo o Estado católico? Ideología, religión y censura en la España de Franco 1937–1941* (Madrid: Ediciones Encuentro, 1997), pp. 134, 161; Archivo Gomá, *Documentos de la guerra civil. 9 Enero-marzo de 1938* (Madrid: Consejo Superior de Investigaciones Científicas, 2006), pp. 302–3, 309–10, 374.

40 Tusquets, *Masones y pacifistas*, p. 257; Mora, 'Joan Tusquets', pp. 238–9; Riera, *Los catalanes de Franco*, p. 127; Canal, 'Las campañas antisectarias de Juan Tusquets', pp. 1208–9.

41 Mora, 'Joan Tusquets', pp. 238–9; Riera, *Los catalanes de Franco*, p. 127; Canal, 'Las campañas antisectarias de Juan Tusquets', pp. 1208–9.

42 Interviews with Lluís Bonada, *Avui*, 28 February 1990, with Mora, 'Joan Tusquets', p. 239, with Subirà, *Capellans*, p. 36.

43 Esther Tusquets Guillén, *Habíamos ganado la guerra*, pp. 153–6, 158–61; Mora, 'Joan Tusquets', p. 234.

44 Arxiu Vidal i Barraquer, *Esglesia i Estat durant la Segona República espanyola 1931/1936*, 4 volumes in 8 parts (Monestir de Montserrat: Publicacions de l'Abadia de Montserrat, 1971–1990), II, pp. 386, 638, 644–6; III, p. 935; Subirà, *Capellans*, p. 21.

45 Subirà, *Capellans*, p. 25 (Dachau), pp. 32–3 (Catalanism); interview with Lluís Bonada, *Avui*, 28 February 1990; interview with Antoni Mora, 'Joan Tusquets', p. 234; with Canal, 'Las campañas antisectarias de Juan Tusquets', p. 1213.

8

Antonio Vallejo Nágera: Heritage, Psychiatry and War

MICHAEL RICHARDS

In recoiling from grievous loss or fending off a fearsome future, people the world over revert to ancestral legacies.[1]

On 26 June 1936, three weeks before the military rebellion which would lead to the Civil War, a grand banquet was held in the Palace Hotel in Madrid to celebrate the awarding of the *Cruz del Mérito militar* (Cross of military merit) to the military psychiatrist Antonio Vallejo Nágera in recognition of his recent work.[2] This grand occasion is noteworthy because of its lavishness, but also because of its proximity to the outbreak of armed conflict and for the impressive list of guests who were present to join the ovation. This included many of the most illustrious figures of the Madrid political, medical and military scene at the time. Among the most important guests were, for example, Antonio Goicoechea, founder of the monarchist political organization *Renovación Española* and instigator in 1934 of an abortive coup against the Republic to be financed by Mussolini; the military officer, Jorge Vigón, part-time historian of Spain, admirer of Adolf Hitler and, like Goicoechea, equally involved in intrigue against the 'communist' government; and anti-liberal intellectual, Ramiro de Maeztu, founder in 1931, with Eugenio Vegas Latapié (who was also present), of the monarchist movement and journal *Acción Española*.[3] Thus, on the eve of war, Vallejo Nágera was already firmly associated with leading anti-republican figures, all of them linked to *Acción Española*, the journal for which he had recently published a series of articles on the 'psychopathology of anti-social conduct'. Such conduct, in Vallejo's scarcely veiled reference to the Spanish Republic, was encouraged by political freedom: 'democracy has the serious drawback that it flatters the lowest passions and gives equal value to the insane, the imbecilic and the psychopathic as it gives the wise and balanced'.[4]

The thesis of these articles, written in the lead-up to the elections of February 1936, is clear and appealed hugely to the anti-democratic movement which was about to be unleashed.[5] The diffusion of 'simplistic political doctrines' was effected, according to Vallejo Nágera, through 'psychic contagion, the true ideological key of peoples, of the political and social milieu of a country'. The clearest and most recent example to be cited was 'the communist epidemic that today afflicts society, because materialism and carnality has weakened the resistance of the social body'.[6] The presupposition was that the human species tends impulsively towards 'animal and instinctive behaviour', particularly in societies and amongst social groups which had not yet become properly civilized.[7] The psychology of 'the crowd' therefore differed little from that of children; thus, there was a need for 'the submission of the crowd to a leader', a process to be carried out through the application of the theory and practice of '*el caudillaje*' (leadership by a caudillo, or warlord).[8]

We should note here that this thesis, constructed on the eve of the Civil War, was related both to arguments in the recent past and to events about to take place in the immediate future. First, Spanish psychiatry had witnessed a significant institutional modernization during the decade prior to the procla-mation of the Second Republic, particularly with the founding of several important specialist journals and the founding of the *Asociación Española de Neuropsiquiatras* (Spanish Association of Neuropsychiatrists), in 1924 and, in 1926, of the *Liga de Higiene Mental* (Mental Health League). By the end of the 1920s there was a developing and internationally recognized movement in Spain of liberal, reformist, psychiatrists, criminologists, educationalists and anthropologists, which argued for the understanding of mental illness to be located within society and its treatment and prophylaxis to be placed in the hands of enlightened public health professionals. It had been a movement for expanded rights and greater political and moral freedom in such areas as birth control, marriage and divorce, and sexuality. This movement had been repressed under the Primo Dictatorship at the end of the 1920s but was supported by the first government of the Second Republic which articu-lated a series of reforms with the aim of achieving adequate mental hygiene provision. The reforms were to be truncated by the onset of the Civil War.

Such crucial questions as the high mortality rate, its relation to 'excessive procreation', and the spreading of infectious diseases were also central concerns of a wider, pre-Civil War, movement of eugenic reform which overlapped with mental hygiene programmes, and such polemical themes as 'defence of the race' were widely discussed.[9] Orthodox Catholics were, in turn, outraged by such neo-Malthusian 'tampering with nature' which was forbidden in the Papal Encyclical, *Casti Connubi* of December 1930, which was highly critical of sterilization laws in other states. Hence the repression of the Spanish eugenic movement before 1931; but Catholic conservatives were far from being averse to ideas about 'perfecting the race'. By 1934, figures like Vallejo Nágera would begin, under the influence of theories and practices in Nazi Germany, to reconfigure both legitimate public health concerns and the modernist fashion for genetics and to turn 'mental hygiene' into what he would call '*racial* hygiene'.

Second, with the political conflict of the period 1934–6 and the ensuing Civil War, Vallejo would develop 'racial hygiene' as the basis for a set of ideas directly related to the repression of liberalism, the Republic and of enemies of 'the Crusade'. His arguments in the cited 1935 articles in *Acción Española* explicitly prefigured the wartime psychiatric experimentation and violent political rhetoric which Vallejo would indulge in on Franco's behalf during the Civil War, contributing to the ideological orthodoxy of those in the Nationalist ranks who believed utterly and blindly in the 'Crusade' and in its repressive programme which continued into the 1940s.

* * *

Antonio Vallejo Nágera, advocate in the 1930s and 1940s of a peculiarly Catholic and authoritarian brand of 'racial hygiene', has become synonymous with the Francoist repression of the early post-Civil War years. He was the most public propagandist in Spain of the theory and practice of biological typology as the basis of a psychiatric ideology and practice to be applied to 'the masses' during the Spanish Civil War and the early 1940s. This mass 'therapy' both reflected the shared ideals of Franco's Crusade and, in turn, influenced and legitimated the Nationalist war effort and its punishment and 'treatment' of those broadly defined as 'the enemy'.

This chapter builds on what we already know and understand about the ideas and political role of Vallejo Nágera.[10] It does so by looking specifically at the period beginning with the inception of the Second Republic in 1931, which, in December 1931, as a rightist response, produced the aforementioned Catholic intellectual review *Acción Española*, and ending in the immediate aftermath of the Civil War. The end of the Civil War did not signal the end of Vallejo Nágera's ideological interventions, by any means. But by the time of the cessation of war in Europe in 1945, the Franco regime had begun a process of political reorientation and Vallejo Nágera was about to begin a slow process of resignation and some level of disillusionment.

Figure 8.1 The young Vallejo Nágera. His most productive periods coincided with the political conflicts of the 1930s.

In the early weeks of the Civil War, Vallejo became director of Franco's military psychiatric services, based in the city of Burgos where the wartime Nationalist headquarters was sited. As such, he was responsible for the administration of 14 psychiatric clinics in the Nationalist zone during the war and conducted a series of experiments on Republican prisoners, combining formal psychological tests, as used in modern psychiatric clinics, and the techniques and theories of forensic medicine, under the influence of anthro-pological measurement and a racial interpretative framework. This research into what he called 'constitutional psychopathic inferiority' clarified, according to Vallejo Nágera, the associations of heredity with criminality, a clarification which could prove useful in the political realm and in the social sciences, perhaps even in 'improving the human condition'.[11] Several problems were identified as being of particular interest; among these were the possibility of ideological 'conversions' as part of a general affective change in prisoners, and identifying the specific relationship between 'the bio-psychological qualities of the subject' and 'democratic-communist political fanaticism'. The European fascist context can be illustrated by the fact that Gestapo officers and Nazi doctors visited the camps at the same time and carried out simultaneous experiments. In return, Vallejo Nágera achieved recognition in Nazi Germany, being awarded honorary membership of the International Congress of Forensic and Social Medicine in Bonn, having presented a paper there in September 1938 on his observations of prisoner subjects.[12] Vallejo Nágera was far from being alone within the Spanish right and the scientific community in his admiration of Germany and his belief, once European war came in September 1939, that the Axis powers represented Europe's future. The conclusions drawn from these studies effectively gave scientific legit-imacy to three notions: (a) that those of a democratic disposition were likely to be suffering from an inherited inferiority; (b) that women were mentally and bodily only suited to traditional feminine roles and moral behaviour; and (c) that social revolution and revolutionary ideology in Spain were best explained on the basis of biology and psychology: the Republican war effort, in effect, was not political but criminal and this 'criminality' could be explained through the biology of body and mind.[13]

The often violent rhetoric of Vallejo Nágera's writings and declarations during and in the aftermath of the war have understandably and legitimately bolstered the case for interpreting the victors' repressive programme in Spain as a form of fascism, closely related, in certain respects, to Nazism in Germany. The comparison is worth making, though it is also problematic, not least because Nazi violence was very obviously based, in the mind of Adolf Hitler and widely in the perceptions of broader society, on questions of race. The link to racial questions was not so obvious in the case of Francoist violence, which was more evidently based on politics. The German–Spanish comparison is justified, however, when we consider the significance of the myths and metaphors of 're-birth', 'purity of blood' and 'regeneration', and the strategies based on such myths, common to both cases.[14] In the published psychiatric work of Vallejo Nágera, much of it based on empirical observation through experimen-tation (though clearly shaped in its conclusions by the ideology of National

Catholicism), we can see a concerted effort, as in Germany, to ground these racial myths, and the repressive political and cultural practices arising from them, in scientific theory: public and personal morality and the resurgence of the nation, it was argued, were founded upon biology and the body as well as upon political ideas and structures. This had profound effects on life during the Franco years and on memories of the period of war and dictatorship.

Franco's victory enabled his regime, the 'New State', to take control of public memory for decades after the Civil War. It is not surprising, therefore, that the history of victory and defeat has become enmeshed in the recent movement in favour of the recuperation of historical memory. One of the most important wartime stories to emerge has been about the sequestration of thousands of the children of executed, imprisoned or exiled opponents of the New State, secretly taken during and after the Civil War, renamed and given to families sympathetic to the new triumphant regime.[15] Whether consciously or not, the brutal process was carried out according to criteria developed in Vallejo Nágera's tracts on 'racial hygiene' and his insistence (in 1938) on 'segregation':

> The New State must take the appropriate social measures of protection against psychopaths ... the most urgent being their segregation into *labour camps* [his emphasis]. There will never be a situation as propitious as the present to take decisions with psychopaths, since those of the liberated zone are either in government prison or sentenced to imprisonment for their crimes. Unfortunately we have to recover many more psychopaths from the unredeemed zone, and realize the danger that they can infiltrate the ranks of honest citizens, since mimicry is one of their best qualities.[16]

The recent recuperation of memory has been necessary and inevitable because the Civil War and early Franco years can still be recalled by those directly affected by the events; such painful experiences inhabit a twilight zone between memory and history. One effect of this, however, is that historical contextualization has often been limited; the history as written and disseminated through the mass media as part of the necessary recuperation of memory has presented the violence within frameworks of 'fascism', 'war crimes' and the violation of 'human rights' which certainly 'speak' to present concerns but are often too simple and do not always attempt analysis and explanation of the past.[17] The question here, therefore, is whether it is possible, or beneficial, to apply the concepts and methods of social and cultural history to the theme of the psychiatric and biological aspects of the Francoist repression in order to explain it. This explanation is possible through interrogation of the closely related concepts of heritage and inheritance.

* * *

The first aim will be to gauge the significance of cultural influences and how they evolved under changing circumstances. Vallejo will be viewed from a biographical perspective to assess the range of influences on his ideology and actions. This first section explores the lineage, familial ethos and social surroundings of our subject, including questions of religion and gender, and his relationship to Castile, Spanish nationalism and a spatial sense of place. These categories will be considered through the concept of 'heritage' (*herencia*). Specifically, when we speak about heritage we are concerned with what is or may be inherited (in cultural, racial and familial terms). It should be noted here that the relation between culture and *herencia* is an underdeveloped question when investigating ideology and doctrine in the history of contemporary Spain. It is also appropriate to consider the influence of inheritance in this case since Vallejo's own works are often preoccupied with questions of marriage, procreation and heredity.[18]

The second aim is to situate Vallejo Nágera as an historical actor through analysis of his reception of and as participant in the development of theories and practices of psychiatry in Spain and Germany. The category of psychiatry will thereby be added to the concept of heritage. These theories and practices merged with the work of psychologists and educationalists and with the doctrine of the Catholic Church. It is important to remember that the specialist discourses and doctrines under analysis – those of medical science and Catholicism – formed part of a continuum going back before and extending long after the Civil War and were prevalent in many other states as responses to culturally constructed 'problems' based on 'social ills', including attacks upon what was considered by elites to be a cultural heritage. The second section thus explores several of *the works* of Vallejo Nágera. At the same time, the analysis also takes into account a range of collective and institutional responses to the dynamics of war fought within a state for 'ownership' of 'the nation'. Thus, to the categories of heritage and psychiatry must be added that of war.

Culture, Family and Heritage

It must be said that the noble class has for a long time been the chief upholder of collective memory ... Nowhere else is found such continuity of life and thought, nor is the rank of a family so clearly defined by what it and others know of its past.[19]

One approach to situating Vallejo Nágera and his way of thinking is through biography, exploring the interaction of the personal and psychological realm with the public life, allowing some sense of *the familial and cultural heritage* to register. The sphere of the family, militarist ethics and the theories and practice of psychiatry can easily be related to Vallejo's father, who was an army officer, and to his uncle, a medical doctor with leanings towards the study of mental illness. Culturally, conflict and division in Spain in the 1930s brought forth a set of ideological precepts which both appealed to the past and, in David Lowenthal's sense, attempted forcibly to make the past a central part of the present; the Civil War would condense the history of centuries in Spain going back to what we call the *Reconquista*. This process of condensing the past – the timelessness of collective memory – had genuine resonance for certain social groups.[20] For those who considered themselves to be the social elite, cultural webs of significance incorporated forebears who long pre-dated those individuals and groups who would invoke constructed memories of them.

Maurice Halbwachs, the first theorist of social memory in the 1920s, attempted to account for these overlapping 'durations' of memory which reinforced various forms of collective identity.[21] Halbwachs emphasized that the traditions by which social class identity was made, for example, were important components of 'the social frameworks of memory'.[22] Halbwachs argued that in contemporary societies, including those where noble title had become formally obsolete, certain spiritual and social activities associated with such titles were perpetuated – time-honoured codes of behaviour, religious practice, marriage patterns, the dissemination of myths, and the grouping together of professional élites. The consequent accumulation of wealth and esteem conferred were analogous to the status enjoyed by former noble classes. As Lowenthal suggests, at moments of crisis, these cultural signifiers become obvious in claims for and defence of a codified heritage. In Antonio Vallejo Nágera's Civil War writings, as we will see, a scientific discourse and discipline was conjoined with what Halbwachs called 'the nobility of race, blood and the sword', represented in a 'continuity of life and thought', and, ultimately, in this case, by Franco's war (the 'Crusade'), drawing on Catholic orthodoxy, faith in Castilian narratives of conquest and *casticismo*, and traditional ideas of family, gender and a personal sense of breeding: a form of certified identity.[23]

* * *

Antonio Vallejo Nágera was born in 1889 in the small town of Paredes de Nava in Castile, close to the ancient city of Palencia, originally a fortified Celtiberian settlement. The orthodox Catholicism and political conservatism for which he would become known were part of both a cultural and familial inheritance. Medical doctors in the Vallejo family can be traced back to 1818, the year of the birth of Vallejo Nágera's grandfather, Antonio Vallejo Sicilia, who studied medicine and became rural doctor in Villaviudas, Palencia, in preference to cultivating his agricultural holdings, and who married a local woman, María Concepción Lobón, who was from the nearby town of Torquemada. Antonio and María had two sons: Félix (Vallejo Nágera's father), who rose to the rank of lieutenant colonel in the cavalry, and Martín, Vallejo Nágera's uncle, born in 1861, who became professor in the faculties of medicine in Cádiz and Barcelona and would prove to be a great influence on his ambitious nephew. As was quite normal in this social environment, the publicly active members of the family, over several generations, were always male. The 'gentlemanly' behaviour of traditional and 'respectable' society 'protected' women; consequent social norms ensured that women would thereby be saved from 'vice'.[24]

Genealogy, the continuity of descent, can be traced through family names and through the relationship of those names to particular places. In the case of noble or influential families, genealogy is an important part of the coming together of family, history and power. According to Fernando Claramunt, former student of Vallejo Nágera and biographer and long-standing companion of Vallejo Nágera's son, Juan Antonio Vallejo-Nágera, also a well-known psychiatrist,[25] such was the case when in 1887 Félix Vallejo, Vallejo Nágera's father, married Consuelo Nágera de la Guerra, a woman from the same town in Palencia, 'joining the surnames of two noble castes'.[26] The name of Nágera de la Guerra would appear to have some association with the Battle of Nájera, fought in April 1367 near the town of Nájera in the region of Rioja Alta. 'Nágera', in Vallejo Nágera's name, was more often spelt with a 'j' – 'Nájera' – suggesting some distant connection to the place, although Vallejo Nágera apparently preferred the 'g' form because he wanted to accentuate his Castilian origins.[27] The battle, of course, was very much to do with Castile, and through it the throne of the kingdom was temporarily returned to Pedro I. The social implications were important, particularly in relation to the Jewish communities, when a long period of anti-Semitism began, culminating in 1412 with a programme of forced conversions, for example, in Vallejo Nágera's home town, Paredes de Nava. Later, from 1492 onwards, a repressive policy of uniformity, with the expulsion of Jews and of the moriscos and conversions, creating what, from post-1939 exile, the cultural historian Américo Castro would describe as distinct 'castes': 'old Christians' and 'new Christians'.[28]

As with much writing about national identity and nationalism throughout Europe in the nineteenth century and during the first third of the twentieth century, lineage, heritage and a sense of shared patrimony was often linked to the land, to landscape, and to the physicality of particular places. A sense of place is symbolized by recurrent cultural signifiers: in this specific example we should mention the Castilian countryside and climate. The harshness of climate and landscape of the Iberian plateau bolstered a sense of character, personality and identity. An identifiable *Weltanschauung* (world-view) or *paisaje interiorizado* (internalized landscape) was shaped by the physicality and perceptions of the daily life as experienced within the physical space and its history which was projected outwards beyond regional and even national boundaries. The kinship between militarism, orthodox Catholicism, the myths of Reconquest, and the glories of Castilla la Vieja, as fundaments of the political right can, in this version of the past, be traced back much further than the fifteenth century. With its extant Visigothic remains of the kingdom of Hispania in the sixth and seventh centuries and a subsequent history effectively as a frontier region during the early and middle periods of the *Reconquista*, as well as being the site of the marriage of El Cid in 1074, Palencia was susceptible to the construction of legends.[29] The settlement which centuries later became Paredes de Nava was inhabited long ago by the Vacceos, a pre-Roman, 'Spanish', people specific to the region, who passed onto local tradition a certain fame for being highly skilled horsemen. Such ancient traditions and legends were still meaningful at the end of the nineteenth century, carried on, not least, in myths perpetuated by the military regiments of the region and in the traditions which these regiments would claim to be defending in 1936. Antonio Vallejo Nágera initiated his own military career with voluntary inscription at the age of 16 in the most ancient cavalry regiment in Spain, the *Lanceros de Farnesio*, and trained at the military equestrian academy in Valladolid, directed by his cavalry officer father.[30] The Moroccan link to ancient Castilian tradition was cemented by war in North Africa in the early twentieth century and the activities of Spanish cavalry regiments there.

Identification of Castile with 'Spanishness' and, specifically, with endurance and stoicism, was not the sole preserve of the political right, of course. Idealization of Castile and the Castilian peasant's way of life was an important element of the left-of-centre intellectuals of the 'Generation of 1898', such as Miguel de Unamuno, Antonio Machado, Azorín (José Martínez Ruiz) and Pío Baroja.[31] While left-of-centre writers mythologized the peasant and the peasant way of life, however, those of the right spread their focus beyond the lowly inhabitants of Castile and perpetuated myths of superiority, of *Séneca* (the 'Spaniard'), of warfare and warrior values, of the mysticism of blood, and the history of Catholic crusades. It has been argued here, therefore, that the sense of continuity, nobility, hierarchy and inheritance, enunciated by the political right in the 1930s in relation to Castile and its values, is essential in explaining the mentality of the conservative, Catholic, right who would come to the fore during the Civil War. The focus on Visigothic roots, uniformity, expulsion and conversion, bestowing a unique *casticismo* and the rhetorical tropes of *estirpe* – the stock, lineage, race and blood – connects the personal, the public and the historical in rightist thought and action.[32]

In Catholic doctrine, the family forms the essential constitutive cell of society. For those who considered themselves 'the select', because of class position, wealth, place of birth, access to elite institutions and professions, the family was also essential to tracing a lineage and defining a particular heritage. The family of Consuelo, Vallejo Nágera's mother, was influential in the social and political life of Paredes de Nava and of Palencia. In the post-1918 period, one relative, Alejandro Nágera de la Guerra, became a leading light in the local political, literary and newspaper scene and was President of the *Federación de Sindicatos Católicos Agrarios de Palencia* (Federation of Agrarian Catholic Trade Unions of Palencia) by the early 1920s. During this period, the *Federación* was able to purchase the newspaper *El Día de Palencia* which became a significant voice in the dissemination of social Catholic ideas. In the face of agrarian conflict in the region, one editorial characteristically declared that 'the salvation of this egotistic and materialist society is in the practice of social doctrine that has its origin in the Gospel'.[33]

Vallejo Nágera was the first-born and became particularly special to his mother; perhaps this closeness explains why, unlike his father and brothers, Vallejo Nágera was not very sportsmanlike. His brother Félix, however, would also become a military doctor, while his other two brothers became army generals, 'men of action', one in the cavalry, the other on the General Staff. The significant point, however, is less the specific profession chosen by each brother than the social milieu or network within which they circulated. When in 1925 Vallejo Nágera was married, to Dolores Botas Rodríguez, daughter of the mayor of Oviedo, it was naturally a union made firmly within a well-defined social stratum and naturally extended the élite social network. The Vallejo and Nágera families were rooted in a Catholic community of shared ideas and material interests. The list of '*abuelos hidalgos*' ('noble forebears') with the name 'Vallejo' registered in the local censuses goes back to 1670. Similarly, there are records of los Nágera, a family with both Navarrese and Castilian roots, in the province of Zamora from around 1500.[34] Indeed, the family history formed a microcosm of the 'condensed' past of which we spoke earlier, its cultural reference points forming part of the timeless narrative of tradition, conservative patrimony and sense of the patria. Such a microcosm was replicated in many other families with similar cultural reference points, reinforcing the process of condensation by embedding it within and defining a particular, networked, social stratum.

This 'select' stratum understood war as a particular function of life and felt the pressure of war in particular ways. As with many leading figures of the Spanish Civil War, Vallejo Nágera grew up in the shadow of war and of cataclysmic events, primarily the military, political and social trauma of 'el Desastre' in Cuba in 1898, and the protracted struggles in North Africa. He began his career in the army's department of health in 1910, thus beginning his professional life shortly before the armed conflicts in Morocco and the European War of 1914–18. As a medical captain he was sent to Spanish Morocco, where he served in the Larache Mountain Rescue, and, according to family memory, 'was distinguished in military action'.[35] On his return, Vallejo Nágera requested a posting in Barcelona, where he could work more closely with his uncle Martín, by this time professor of pathology at the university, and it was under his uncle's sponsorship that Vallejo Nágera, in April 1917, gave his first paper on 'the prophylaxis of malaria in Morocco'.

Martín Vallejo Lobón was a highly driven, conservative Catholic, a monarchist and traditionalist; but these ideological positions were not the only influences imparted by him to his nephew. The sentiment behind the words of his inaugural lecture in June 1908 to the Real Academia de Medicina y Cirugía de Barcelona (Barcelona Royal Academy of Medicine and Surgery) seems to have rubbed off on Vallejo Nágera who was 19 at the time, an impressionable youth, completing his medical studies:

> Going through the pages of history, and studying comparatively and individually the qualities that have decorated as many men who have earned the honours of posterity … we find one that is common to all, and therefore must be indispensable for great undertakings: assertive will.[36]

Much later the young Vallejo Nágera would seize his moment in the midst of the political tumult of Spain in the 1930s and become the most prominent psychiatrist during the 'great undertaking' which was the Civil War, dominating public psychiatric discourse in the repressive era of economic and cultural autarky in the 1940s. In fact, if he had been able to predict the future, Martín Vallejo might legitimately have added the quality of opportunism to his moral prescription to pursue 'assertive will', given the political nature of career advancement, at the expense of the politically dubious and 'the defeated' in the era of the Civil War. The period of purges following the war had a profound effect on the medical profession in post-war Spain.[37] It was war which provided the opportunity for members of the traditional right to rise to the pinnacle of influence, whether in politics, intellectual life or the professions. In Vallejo Nágera's case, war had been an intermittent feature of life and on several occasions this meant a strengthening of already important German influences.

Returning to 1918, Vallejo Nágera was able to broaden his experience in a significant way when he was approached to become one of a team of delegates to the military commission of the Spanish embassy in Berlin.

Figure 8.2 The military psychiatrist Antonio Vallejo Nágera (1889–1969).

This commission was charged with inspecting the prisoner of war camps throughout Germany as part of Spain's diplomatic and humanitarian role as a neutral power on behalf of a number of belligerent nations. Vallejo Nágera had already begun to acquire a skill in the German language before the war of 1914–18 when he was studying in Barcelona with two of his brothers, probably recognizing the importance of German scholarship in psychiatry at the time. During the mission to Germany, the task of Vallejo Nágera, who was dispatched to Munich, was without doubt an arduous one and in recognition he was made a Knight of the Order of Isabella the Catholic by Alfonso

XIII in June 1919.[38] There were truly appalling conditions in Germany, with epidemic disease and great hunger. Reference to relatively few data suggest the shocking nature of the situation: the city of Dusseldorf, for example, was suffering an 80 per cent infant mortality rate in 1918; 1.75 million German soldiers died in the influenza epidemic of the time. Moreover, and significantly in suggesting influences upon Vallejo Nágera, some 72,000 people died in German psychiatric asylums during the war from hunger, disease or neglect.[39] It was thus at a time of great crisis in Germany, as the empire was about to disintegrate, that Vallejo Nágera absorbed the organic bent of psychiatry in that country, an influence which was to become evident during Spain's Civil War.[40]

To many pro-German Spanish psychiatrists, including Vallejo Nágera, the First World War and concurrent revolutions had produced a misery and disgrace of patriotic spirit across Europe that was related to mass psychoses and mental disequilibrium.[41] The dominant figure in European psychiatry at the time of the First World War was Emil Kraepelin, in political terms, a right-wing authoritarian, who established a psychiatric institute in Munich which popularized a nationally-oriented biological approach to psychiatry.[42] This form of conceptualizing psychiatry had social implications. Kraepelin believed that the rigid stratification of Imperial German society was genetically determined and that the 1918 revolution, which threatened to overturn the social hierarchy, was essentially the result of the hysterical mental disorder of the ignorant masses.[43] After the war, therefore, there was a significant anti-liberal reaction in Europe which, again, was often expressed in gendered terms. Because of the war, it was claimed by Spanish observers, women had been made 'slaves of the factory', free rein had been granted to personal, endogenous reactions (like hysteria) and psychopathic cruelty had been justified ideologically by positivist psychiatrists using the 'doctrine of social crime'.[44]

Cultural and familial myths therefore overlapped with each other in the perpetuation of networks of significance and, in Vallejo Nágera's case, this context was coloured by German intellectual and cultural stimuli and by war and revolution. These cultural and familial myths which formed the essential background seeped through into the surface of the family narrative. Thus, alongside unspoken myths to do with family breeding and heritage there was also the exchange of 'tall tales' told by family members to each other, across generations, perpetuating inaccuracies and confusions, which could, in changed circumstances, act as propaganda. For example, uncle Martín appears unwittingly to have played a retrospective role in the relativization of the politics and politicized psychiatric practice of Vallejo Nágera. So close has the identification between the two figures within the family narrative been that they occasionally merge into one and the same person. The quality of 'flexiblity', for instance, has been somewhat dubiously attributed to both

Martín and Vallejo Nágera. They were both certainly eclectic in the way they tended to flit from one set of theories to another in the course of their work, but there is little real evidence to support the argument of Claramunt, based on conversations with family members, that neither of them fell into 'fanaticism' or 'intransigence'.[45] Both men, he also argues, maintained friendships with known free-thinkers, although clearly they were not themselves in the least bit liberal. It has even been claimed that in the 1920s Vallejo Nágera enjoyed a feeling of reciprocal respect with Manuel Azaña, political figurehead of the Republic, although there clearly existed a political gulf between them.[46] The retrospective claim of mutual respect between Vallejo Nágera and Azaña ought to be viewed as a way of suggesting the reasonableness and openness of Vallejo Nágera, constructing a myth to gloss over his ideological critique of democracy during the 1930s when he described 'social agitators' and 'the directors of revolutionary movements' as the 'original bacilli of psychic epidemics'.[47]

Psychiatry and Heritage

We give thanks to the philosopher Nietzsche for the resurrection of the Spartan ideas regarding the extermination of inferior organisms and psyches, of those he calls 'parasites of society'. Modern civilization does not support such cruel postulates in the material order, but in the moral it is not afraid to put into place bloodless measures that will put the biologically defective in conditons that render impossible their reproduction and the transmission to the progeny the defects which so affect them.[48]

The weak Spanish state relied on the support of militarism and religion during modernization from the second half of the nineteenth century as the process of urbanization gathered pace. Although collective doubts remained about the value of science, the tensions inherent in modernity were seen as resolvable partly through an understanding of the modern mind. There were two identifiable psychiatric movements by the latter half of the nineteenth century in Spain: the 'mentalist' (or psychological) school and the 'organicist' (or somatic) tradition. Catholicism and militarism, as well as liberal positivism, would influence the development of these movements. Both the mentalist and the somatic schools relied to some extent on the influence of heredity and by the early twentieth century, there was a shift towards an organicist understanding of mental inheritance. While Spanish criminologists were cradled by Italian positivism, virtually all Spanish psychiatrists of the first half of the twentieth century, and not least military psychiatrists, became steeped in German organic psychiatry. The military group of psychiatrists was associated with the organic, histological, school of psychiatry, centred on Madrid, which existed in some tension with Barcelona where theory and practice, exemplified in the work of Emilio Mira López (1896–1964), an early Spanish exponent of psychoanalysis, had, by contrast, a strong psychological direction.[49] It was particularly the organicist tradition in Spain which converged with the kind of racial hygiene which Vallejo Nágera was to espouse.[50]

We have indicated how influential Antonio Vallejo Nágera's uncle, Martín Vallejo Lobón, had been from an early stage. Gradually, Vallejo Lobón was to move away from his specialism of internal medicine and become increasingly interested in psychiatry and related areas, from both an organic and Catholic point of view. In 1911 he was instrumental in reviving the journal *Revista Frenopática Barcelonesa* and he would contribute a number of papers, including one published in 1913 on the theme of 'moral madness'.[51] He was also a member of the founding junta of the Barcelona Society of Psychiatry and Neurology (*Sociedad de Psiquiatría y Neurología de Barcelona*). His nephew could hardly fail to be influenced by this turn towards medicine of the mind by one of his closest mentors. Martín was primarily known as an effective teacher and was less a brilliant or prolific academic scholar than a pedagogue and administrator. He did, as we have seen, publish a number of works which indicate his influence on Vallejo Nágera, however, especially where he attempts to reconcile orthodox religious moralism with modern scientific principles. Several of his papers were published in Catholic journals. One of them demonstrated an attempt to relativize the role of Darwinist evolutionism, arguing, as his nephew was more or less to do three decades later, for 'the perfect harmony between scientific truth and revelation, between the truths known by faith and those that we are provided by dispassionate and rational observation'.[52]

With the death of Martín Vallejo in 1919, Vallejo Nágera had been transferred to Madrid where he was involved in medical and psychiatric examinations of military recruits, until, in 1926, he became assistant director of the Ciempozuelos Military Psychiatric Clinic near Madrid. This position stimulated Vallejo Nágera's interest in both experimental and clinical activities, and in 1930 he was made director of the clinic. The following year he was named Professor of Psychiatry of the Military Medical Academy. This was the beginning of the most prolific period of Vallejo Nágera's career, coinciding with the decline of the monarchy and the political shift to the left represented by the Second Republic. This shift was of course felt by conservative Catholics like Vallejo Nágera as a brusque and unnecessary political change of direction for the country. The generalized sense of fear of modernity and reform and the threat this was seen as posing to the national heritage and patrimony were felt deeply by Catholic elites and their response took the form of a reversion to 'ancestral legacies', as suggested in the argument of David Lowenthal. In Vallejo Nágera's case, this was exemplified by the series of articles from 1935, published in *Acción Española*, on the 'psychopathology of anti-social behaviour', which were referred to earlier.

During the pre-war period of the Republic, as director of the Clinic in Ciempozuelos and as a military man and orthodox Catholic, Antonio Vallejo was somewhat removed from the more politically enlightened and reforming currents within the medical profession. The National School of Health, for example, was founded a few months before the arrival of the Republic. It was run and supported by a number of leading Republicans, including Marcelino Pascua, Gregorio Marañón and Juan Negrín.[53] Vallejo Nágera was meanwhile becoming an ever more prominent critic of the Republic, as his contributions to *Acción Española* and his association with leading anti-republican plotters in June 1936 confirm, and he was feeling the need to propagandize on behalf of his work at Ciempozuelos.[54]

Although Vallejo Nágera was above all eclectic in his research, his writings contributed to experimentation and debate in two identifiable areas. The first was essentially focused on the meeting point of psychiatry and biology; we can sum this up as an organic approach to psychopathology, initially designed for consumption by scientific peers, but with increasingly clear political implications in the conflictive 1930s. The second area was more immediately ideological and appealed to a broader audience. These more popular works were based rhetorically on scientific argumentation and therefore had a veneer of scientific authority. Thus, it is not possible to view Antonio Vallejo's professional work in isolation from his political fixations. Psychopathology, conservative nationalism and a Catholic concern with conscience and the soul came together in his work, as a broadly chronological account of his work will demonstrate.[55]

Vallejo Nágera's doctoral thesis of 1930 dealt with simulated mental syndromes, reflecting a career-long interest in simulation and the moral underpinnings of the imitation of pathological states, which was founded on his involvement in military conscription and recruitment. Simulators, according to his findings, had certain identifiable and innate qualities and bodily (or 'constitutional') features which predisposed them to 'tenacity' and 'insensibility' with the objective of defrauding clinicians and benefiting economically.[56] Such arguments would influence his later warnings about revolutionaries (and revolutionary women, in particular, as well as the children of republicans) and their alleged propensity to mimicry, a way in which revolutions spread and became more dangerous.[57]

The coming together of the medical and the political in Vallejo Nágera's publications coincided with the most conflictive period of the Second Republic, especially from 1934. There was a hardening anti-democratic tone from this time, but Antonio Vallejo seems not to have been a ubiquitous figure in terms of public and explicit anti-Republican statements prior to July 1936. However, the long and often overlooked article on the pathology of 'anti-social behaviour', written in 1935 and published in three parts in *Acción Española*, can be viewed as one of his key works because it explicitly brought psychiatric observation and politics together, in the context of the political strife of the Republic.[58] Here the notion of 'behaviourism' was introduced as a key to understanding the individual personality. Once behaviour was observed, it was argued, the role of inheritance and of physical constitution all became crucial in determining temperament, character and intelligence. Vallejo Nágera would take advantage of the conditions of Civil War to develop this bio-typological approach to encompass society and the collective mind.[59]

As we saw at the beginning, the Second Republic provided a wide arena for a renewed interest in 'the health of the race', largely because many prominent liberals believed that social ills could be resolved through the application of eugenic theories. Many of these intellectuals became politically active in 1931. Vallejo Nágera was a close observer of these developments, but was less interested in the modernizing potential of measures of medical and mental hygiene than in the specific role of heredity in individual and collective pathology which threatened the social status quo and traditional values. As an orthodox Catholic he adhered to papal teachings on sterilization.[60] Contrary to some observers, this did not mean that Vallejo Nágera was particularly critical of the Nazi regime in Germany;[61] as we have seen, he was steeped in German militarist-authoritarian and psychiatric thinking and remained so long after the Spanish war. Vallejo Nágera's brand of racial hygiene was an offshoot of the Latin eugenics movement (including France, Italy and South America), however influenced by the environmental realm indicated by Catholicism and Lamarckism, and distinct from the 'Nordic eugenics' of Britain and Germany which followed the more rigid Mendelian 'laws of inheritance'.[62] Rather than bringing forward 'negative' measures to restrict the fertility of 'moral imbeciles', the emphasis was on 'positive' eugenics to encourage 'healthy' marriages and births. Inevitably, even this 'softer' version of race hygiene involved ideological incentives to follow the prescribed moral path, particularly for women.[63]

Vallejo Nágera agreed with the National Socialists in Germany that each race has a particular cultural significance and heritage, and warned of the danger to Spain of degeneration in 1934:

> Either we can let ourselves be drawn by the positivist and materialist currents that dominate in the greater part of the world, or, with the Italian and German people, we [can] return to the foreground, to demand the recuperation of our spiritual and racial valour that allowed us to civilize

immense lands still linked to the Spanish Motherland, after a century of material independence, by racial and cultural ties.[64]

He argued that the modern eugenic positivists of the Republic 'nullify' the individual and threaten to destroy the family. His distinction between eugenics and racial hygiene was based on the argument that the former had a 'reduced horizon', limiting itself 'to the conservation of the healthy genes of all the people', while the latter was preferable because it aimed for 'high spiritual values', to perfect the men within the pueblo who were 'superior'.

These factors were important in the development of the conservative ideology of those who would become the rebels in July 1936 which would ascribe particular meanings to allegiances of social class and other forms of identity, including political identities. Vallejo Nágera's *Eugenesia de la hispanidad*, published in 1937, but at least partly written as early as March 1936, is a case in point in the way it advocates 'segregation'. It is illustrative, indeed, of the way in which heritage can become 'a byword for bellicose discord, exalting rooted faith over critical reason':[65]

The war will create the lineage of Knights that are needed in the New Spain, and will revalue the pedigree of spiritual nobility. Distinctive of the sides in the fight will be aristocracy in the thought and feeling of the Knights of *Hispanidad* [Spanishness]; moral plebeianism in the foot-soldiers of Marxism.[66]

Pre-war social distinctions, between believers and unbelievers, deserving and undeserving, and good and evil, were activated by the new correlation of social forces unleashed by war, and the ideas of Vallejo Nágera came fully into their own.[67] German romantic nationalism was an inevitable storehouse for manipulation, as illustrated in Vallejo Nágera's homage to Nietzsche, cited at the beginning of this section, where the focus on inheritance potentially placed children at the centre of the perceived threat from the 'dangerous classes'.

The context of warfare and mass imprisonment made possible the psychiatric studies of republican prisoners directed by Antonio Vallejo Nágera, referred to earlier. The theories behind the studies were not new: as we have seen, bio-criminological ideas had been significant in Spain and internationally since the nineteenth century, widely discussed by both liberals and conservatives, including Catholics, before the 1930s. What had changed was the political situation and the nature of the nascent Francoist state. In this context, the psycho-anthropological experiments on prisoners had the effect of confirming and legitimizing the degrading segregation of those who had been conquered and captured. The studies provided an opportunity for

Vallejo Nágera to test the validity of his previous postulates about a number of questions: the reliability of existing typologies of mind and body; the variation in psyche according to constructed ethnic, geographic and racial heritage; the role of sex in revolutionary allegiances and behaviour; the extent of simulation and revolutionary mimicry; and of 'degeneracy' and 'mental deficiency'; and the effects of wartime conditions on subjects of varying cultural background and religion.

The subject matter of these studies was composed primarily of groups of male political prisoners: 'Spanish Republicans' ('the agents and propagandists of Marxism'); Basque 'separatists' (of unique interest because they 'unite political and religious fanaticism'); Catalan 'Marxists' (within whom were found both Marxist and 'anti-Spanish' fanaticism); and foreign Republican prisoners (volunteers of the International Brigades) from Latin America, Britain, Portugal and the United States. The examinations combined bio-metric investigation with psychological typification. These included detailed measurements of the length, breadth and depth of the skull, the genitals, the distance between the eyes, the length of the nose, the abundance and placement of body hair, and description of skin colour, indicating any 'morphological stigmatization'. Spoken responses to questioning were used to identify the type of primary temperamental reaction of subjects, sorting them into the 'introverted' and 'extroverted', and 'mental age' was determined by adaptation of a psychological intelligence scale. The 'moral activity' of each subject was gauged by completion of a 200-item questionnaire with information about family, sexual, political, religious and military antecedents. These were based on the form of interrogation introduced in Nazi-run centres of biological-criminal investigation, principally in Munich, which graded political prisoners and racial enemies according to a 'biological-hereditary inventory'.

Investigation of the 'family tree', including parents and siblings, with questions referring to drunkenness, criminality, social position, spiritual predispositions, state of mind, and characterological properties, such as temperament, level of education, types of psychic reaction, and familial conduct, indicated the familial heritage of subjects. Other 'anomalies' of the family, such as 'pauperism', emigration, illegitimacy, economic crises and mental illness, were minutely annotated. Questions referring to the record of the female parent as housewife and mother, miscarriages or abortions, her reputation in the neighbourhood, her moral and educating qualities and her inclination to controversy and to adorning her person, completed this part of the process. Then, the prisoners' own education, religiosity, propensity towards begging, moral background relating to crime, alcohol, work, family break-ups, conduct during military service, spouses, children (their antecedents, state of mind, criminality), health (from childhood), type of behaviour when inebriated, and personal attitudes towards crime were recorded. It was found that the majority in all of these groups were 'degen-erate', and it was concluded that the materialism of Marxism was attractive to 'mental retards': 'The simplicity of Marxist ideology and the social equality it advocates promotes its uptake by the mentally deficient, who find in the material goods offered by communism and democracy the satisfaction of the lowest human appetites.'[68]

A further study into the 'psyche of Marxist fanaticism' of 50 of the 900 women held in the provincial prison of the occupied city of Malaga completed the series of investigations.[69] Vallejo Nágera maintained that study of the 'criminal pathological form' during the Civil War confirmed 'the feminine cruelty of woman' when she had lost her religious sentiments and 'operates exclusively stimulated by her natural tendencies'.[70] These female 'Marxist delinquents' had been tried by councils of war, according to the preamble to the study's findings, for 'horrific murders, burnings and sackings' and 'egging-on' their men folk to all kinds of disorders. Thirty-three of them had been sentenced to the death penalty by a military court for crimes against the patria, although the 'magnanimous' General Franco commuted the death sentences to life imprisonment (30 years) for those who took part in the experiments. In fact, most women were in prison because of some political association – attending political meetings of the left, encouraging the so-called 'rebels' (i.e., Republicans), 'making statements hostile to the Glorious National Movement' – or for transgressing social norms – being 'talkative', 'inciting to rebellion', giving shelter to 'fugitives', going beyond 'normal' female behaviour. Virtually all of the women in prison for 'political crimes' in Malaga were from the very poorest areas and many of them were young. Domestic maids were frequently caught up in the repressive aftermath of the occupation and female servants were consciously targeted for religious education and spiritual exercises in the early years of 'liberation'.[71]

The roots of the mental conditions from which the 50 Malaga women prisoners were said to be suffering were 'confirmed' in the experiments as hereditary and 'genetic'. Among the parents, siblings and other blood relations of the subjects were a high proportion of 'mentally sick', 'psychopaths', 'criminals', 'bigots', 'vagrants', 'homosexuals', 'alcoholics' and 'suicides'. Many were 'revolutionaries' or 'non-Catholics', and this 'in a country which had fought for Catholicism' and in which the racially 'select' were 'esteemed as Catholics'. It was concluded that 36 of these women (72 per cent) had 'degenerative temperaments'. Some revealed defects which were the 'collateral inheritance of schizoid or cycloid bases', but most were drawn to 'hysteroid criminality', a category not used in the male studies.[72] Only 11 (22 per cent) had 'normal' female personalities, which meant 'being moral', working, living a social life without conflicts, being non-delinquent, and not given to 'sexual perversity', kept on the path of virtue by piety, maternity and constitutional weakness. Thirteen were 'born revolutionaries', a variant of the questionable positivist category of 'innate criminality'. In other words, the women instinctively sought to overturn the social order because of the congenital peculiarities of their bio-psychic constitutions. Twelve were described as 'anti-social psychopaths' and drastic implications were spelled out: 'If participating in Marxism is the preference of anti-social psychopaths, as is our idea, the segregation of these subjects from infancy could rid society of such a frightening plague.'[73] Those remaining without categorization were part of the multitude of uncultivated, crude, 'suggestible beings', lacking spontaneity or initiative, 'who form the majority of anonymous people', and were condemned as 'social or moral imbeciles'. Overall, while the masses in rebel Spain displayed 'constructive affective factors of the New Spain', the republican multitude was possessed of a 'infantile psychology' and its actions determined by 'human passions' rather than spiritual values.[74]

* * *

Dedication to the rebel war effort catapulted Vallejo Nágera to the top of his profession. In January 1939 he was made Head of Military Health in the recently occupied territory of Barcelona, before being moved to Madrid in April as head of the neuro-psychiatric services of the Military Hospital. Somewhat controversially, he was appointed first Professor of Psychiatry in Madrid in 1942, being favoured above Juan José López Ibor who was considered to have monarchist sympathies.[75] Vallejo Nágera was also an official ministerial advisor to the Spanish government in the early 1940s, on education policy (from 1941) and on health (from 1943) and became President of the Spanish Association of Neuropsychiatry in the early 1950s.

As the Second World War drew to an end, Vallejo Nágera refused bluntly to believe that the horrific atrocities committed by Germans, and in the name of Germany, in the wartime extermination camps had really happened. His experience of German prisoner of war camps during the First World War had demonstrated, as he saw it, the gentlemanly, military spirit of German officers which made such happenings simply impossible; the claims of the Allies in 1944 were, as he saw it, simply politically motivated calumnies. News filtered into Spain, however; the tragic scenes accompanying the liberation of the camps were detailed minute by minute through the radio and the truth could not be denied: 'In 1945, the Berlin Bunker sinks and the rubble of cement and twisted iron falls above the head of Don Antonio.'[76] There is a certain irony in the fact that, as his influence reached its zenith, many of Vallejo Nágera's ideas became somewhat discredited and he entered a period of professional life marked by resignation rather than celebration, though his influence was kept alive because he had reached a place of prominence at the high-point of the

Figure 8.3 Antonio Vallejo Nágera's racist ideas became partially discredited and his political influence diminished after 1945.

'Crusade'. Although he continued to maintain an ideologically-informed belief in pro-natalism, after 1945 his works show signs of a half-hearted concern with matters to do with the mundane problems of peace and reconstruction.

Conclusions

The determinism of the concepts of 'Nation' and 'race', invariably accompanied by myths of blood, heritage, and inheritance, can be illustrated by exploring the intersection of science and the state. If something is said to be 'in the blood' or 'in the genes', it is claimed to be immutable and there is no easy counter-argument to be put against it, especially if it is supported by scientists. The truism of blood determinism applies both to the public and the private sphere. Biology (backed up by history) seems to be more powerful than sociology; claims to racial purity or superiority are deemed to be more determinant than those of social class, of socio-economic inequality, or political ideals, such as democracy. Franco's mythical Crusade drew upon primordial cultural reference points; several of these were present in the psychiatric discourse discussed in this chapter. The psychiatric and biological postulates developed by Vallejo Nágera were founded upon the traditions, symbolism and history which formed the cultural strands which bound together the network of shared beliefs and understandings of the Nationalist Catholic elite of which he was a member. This milieu of values, social relationships and practices, which seemed to have existed since time immemorial, were placed in danger of degeneration by 1931 with the arrival of the Second Republic. Vallejo Nágera thus became publicly involved with the struggle to defend all that was 'natural' and 'pure'; all of that which formed a particular national patrimony and familial inheritance.

The anti-reform struggle is also explicable, in fact, through analysis of the domestic or private realm, a microcosm of the broader cultural realm. The pride in lineage is palpable in the history of families of a particular class, a lineage which is deeply immersed in Catholic faith, in material values and interests, and in the very idea of the family as the moral, 'genetic' or 'bodily' wellspring of a hierarchical and value-laden idea of the nation and of community. This applied not merely to an aristocratic few but to substantial sections of the urban, rural and provincial middle classes. Antonio Vallejo Nágera was a product of a family of soldiers and doctors (and female child-bearers and rearers) which daily, through time-honoured practices, put eternal values into operation and reinforced and linked those living in the present with past generations and, it was assumed and hoped, with generations to come. Catholic, middle class, family life bonded a numerous and influential section of society to a conservative sense of patriotism. In its hymning of this peculiar heritage, the Civil War and its trials and torments cemented the process and its aftermath shaped the inward and backward-looking, nationalist doctrine of Francoism, reliant on a restrictively narrow inheritance. This inheritance would mire Spanish society for two decades in the obsolescence of National

Catholicism, until the desires of mass consumerism and modernity would lead, if not to political freedom, at least to the 1960s' cultural escape from the past.

Endnotes

1   David Lowenthal, *The Heritage Crusade and the Spoils of History* (Cambridge: Cambridge University Press, 1998), p. xiii.

2   *ABC*, 27 June 1936, 28. The award was specifically in relation to the book *Propedéutica clínica psiquiátrica* (Barcelona: Labor, 1936), which explored the biological roots of temperament and behaviour. *Gaceta de Madrid*, 28 June 1936, No. 180, 2722. Vallejo Nágera had received similar decorations before, although this latest was more prestigious because it came with a pension.

3   Those involved in intrigue against the Republic, all associated with *Renovación Española* and *Acción Española*, took advantage of such social occasions to meet and discuss. See, e.g., Paul Preston, *Franco* (London: HarperCollins, 1993), p. 110. After the assassination of Calvo Sotelo in July 1936, Vegas Latapié became heavily involved in a reprisal plot to murder the President of the Republic, Manuel Azaña. Hilari Raguer, *La pólvora y el incienso: la Iglesia y la guerra civil española, 1936–1939* (Barcelona: Ediciones Península, 2001), p. 63.

4   Antonio Vallejo Nágera, 'Psicopatología de la conducta antisocial', I, *Acción Española*, No. 82, December 1935, 520. Parts II and III, in *Acción Española*, Nos 83–4, January–February 1936.

5   These articles received a wider dissemination when published in book form at the height of the Civil War: *Psicopatología de la conducta antisocial* (San Sebastián: Editorial Española, 1938). Pre-war 'findings' about the alleged link between democracy and the left and psychopathology would achieve greater legitimacy amongst adherents to the 'Crusade' once the level of violence increased hugely with civil war. To reinforce the point, sections of the pre-war 1935 articles appeared unchanged in other wartime works. See, e.g., *La locura y la guerra: Psicopatología de la guerra española* (Valladolid: Santarén, 1939).

6   'Psicopatología de la conducta', III, 289–90.

7   'El pecado original no es un mito, es un fenómeno biológico', *ibid.*, 285–6.

8   *Ibid.*, 288, 295.

9   For concerns that in order to avoid high infant mortality rate women should have fewer births, see Gregorio Marañón, *Tres ensayos sobre la vida sexual* (Madrid: Biblioteca Nueva, 1926).

10   The first, rather isolated, paper by a historian on Vallejo Nágera's Civil War activities consisted of a reproduction of a report of wartime psychological experimentation in Málaga with a short commentary authored by Antonio Nadal Sánchez: 'Experiencias psíquicas sobre mujeres marxistas

malagueñas: Málaga, 1939', in *Las mujeres y la guerra civil española* (Madrid: Ministerio de Cultura, 1991), pp. 340–50. Nadal's paper was the inspiration for the attempt to ground the Málaga experiments in social and cultural history in Michael Richards, 'Morality and Biology in the Spanish Civil War: Psychiatrists, Revolution and Women Prisoners in Málaga', *Contemporary European History*, 10, 3 (November 2001): 395–421. Vallejo had not figured prominently even in the historiography of medicine in Spain. An early post-Franco account (1977) which mentions him critically is by a psychiatrist: Carlos Castilla del Pino, 'La psiquiatría española (1939–1975)', in Castilla del Pino, ed., *La cultura bajo el franquismo* (Barcelona: Ediciones de Bolsillo, 1977), pp. 79–103. For a survey of mental medicine during the Civil War, see Antonio Carreras Panchón, 'Los psiquiatras españoles y la guerra civil', in *Medicina e historia*, 13 (1986): i–xvi. For later media interest in Vallejo's programs of tests on Civil War prisoners, see, e.g., Rodolfo Serrano, 'En busca del "gen rojo"', *El País*, 7 January 1996, which was loosely based on a short academic paper: Javier Bandrés and Rafael Llavona, 'La psicología en los campos de concentración de Franco', in *Psicothema*, 8, No. 1 (1996): 1–11. Media reports were taken up in other countries in a misleading manner. See, e.g., 'Du marxisme considéré comme une maladie mentale', *Le Monde*, 25 January 1996, reproduced in *The Guardian*, 31 January, 1996. For Vallejo interpreted as part of a broad 'culture of repression', see Michael Richards, *A Time of Silence: Civil War and the Culture of Repression in Franco's Spain* (Cambridge: CUP, 1998). With later access to archives, monographic study of related themes has been possible. See, e.g., Javier Rodrigo, *Cautivos: Campos de concentración en la España franquista, 1936–1947* (Barcelona: Crítica, 2005), pp. 128–66.

11 Vallejo Nágera had previously conducted hundreds of psychiatric and forensic examinations as a military psychiatrist. *La locura y la guerra: psicopatología de la guerra española* (Valladolid: Librería Santarén, 1939), p. 52.

12 'Psychiatrische beobachtungen im Spanischen krieg', *Internationaler Kongress für gerichtliche und soziale Medizin* (Bonn: Scheur, 1938), pp. 512–17.

13 Richards, 'Morality and Biology'.

14 For the ideological common rationale, based on palingenetic myth, of various fascist regimes and movements, see Roger Griffin, *The Nature of Fascism* (London: Routledge, 1991). For the concept of racial regeneration in Vallejo Nágera's work, see *Eugenesia de la hispanidad y regeneración de la raza* (Burgos: Editorial Española, 1937). For Griffin's selection of a passage from Vallejo Nágera's book, see Griffin, ed., *Fascism* (Oxford: Oxford University Press, 1995), pp. 190–1.

15 See Ricard Vinyes et al., *Los niños perdidos del franquismo* (Barcelona: Plaza y Janés, 2002) and the associated television documentary, *Els nens perduts del franquisme*, shown by Catalan television (TV-3), which played an important part in reuniting republican families split apart by the war. For the psychological, eugenic and European context, see Michael Richards, 'Ideology and Psychology of War Children in Franco's Spain, 1936–1945', in Kjersti Ericsson and Eva Simonsen, *Children of World War II: The Hidden Enemy Legacy* (Oxford: Berg, 2005), pp. 115–37.

16 Antonio Vallejo Nágera, *Política racial del nuevo estado* (San Sebastián: Editorial Española, 1938), p. 90.

17 Taken to extremes, Vallejo Nágera can be depicted in simple terms as a figure associated with 'evil' and, therefore, as an aberration rather than a phenomenon explicable in historical terms and in relation to broader phenomena which made such acts possible: '*el doctor Mengele de la psiquiatría franquista*'. See Joan B. Culla i Clarà, 'La historia, ese viejo estorbo', El País, 1 February 2002.

18 On 'healthy' marriage, see, e.g., *Higiene de la raza: La asexualización de los psicópatas* (Madrid: Ediciones Medicina, 1934); *Eugamia: Selección de novios* (San Sebastián: Editorial Española, 1938); *Antes que te cases* (Madrid: Editorial Plus Ultra, 1944).

19 Maurice Halbwachs (ed. Lewis A. Coser), *On Collective Memory* (London: University of Chicago Press, 1992), p. 128.

20 See Richards, *Time of Silence*, p. 9.

21 Halbwachs' use of the notion of 'duration' originated in his pre-Durkheim period when he studied with Henri Bergson and his interest in *place* as a determinant of memory (to be explored later) originated in his association with the Annales school of history in Strasbourg.

22 Maurice Halbwachs, *Les cadres sociaux de la mémoire* (Paris: Presses Universitaires de France, 1925).

23 Halbwachs (ed. Coser), *Collective Memory*, p. 128.

24 For '*el caballero cristiano*' as '*un tipo ideal*' in Spain and the '*culto del honor*' as the '*el fondo mismo de la psicología hispánica*', see, e.g., Manuel García Morente, *Idea de la hispanidad* (Madrid: Espasa Calpe, 1947 (originally, 1938)), pp. 55–7; 74–7.

25 Fernando Claramunt first met Antonio Vallejo Nágera, of whom he was clearly a great admirer, in 1953 when he became the professor's doctoral student.

26 Fernando Claramunt, *Juan Antonio Vallejo-Nágera* (Madrid: Espasa Calpe, 1993), p. 25.

27 Nájera (with a 'j') also has historical links to Castile, however. The Camino de Santiago, for example, links Nájera, one of the route's stages, with Burgos.

28 See Américo Castro, *España en su historia: Cristianos, moros y judíos* (Buenos Aires: Losada, 1948), revised as *La realidad histórica de España* (Mexico: Porrúa, 1954), works of cultural history, but ultimately a response to Spain's Civil War.

29 For the critique of the simple, racially-founded, warrior myths, see Castro, *La realidad histórica*.

30 Hoja matriz de servicios. See Carlos Molero Colina, *Lanceros de Farnesio* (Valladolid: Diputación, 2000).

31 José Enrique Martínez, *Generación del 98: Antología* (Zaragoza: Luis Vives, 1991); Miguel de Unamuno, *En torno al casticismo* (Madrid: Espasa Calpe, 1943 (original, 1895)); Antonio Machado, *Poesías completas* (Madrid: Espasa Calpe, 1987).

32 Some of the following data relies on the biography of Vallejo Nágera's son, Juan Antonio, also a psychiatrist, by Fernando Claramunt (*Juan Antonio*), based largely on conversations with surviving family members. For the mythical '*paisaje interiorizado*', see pp. 21–4.

33 See José-Vidal Pelaz López, 'Prensa, poder y sociedad en Palencia, 1808–1941', doctoral thesis, University of Valladolid, 1998. This citation, p. 581. See also p. 647. In 1927 Alejandro Nágera de la Guerra was a candidate for the National Assembly established by General Primo de Rivera. Luis Nágera de la Guerra was provincial counsellor in Palencia during the years of the Second Republic.

34 Claramunt, *Juan Antonio*, p. 25. For the *escudos de armas de linajes de los Vallejo y los Nágera, see p. 88*.

35 'Antonio Vallejo Nágera. Hoja matriz de servicios, 1910–1952', Ministerio de Defensa, Archivo General Militar de Segovia, Legajo B-382. The claim to disitinction in action, in Fernando Claramunt, *Juan Antonio*, p. 28.

36 Martín Vallejo Lobón, *La voluntad como recurso higiénico* (Barcelona: Real Academia de Medicina y Cirugía de Barcelona, 1908), p. 8, cited in José Manuel López Gómez, *Don Martín Vallejo Lobón: El médico y el hombre* (Barcelona: Universidad de Barcelona, 1988), p. 114.

37 See, e.g., Pedro Laín Entralgo, *Descargo de conciencia (1930–1960)* (Barcelona: Barral, 1976), p. 283.

38 Orden de Isabel la Católica, 2 junio 1919, Archivo del Ministerio de Asunto Exteriores, Cancillería, sig. C305 exp. 002. Vallejo Nágera also received campaign medals from Morocco and the Civil War.

39 Michael Burleigh, *Death and Deliverance: 'Euthanasia' in Germany, 1900–1945* (Cambridge: Cambridge University Press, 1994), p. 11.

40 Vallejo Nágera translated several German works on psychiatry, including Robert Gaupp's *Psicología del niño* (Barcelona: Labor, 1927).

41 Antonio Vallejo Nágera, 'Psicopatología de la conducta antisocial', I, 519; II, *Acción Española*, 83, January 1936, 169–94; III, 84, February 1936, 300; Vallejo Nágera, *Locura*, p. 53.

42 See Eric J. Engstrom, 'Emil Kraepelin: psychiatry and public affairs in Wilhelmine Germany', *History of Psychiatry*, 2 (1991): 111–32.

43 See particularly Emil Kraepelin, 'Psychiatric Observations on contemporary issues', (originally, 'Psychiatrische Randbemerkungen zur Zeitgeschichte', *Suddeutsche Monatshefte*, 16, 2 (1919): 171–83), translated with introduction by Engstrom, *History of Psychiatry*, 3 (1992): 253–69.

44 Tomás Maestre, 'Neurosis y psicosis colectivas', *España Médica*, 632 (May 1933): 6; Michael Richards, 'Spanish psychiatry c. 1900–1945: constitutional theory, eugenics, and the nation', *Bulletin of Spanish Studies*, 81, 6 (September 2004): 823–48.

45 In Claramunt, *Juan Antonio*, p. 26.

46 Claramunt, *Juan Antonio*, p. 31. The two met on official business later during the period when Azaña was Minister of War in 1931. The story may well originate in the simple fact that Vallejo Nágera, like many monarchist men of letters at the time, was a socio of the Madrid Ateneo in the 1920s, during a period when Azaña was a leading light there. Ateneo Científico, Literario y Artístico de Madrid, *Lista alfabética de los señores socios*, 1922: Antonio Vallejo Nágera: Socio de número, No. 10.119.

47 'Psicopatología', III, 301.

48 Vallejo Nágera, *Eugenesia de la hispanidad*, p. 49.

49 Diego Gracia Guillén, 'Medio siglo de psiquiatría española, 1885–1936', *Cuadernos de Historia de la Medicina Española*, 10 (1971): 305–39. Mira, *La psicoanàlisi*, 2 vols (Barcelona, 1926, abridged 3rd edn, Barcelona: Edicions 62, 1974).

50 Richards, 'Spanish psychiatry'.

51 Martín Vallejo Lobón, 'Locura moral', *Revista Frenopática Barcelonesa*, Año VIII, No. 18, Nov–Dec (1913): 229–44.

52 Martín Vallejo Lobón, 'Errores modernos sobre el orígen y evolución de los seres vivos', *El criterio católico*, Año VII, No. 75 (March 1904): 65–77, cited in López Gómez, *Don Martín Vallejo Lobón*, pp. 104–5. Martín was also a member of the *Junta de honor del Primer Congreso Hispano-Americano de las Congregaciones Marianas* in November 1904.

53 On the other hand, Vallejo Nágera was Vice-President of the prestigious (and politically conservative) *Academia Médico-Quirúrgica Española* in the early 1930s.

54 See, e.g., 'Una interesante visita al manicomio de Ciempozuelos', *ABC*, 6 February 1931, 12–13.

55 Before 1931, Antonio Vallejo Nágera was occasionally positive about Freudian techniques. See 'Locuras curables y locuras incurables', *El Siglo Médico*, 86 (1930): 85–6. Later he was more often explicitly anti-Freudian.

56 *Sindromes mentales simulados* (Madrid: Editorial Labor, 1930).

57 For example, *Divagaciones intrascendentes* (Valladolid: Editorial Española, 1938), p. 84; *Política racial*, p. 90; *Niños y jóvenes anormales* (Madrid: Sociedad de Educación 'Atenas', 1941), pp. 47–8.

58 'Psicopatología de la conducta antisocial', I, II, and III, *Acción Española*, 82–4, December 1935–February 1936.

59 These theories were based heavily on the internationally well-known work of the Professor of Psychiatry at the University of Marburg, Ernst Kretschmer (1888–1964), outlined in his influential post-First World War study, *Körperbau und Character* (Berlin: Julius Springer, 1921). For reception in Spain, see Kretschmer, 'Genio y figura', *Revista de Occidente*, August 1923, 161–74; José María Sacristán, *Figura y character: Los biotipos de Kretschmer* (Madrid: Imp. Ciudad Lineal, 1926). See Richards, 'Morality and Biology'.

60 For example, 'Ilicitud científica de la esterilización eugénica', *Acción Española*, I, 2 (1 January 1932), 142–54, and I, 3 (15 January 1932), 249–62. Indeed, Vallejo Nágera felt that the Republic would follow the German example and introduce a sterilization law. *Higiene de la raza*, p. 7.

61 See Benjamín Rivaya, 'La reacción contra el fascismo. (La recepción en España del pensamiento jurídico nazi)', *Revista de Estudios Políticos*, 100 (1998): 153–77 and 154.

62 Nancy Leys Stepan, *The Hour of Eugenics: Race, Gender, and Nation in Latin America* (Ithaca NY: Cornell University Press, 1991), esp. pp. 189–92.

63 Richards, 'Spanish Psychiatry'.

64 Vallejo Nágera, *Higiene de la raza*, p. 1.

65 Lowenthal, *Heritage*, p. xiv. Vallejo Nágera, *Eugenesia*, pp. 49–51.

66 *Eugenesia de la Hispanidad*, pp. 5–6.

67 Vallejo Nágera's most populist wartime writings, many of them originally appearing in the press, were collected together as *Divagaciones intrascendentes* (1938).

68 Vallejo Nágera, *Locura*, p. 52, taking up a similar argument made in 1935: 'Psicopatología de la conducta', III, 289–90.

69 Richards, 'Morality and Biology'.

70 Vallejo Nágera, *Psicología de los sexos* (Bilbao: n.p., n.d., 1945?), p. 34.

71 For example, *Sur-¡Arriba!*, 20 February 1937; *Sur*, 25 September, 1937, 3; 29 September 1937, 10; *Boinas Rojas*, 30 September, 1937, 2.

72 *Locura*, p. 223.

73 *Locura*, p. 52.

74 See, e.g., *La locura y la guerra. Psicopatología de la guerra española* (Valladolid: Librería Santarén, 1939); *Sinfonía retaguardista* (Valladolid: n.p, 1938).

75 See Laín Entralgo, *Descargo*, p. 301; Antonio Carreras Panchón, 'Los psiquiatras españoles y la guerra civil', *Medicina & Historia*, 13 (1986): 7; Gonzalo Moya, *Gonzalo R. Lafora: Medicina y cultura en una España en crisis* (Madrid: Universidad Autónoma, 1986), p. 122.

76 Claramunt, *Juan Antonio*, p. 35.

Illustration and Translation Credits

Illustration Credits

Ministerio de Cultura (MCU), Archivo General de la Administración (AGA), Fondo de Medios de Comunicación Social del Estado (MCSE): Antonio Maura (F-03580-08-001, F-03580-08-003, F-03580-10-001); Miguel Primo de Rivera (F-03710-27-004, F-03710-28-003, F-03710-26-003); José María Gil Robles (F-03360-01-001, F-03360-01-008, F-03360-02-001); José Antonio Primo de Rivera (F-03710-13-001, F-03710-19-001, F-03710-16-001); Francisco Franco (F-03926-011-001, F-03301-021-001, F-03928-005-001); Juan Antonio Suanzes (F-03839-34-005, F-03839-34-010, F-03839-34-011); Juan Tusquets (F-03697-21-005); Antonio Vallejo Nágera (F-03878-37-001, F-03878-37-002, F-03878-37-003).

Translation Credits (into English)

Chapter 2: Maria Thomas
Chapters 3 and 6: Daniel Evans
Chapter 5: Alison Pinington

Index